MONEY MAKERS

INSIDE THE NEW WORLD

OF FINANCE AND BUSINESS

DAVID SNIDER AND
DR. CHRIS HOWARD

The views expressed in this text are those of the authors and the interviewees
cited and do not necessarily reflect the views of the organizations for which
they currently work or have previously been employed.

First published in 2010 by PALGRAVE MACMILLAN® in the U.S.—a division
of St. Martin's Press LLC, 175 Fifth Avenue, New York, NY 10010.

Where this book is distributed in the UK, Europe and the rest of the world, this
is by Palgrave Macmillan, a division of Macmillan Publishers Limited,
registered in England, company number 785998, of Houndmills, Basingstoke,
Hampshire RG21 6XS.

Palgrave Macmillan is the global academic imprint of the above companies and
has companies and representatives throughout the world.

Palgrave® and Macmillan® are registered trademarks in the United States, the
United Kingdom, Europe and other countries.

ISBN: 978–0–230–61401–7

Library of Congress Cataloging-in-Publication Data
Snider, David.
    Money makers : inside the new world of finance and business / David Snider
and Chris Howard.
        p.   cm.
    ISBN-13: 978–0–230–61401–7 (hardcover)
    ISBN-10: 0–230–61401–9 (hardcover)
    1. Investments.   2. Venture capital.   3. Hedge funds.   4. Banks and
banking.   I. Howard, Christopher, 1970–   II. Title.
HG4521.S71134   2010
332.092'273—dc22   2009025885

A catalogue record of the book is available from the British Library.

Design by Letra Libre, Inc.

First edition: February 2010
10   9   8   7   6   5   4   3   2   1
Printed in the United States of America.

CONTENTS

Conclusion   203

FOREWORD

This book is being published at an extraordinary time. The financial markets and the economy in the United States have been through a remarkably destabilizing period. Today we are evaluating the damage, seeking to understand the root causes, and thinking about how public policy should be adjusted for the future.

In this book, the authors take an in-depth look at six of the fields driving the economy, many of which were key actors in this recent drama: investment banking, venture capital, private equity, hedge funds, management consulting, and the management of important U.S. corporations. The perspectives and conclusions offered are the result of scores of interviews with the most important and knowledgeable people in each of these areas. This unusual access, combined with the authors' clear analysis, provides an excellent narrative for all types of readers.

My own professional history has touched many of the areas this book considers. I began my career in asset management then enjoyed almost three decades in investment banking before having the privilege to serve as under secretary of the U.S. Treasury and then, for a brief period of time, manage a major commercial bank. During this period, the position of alternative investing (including venture capital, private equity, and hedge funds) grew tremendously, increased trade, created global markets and technology, and became an offensive tool as well as a key part of business strategy. *Money Makers* provides important background and perspective on these shifts and how our current financial landscape evolved as it did—both to enable so much prosperity and to put it all at risk.

I have always believed that well-functioning capital markets are a critical factor in successful economies. When providers and suppliers of capital meet and make informed decisions, in their own self interest, both the economy and the citizenry win. Capital is allocated in a superior way and results in increased growth for the economy. There must be clear rules and regulations that make this supplier-provider engagement fair, predictable, and confidence-building. But professional participants are also a key ingredient for this process to produce the best result.

Indeed, several of these activities—venture capital, private equity, and hedge funds in particular—are very young industries, really only about a generation old. Surely given their recent rapid growth and visibility, the future of these industries will be characterized by greater transparency, more oversight and, in general, greater scrutiny. While the other activities considered here, such as investment banking, management consulting, and the leadership of Fortune 500 companies, are more established, they, too, have transformed substantially in the last few decades and experienced significant disruption in the wake of recent events. *Money Makers* provides a timely explanation of these components of the economic landscape.

There is no question that recent events have shaken everyone's confidence in many parts of our system. It is very fair to ask hard questions about what went wrong, what went right, and how we should adjust public policy goals and the attendant regulation. But to arrive at the right answers we need to understand who these industry players are, the rules they have been playing under, and how their own practices and cultures have been rapidly changing. *Money Makers* will be an important source of perspectives in that effort.

Robert K. Steel is the former president and CEO of Wachovia Corporation. He joined the board of directors of Wells Fargo & Co. upon the firm's merger with Wachovia. He previously served as under secretary of the Treasury for domestic finance. In this role, he worked as the principal advisor to the secretary on matters of domestic finance and led the department's activities with respect to the domestic financial system, fiscal policy and operations, and governmental assets and liabilities. Prior to becoming under secretary, he was vice chairman of Goldman Sachs & Company.

INTRODUCTION

Billionaires Julian Robertson and Henry Kravis did not inherit large sums of money. They have never invented a new product or built companies that serve millions of customers. Yet by pioneering new ways to successfully invest, they have taken investors' money, produced large returns, and, in the process, made themselves extremely wealthy. But how did they do it and what are these industries that they have helped to create?

Although the elite fields of business and finance play large and dynamic roles in the global economy, how they work remains a mystery to most outsiders. Just over a decade ago, "hedge funds," "private equity," and "venture capital" were finance terms rarely discussed in the mainstream media. Today, they receive full-scale coverage. A recent "*Time* 100: People Who Shape our World" included a publicity-shy hedge-fund trader, a New York leveraged-buyout veteran, and a West Coast venture-capital financier, along with assorted entrepreneurs and Fortune 500 CEOs.

This book describes the inner workings of the highly selective and often secretive industries of the private sector: investment banking, venture capital, private equity, hedge funds, management consulting, and the management of Fortune 500 companies. It reveals them from the perspectives of leaders in each field, who share insights, anecdotes, and recommendations that can be valuable to anyone with an interest in finance and business.

These six industries alone do not represent the entire business universe. Real estate developers, accountants, commercial bankers, mutual-fund and institutional money managers, as well as government regulators (among others) play important roles in the economy. However, the descriptions of the businesses described here provide a broad understanding of the key players in the financial industry and many of the routes to power and monetary success.

THE PERIOD OF FINANCIAL RECKONING

September 2008 through the first half of 2009 was one of the worst periods for business and finance in history. Trillions of dollars in the market value of U.S. businesses disappeared, and with it went a commensurate amount of average Americans' and professional investors' money. Although investment bankers, hedge-fund managers, and CEOs of struggling businesses all received a huge amount of scrutiny for creating an economic mess, only a fraction of the people in these fields took actions that directly contributed to the recession.

The downturn was as brutal as it was unexpected. Through the first half of 2008, many major sectors of the economy were growing. Nevertheless, a rapid succession of financial events wrought destruction across the economy that autumn. Some of the largest and most-respected firms on Wall Street disappeared in a matter of months. Bear Stearns, Lehman Brothers, and Merrill Lynch—all investment banks operating multiple lines of business—were forced to sell themselves or go into bankruptcy. Their fall was based, in part, on housing-related financial products. The ambiguity concerning the value of these financial instruments (such as collateralized mortgage debt and credit default swaps) created so much uncertainty about the banks' capacities to absorb investment losses and honor their financial commitments that they were not able to continue operating as independent financial institutions.

Fortune 500 companies went bankrupt, as did businesses owned by private equity firms. The hedge-fund industry, which had recorded year after year of impressive results, saw its returns decline by 18 percent in 2008. On top of that, the market was confronted with outright fraud. Hedge-fund operator Bernie Madoff acknowledged that the $50-billion hedge fund he ran was a Ponzi scheme. Billionaire financier Allen Sanford, who promised investors safe, reliable returns, allegedly poured his clients' money into risky enterprises and his own lavish lifestyle. Although these criminal activities hurt investors, this illegal behavior was not the core reason for the recession.

At the center of the economic debacle was the bursting of a debt-based bubble. It was inflated not only by the recent prevalence of greed and bad decision making, but also by years of too much borrowing and too little capital throughout the United States. This permeated the financial system, in which investment firms used large amounts of leverage. It was exacerbated by the U.S. government's huge budget deficits and by the millions of consumers who spent in excess of their savings. As President Barack Obama remarked in June 2009, "A culture of irresponsibility took root from Wall Street to Washington to Main Street."[1]

MOVING FORWARD

The face of business and finance has been changed irrefutably, but the key industries and the functions they serve will persist. Fortune 500 companies remain the driving forces for jobs, products, and services throughout the world. Investment banks and management-consulting firms continue to advise large corporations and private equity firms on their operations and financial transactions. Private equity, venture capital, and hedge-fund firms all still manage huge investment vehicles and seek to allocate capital to dynamic businesses and financial assets. Although their worlds have been shaken, these industries are again money makers. Investment banks as well as management consultants are developing strategies to generate wealth and growth for their clients. Venture capital, private equity, and hedge funds are seeking to make money for their investors, and Fortune 500 companies are working to produce profits for their shareholders.

The most successful of these institutions emphasize ethics and understand the implications of their actions. The absence of those considerations has historically led to economic misfortune, for both the principal actors and the larger community. Many private equity firms that added no value to portfolio companies and over-leveraged them went out of business in the late 1980s. Venture-capital firms that invested in unsound companies in order to take them public during the 1990s technology boom have disappeared. Investment bankers and hedge-fund operators who recently took too much risk or who broke the law are out of work or in jail. Business schools have been reminded of the importance of emphasizing principles beyond the profit motive, and thousands of students have taken a professional oath that emphasizes responsible value creation.

Investment firms are often criticized for the massive salaries and bonuses that their leaders receive. The huge amount of money that these executives make is a function of their capacity to raise capital from investors and to rapidly and consistently increase that money. Investors are never forced to place their money with a particular manager; they choose to pay high investment fees because they believe that those fees are justified by the acumen of the investment professional. Finance is Darwinian; those who do not produce generally do not survive. Those who create profits reap large benefits.

All six of the industries described in this book, when they conduct themselves well, produce wealth and success that reach far beyond those directly involved. They make our economy operate more efficiently, produce returns for investors of all kinds (including pension-fund participants and nonprofits), allocate capital to generate economic growth, and create life-changing product innovations.

THE AUTHORS

The contrasting experiences of this book's two authors gives their collaborative work a unique perspective on the world of business. Chris grew up in Plano, Texas; David in the suburbs of Boston. Chris was a Bowl-winning college running back at the Air Force Academy. David's athletic career peaked in middle school. Chris's first job was in the military; David's was on Capitol Hill. They each explored a number of different opportunities in the nonprofit sector, yet both ended up pursuing a career in business. David took a position in management consulting at Bain & Company before heading to the private equity firm Bain Capital. After graduate school and time in the military, Chris attended Harvard Business School. He chose to work at Fortune 500 companies, taking a job in an international project management group at Bristol-Myers Squibb and later in the Corporate Initiatives Group at General Electric.

They met when Chris was at GE and David was a student in high school. Their relationship evolved from one of mentor-mentee to a longstanding personal and professional friendship. As Chris transitioned from business to academia, David entered the private sector. Throughout that time they maintained a discussion on the evolving financial world. David's search to understand finance (in order to get a job within it) was, in part, the genesis for this book. Chris wanted to work on this project to provide a text for students and young professionals curious about these fields as well as the people, who, like him, developed an interest in business later in life. They both believed that, given the hugely important position that these select industries occupy, there ought to be a book that explored them from the inside out.

THE CONTENTS OF THIS BOOK

Chapter 1 examines the investment-banking industry, which played the most public role in the recent economic crisis. The industry continues to serve critical financial functions that enable capital markets and the broader economy. Chapters 2, 3, and 4 describe the major financial industries beyond Wall Street: venture capital, private equity, and hedge funds. Each industry controls billions of dollars on behalf of investors and has a huge influence on the development of new companies, the operations of business, and the movements of public financial markets. Chapter 2, on venture capital, also discusses the experiences and challenges of entrepreneurship, because that is so intricately linked to the venture business. Chapter 5 explores management consulting and bridges the divide between the "financial" economy and the "real" economy. Although under the radar, consultants play an important role in advising key corporate and financial decision makers on most mergers, acquisitions, and new, strategic business initiatives. Chapter 6 discusses the management of Fortune 500 companies. These large institutions employ millions, produce thousands of products and services on which we depend, and play important roles in the five other fields.

INSIDER INSIGHTS:
INTERVIEWS CONDUCTED FOR THIS BOOK

The contents of this book come from research, the authors' experiences, and the insights of industry insiders. Associates at top firms as well as industry leaders were interviewed for every chapter to provide a robust perspective on the field. Their insights are interwoven into the chapters, and there are some short profiles and interviews to provide context for people's personal experiences. The education and professional backgrounds of those highlighted are included in appendix B. The careers of a few of those interviewed have been controversial, but this is not a book about leadership practices; it is about understanding how these industries work and how fortunes and reputations can rise and fall within them. Everyone interviewed has reached the pinnacle of one or more areas of business.

Some interviewees preferred that their insights stay anonymous; however, the list below provides a sense of the range and depth of expertise that contributed to the text:

- Alan Schwartz, executive chairman of Guggenheim Partners, former CEO of Bear Stearns
- Ben Casnocha, entrepreneur (founder of Comcate), recognized as one of *Business Week*'s top entrepreneurs under twenty-five
- Bill Meehan, former managing director of McKinsey & Company and founder of the firm's private equity and venture capital practice
- Bill Shutzer, senior managing director of Evercore Partners, former managing director of Lehman Brothers
- Bruce Evans, managing director of Summit Partners
- Chuck Farkas, senior director of Bain & Company
- Chuck McMullan, executive director at UBS Investment Bank
- Chris Galvin, former CEO of Motorola, chairman of Harrison Street Capital
- Craig Foley, founder of Chancellor Capital Management, first institutional investor in Starbucks

- David Rubenstein, cofounder of The Carlyle Group
- JB Cherry, managing director of One Equity Partners
- Jamie Dimon, CEO of JPMorgan Chase & Co.
- Jamie Irick, general manager at General Electric
- Jeff Hurst, cofounder and managing partner of Commonwealth Capital Ventures
- Joe Fuller, cofounder and CEO of Monitor Group
- Joyce Johnson-Miller, cofounder of The Relativity Fund, former managing director of Cerberus Capital
- Julian Robertson, founder of Tiger Management, hedge fund pioneer
- Ken Weg, former vice chairman of Bristol-Myers Squibb
- Kip Frey, partner at Intersouth Partners
- Megan Clark, former vice president of technology at BHP Billiton, former director of N. M. Rothschild & Sons
- Noah Glass, entrepreneur (CEO of GoMobo), recognized as one of *Business Week*'s top entrepreneurs under twenty-five
- Peter Nicholas, chairman and cofounder of Boston Scientific
- Richard Bressler, managing director and head of the Strategic Resource Group at THL Partners, former CFO of Viacom
- Rick Wagoner, former CEO of General Motors
- Ron Daniel, former worldwide managing director of McKinsey & Company
- Sam Clemens, entrepreneur (CEO of Models from Mars), former associate at Greylock Partners
- Seth Klarman, president of The Baupost Group, famed value investor
- Shona Brown, senior vice president of Business Operations at Google, member of the executive committee
- Steve Pagliuca, managing director of Bain Capital
- Suzanne Nora Johnson, former vice chairman of Goldman Sachs
- Tim Jenkins, cofounder of Marble Arch Investments, former associate at Tiger Management and Madison Dearborn Partners

CHAPTER ONE

THE BILLION-DOLLAR BROKERS AND TRADERS OF INVESTMENT BANKING

Banking has created more success stories and millionaires than probably any other profession.

—*A former Lehman Brothers banker*

A HISTORY AND DESCRIPTION
OF INVESTMENT BANKING

On Saturday, March 15, 2008, a team of investment bankers from J.P. Morgan was analyzing the financial documents of a business that the bank was considering purchasing. It was not uncommon for the bankers to be working on a weekend. The demands of advising on mergers and acquisitions often involved long days and weeks that lacked the punctuation of relaxing weekends. The diligence had begun late Thursday night, when CEO Jamie Dimon called the heads of J.P. Morgan's investment-banking division about the deal.[1] Immediately afterward, executives and analysts began receiving urgent calls and BlackBerry messages. They quickly hailed cabs or called town cars and returned to work. Steve Black, J.P. Morgan's co-head of investment banking, arranged for a chartered plane to fly him to New York from the Caribbean island of Anguilla. By 11 P.M., a team was assembled.[2]

As with many such deals, there were other potential buyers examining the same documents in order to determine whether they would make bids and, if so, for what amounts. In this case, the other serious potential buyers were two private equity firms: Kohlberg, Kravis, Roberts & Co. and J. C. Flowers. There was a great deal of bustle in the executive suite at the target company's offices at 383 Madison Avenue. The J.P. Morgan bankers were trying to determine the true value of the target company's $400 billion in assets and operating businesses as well as the risks posed by the financial products held on its balance sheet.[3] There was palpable anxiety among both analysts and senior bankers as they tried to understand the business and its current financial state. The analysts were creating Excel models to value elements of the business based on current market prices and to evaluate what would happen if the market eroded further. Senior bankers were using their knowledge to inform the assumptions underlying the financial models.

Like most deals on which the bankers worked, absolute confidentiality was required, as leaked news of a deal could move stock markets or pose issues of insider trading (a type of securities fraud that occurs when someone buys or sells a stock with company information not available to the public). However, this deal was, in many ways, unlike anything the bankers had ever seen and required extreme secrecy. The potential acquisition target was one of J.P. Morgan's competitors, Bear Stearns. The imminent timing was not a result of the normal pressures of a competitive process but of a fear that, without a buyer, Bear Stearns might be forced into bankruptcy, which could incite a global financial panic. It was not only the CEOs of Bear Stearns and J.P. Morgan, Alan Schwartz and Jamie Dimon, who were closely following the deal, but also U.S. Treasury Secretary Hank Paulson, Federal Reserve Chairman Ben Bernanke, and the president of the New York Federal Reserve Bank, Tim Geithner.

On March 16, J.P. Morgan rejected the potential acquisition, seeing it as too risky because of the potential losses from some of Bear Stearns's investments—notably its mortgage-related holdings. Yet strong encouragement from the Treasury Secretary and the Federal Reserve's guarantee to finance and assume roughly $30 billion of Bear Stearns's mortgage assets led to the unprecedented acquisition. Many in the industry believed that the deal represented the avoidance of a major financial crisis. In fact, it was just the beginning of one.

IN 2008, the investment-banking industry lost hundreds of billions of dollars, saw many of its institutions disappear, laid off thousands of employees, and—in its own demise—precipitated a global recession. How could one industry nearly cause a worldwide depression? Why did the U.S. government believe that stabilizing U.S. banks merited allocating $700 billion to the industry? The answers to these questions are found in this chapter.

THE HISTORY OF INVESTMENT BANKING

The U.S. investment-banking industry dates from before the Civil War, when Jay Cooke sold shares of government bonds to individual investors through a network of salesmen.[4] In the late 1800s, J.P. Morgan and other investment houses played a large role in the industrial mergers and restructurings of the railroad and steel industries. The prosperity of the 1920s led to a massive expansion of investing and financial services, and average Americans began to invest (or speculate) in the stock market. Although the period culminated with a run on the banks, a stock-market crash, and the Great Depression, in the following decades the investment banks that survived expanded along with American business. As companies grew larger, so did their initial public offerings (IPOs), debt issuances, and other financial needs. With those increased capital demands came greater profits for the investment banks.

Banking firms continually sought to take advantage of new markets and changes in regulations, such as a 1981 law that, for the first time, permitted savings and loan (S&L) banks to sell the loans they issued to other financial institutions. This legislation laid the groundwork for much of the housing mess that boiled over twenty-six years later. Prior to 1981, S&L banks carefully evaluated potential borrowers, knowing that they were on the hook if those borrowers defaulted on their loans. The change in the law allowed the banks to sell the loans (and the interest those loans generated). Although not an intention of the regulatory change, S&L banks suddenly had less incentive to conduct thorough diligence on loan applicants, because they did not carry all the risks if the borrowers defaulted. Investment banks could now convert the loans they purchased into mortgage-backed securities and sell them to other investors.

Another financial innovation in the 1980s was the high-yield bond. High-yield bonds were an important development because they allowed companies that were perceived by investors as being somewhat financially risky to have access to debt capital from public markets. The pioneer of the debt instrument was Michael Milken, who built the business for the investment bank Drexel Burnham Lambert. Prior to Milken, Drexel Burnham was a mid-size bank. By "creating," developing, and virtually monopolizing the high-yield debt market, Milken elevated Drexel Burnham to a central role in finance and disrupted the informal rules and hierarchy that had characterized the investment-banking industry for decades. He and the firm left a lasting legacy on Wall Street: pioneering new financial products is critical to rising to the top of investment banking.

In 1990, however, Drexel Burnham was forced into bankruptcy because of losses and criminal charges related to its high-yield practice.
Milken pled guilty to securities violations stemming from charges of
insider trading and stock price manipulation, and served time in jail.
Though particularly high profile, the incident was certainly not the
only scandal in the investment banking industry during the last couple
decades.

In 1991, Salomon Brothers was tarnished by charges that the head
of the government bond-trading department made illegal bids for U.S.
Treasury securities, an incident that led to the ouster of the firm's CEO
and other members of the senior management.[5] Warren Buffett, who
was one of Salomon Brother's largest shareholders at the time, stepped
in and ran the company for a few months to ensure that the firm survived the market's brief loss of trust. In 1994, Joseph Jett of Kidder
Peabody allegedly manufactured over $300 million in fictitious profits
to hide actual investment losses and garner huge bonuses for himself.[6]
Nevertheless, in spite of such bumps along the way, the investment-
banking industry grew in size and profitability throughout the twenti-
eth century.

In 2001, however, banks began to face a number of difficulties.
Most noticeably, the United States was entering a recession on the
heels of the tech bubble. Not only was the economy headed downward, but the large pool of IPOs that banks had facilitated for new
technology companies dried up. Additionally, Internet technologies
made it easier and less expensive to trade securities, which put downward pressure on the transaction fees that banks received from bro-
kering such trades. One of the few bright spots was the low cost of
borrowing money. The U.S. Federal Funds rate, which largely deter-
mines the cost of borrowing for banks, was set at historically low levels. Banks seized the opportunity and began to borrow more heavily
from other banks in order to increase their leverages and, in turn,
their profitability. By expanding the amount of money they could
trade and lend, banks could boost their profits, as long as the additional uses of money yielded higher returns than the costs of the
loans. Many also increased their lending to private equity firms,
commercial real estate developers, and hedge funds—all leveraged

investors. Furthermore, new banking regulations, under the international Basel II agreement, allowed banks to use more leverage than they previously could. The Basel II rules were reliant on credit ratings, which proved inaccurate mechanisms for valuing the risks of many assets.

Although stocks and bonds decreased in value during the 2001 recession, home prices continued their long upward trajectory. Investment banks saw the U.S. housing market as an area with significant profit potential, given that increasing home values led to a very low default rate on mortgages. The banks increased the amount of resources that were focused on residential real estate, buying up mortgages and expanding the use of financial instruments, such as mortgage-backed securities, which could be bought and sold easily. Aggressive lending, home building, and speculative-investor home buying drove up real estate prices and created millions of new mortgages for banks to purchase and securitize. Banks valued these assets and the risks they posed with complex models based on historical fluctuations in home prices and mortgage default rates. They began to believe—and to act—as if home prices could only go up.

However, in 2006, the U.S. housing market began to experience turbulence. Lenders who issued mortgages to highly risky borrowers (those with bad credit histories) experienced defaults. They began to cut back on risky lending and to increase mortgage rates for existing borrowers. Higher rates meant more defaults, and tighter lending policies decreased demand for new homes. Housing prices started to decline at rapid rates, and property owners who had adjustable-rate mortgages they couldn't afford (often subprime borrowers), as well as real estate speculators, started to default on loans.*

The declines in home prices and the increasing default rates were far greater than the financial models had indicated was possible, and

---

*Subprime mortgages are mortgages issued to less credit-worthy people. Often these individuals have histories of failure to pay back debt or have declared bankruptcy. An adjustable-rate mortgage (ARM) is a home loan for which the interest rate can vary over the course of the loan, often starting at a low rate and increasing over time.

the banks found themselves holding trillions of dollars in securities related to the housing market, with prices dropping. Soon after, banks began seeing the values of their investments in commercial real estate decline as well.

Banks' advisory business divisions, which facilitate corporate mergers and acquisitions (companies buying other companies) as well as other capital market transactions (for example, IPOs and debt issuances) also experienced declines. Furthermore, the banks' exposure to private equity transactions created additional pressure on the stability of some institutions. Between 2004 and 2007, private equity firms constituted a large and increasing share of financial deals. Because of the amount of debt that had to be raised for the financing of these transactions, private equity deals were generally more profitable than corporate mergers. However, as a result of the debt used by private equity firms to purchase companies, banks were often left with billions in loans (if the banks did not sell all the debt associated with the deals). As the economy soured in late 2007, the market's expectation of the likelihood of a default on that debt increased, and the market price of the loans fell to only a fraction of their initial value. The banks had to write down the value of the loans, which decreased the strength of their balance sheets.

In autumn 2007, due to housing market financial products and other debt related holdings, investment banks began to take multibillion-dollar write-offs, acknowledging that the assets they held had declined in value. Unfortunately, the write-offs did not solve the banks' problems. Many had used borrowed money to purchase investments; the amount of borrowing (as much as thirty dollars for every one dollar of equity) used to boost gains, ended up magnifying losses. Declines in asset values of only 4 percent wiped out many banks' equity in some investments, exposing them to large potential losses. With little demand for the banks' debt investments, the values of the assets continued to decline, creating further strain on the banks' financial stability. With no buyers, banks could not get liquidity (cash) from their investments. That downward spiral led to concerns that perhaps banks did not have adequate capital to maintain operations.

In March 2008, a rumor began to circulate on Wall Street that Bear Stearns, the smallest of the major investment banks, might be in an unstable position because of its large exposure to the mortgage market. The previous summer, two of its internal hedge funds had been devastated by losses stemming from mortgage-related investments. The hedge funds had purchased mortgage-backed securities and applied huge amounts of leverage; when the investments went down, the funds were nearly wiped out. In March the firm still had $18 billion in cash, an adequate amount to function (although less than one-twentieth of the total amount of the bank's assets).[7] However, Wall Street banks depend on more than cash to function; they rely on the confidence of other Wall Street firms and their customers. Suddenly Bear Stearns lost the confidence of both groups. Investors began to withdraw funds, thereby depleting Bear Stearns's cash supply. Wall Street firms—which Bear Stearns needed to borrow money from and clear trades with—pulled back in order to limit their exposure. In an attempt to stabilize the worsening situation the Federal Reserve and J.P. Morgan provided Bear Stearns with secured lending, but singling it out for assistance unintentionally further eroded confidence in the institution. The firm was left with few options, and the federal government eventually had to step in and broker a merger with J.P. Morgan. The government determined that, given all the interrelated deals and lending between Bear Stearns and other investment banks, Bear's collapse into bankruptcy could pose a systemic risk to the entire U.S. banking system.

Nevertheless, in September 2008, when Lehman Brothers faced similar liquidity issues and a loss of investor confidence, the federal government declined to provide financial backing for a merger deal. Barclays, the British investment bank, was prepared to buy Lehman for $5 billion plus the assumption of $75 billion of debt, but it needed approval from its shareholders before completing the transaction. The U.S. government refused to support Lehman Brothers financially for the three months required for Barclays to close on the transaction, fearing that things would get worse and that, consequently, Barclays would walk away from the deal.[8] Faced with no access to capital and no banks willing to purchase it without guarantees from the U.S. government, Lehman filed for bankruptcy.

Lehman Brothers, the counterparty on thousands of transactions with other banks, was larger and more interconnected than Bear Stearns. Key financial players felt that, if an institution that big could fail, others could too. Investment banks stopped lending, and even the largest and most stable companies could not get short-term loans. Adding to the sense of market chaos was the potential failure of AIG—then the world's largest insurance company—and a forced government takeover of the mortgage-lending institutions Fannie Mae and Freddie Mac. To avoid a full-scale financial meltdown, the secretary of the Treasury and the chairman of the Federal Reserve asked the U.S. Congress for $700 billion to buy the troubled assets that were weighing down the investment banks and inhibiting the ability of the credit markets to function. In the end, the Treasury Department decided to use the money allocated by Congress for the Troubled Asset Relief Program (TARP), in order to make capital injections into the banks. Some banks did not require capital injections to stay solvent. However, Treasury Secretary Paulson felt that it was important for all nine of the major banks to accept the funds to avoid those who voluntarily took government money from being stigmatized. "We did not need the TARP money," notes J.P. Morgan CEO Jamie Dimon. The government "asked the nine banks to take it. Some of those firms may have needed it to survive. Some probably needed it for comfort. We were in neither of those camps, but I think there was a coherent argument that these nine banks take it, in order to help stabilize the system and help those other banks to take it. We didn't think that J.P. Morgan should be partisan or parochial and stand in the way of doing something that was good for the country and, in fact, for the financial system of the world."

To be proactive and avoid further issues, Merrill Lynch sold itself to Bank of America. On September 22, 2008, seven days after Lehman declared bankruptcy, Goldman Sachs and Morgan Stanley became bank holding companies. This change allowed them to raise money by collecting deposits in the same way as traditional banks and to access funding from the U.S. government. Although some institutions were forced to liquidate or sell, a catastrophic collapse of the banking business and the world economy was avoided.

TWO TRENDS THAT SPURRED THE DOWNTURN

Two trends in banking over the last decade helped to exacerbate the recent downturn. The first is the globalization of banking. The involvement of European banks in the U.S. market has increased, as has the role of U.S. financial products in emerging markets, such as Russia, India, and China. Historically, financial disruption in the U.S. was relatively contained to its banks and investors. However, in this instance, rather than only U.S. banks holding toxic debt from homeowners or highly leveraged commercial real estate loans, investors around the world took massive losses. Developing economies that had seen massive inflows of private capital, facilitated by new investment products, experienced sharp declines in their stock markets. Negative and interconnected currents fed on themselves. Investors simultaneously experienced massive losses in their U.S. and international stock portfolios, which motivated them to pull back on new investments. U.S. corporations experienced fewer sales from domestic and international markets, which forced them to lay off people and shutter some overseas operations. Job losses, investment declines, and decreasing housing prices led consumers to spend less. Their decreased consumption impacted countries that were dependent on exporting goods to the U.S. The virtuous cycle of increasing wealth driving increasing consumption and growth was thrown into reverse, and much of the economic value creation of the previous decade was undone.

The second trend is the increasing use of quantitative models to make trades and measure risk. As computing power became greater and greater, the number of investment decisions that were made algorithmically kept growing. "In our business, there are no patents to speak of, so everything is about staying in front of the curve and creativity. We keep creating new areas of high-profit margin. When they get created, they become commoditized, and then you have to find the next area of opportunity," explains Alan Schwartz, executive chairman of Guggenheim Partners and former CEO of Bear Stearns. The problem was that banks' risk management did not always evolve as quickly as the products that traders were creating and banks were selling. In many cases, the banks' policy makers did not have a deep understanding of the risk the banks were exposed to and, as a result, they were blindsided in late 2007 and in 2008, when things started to fall apart. "By 1999 when Glass-Steagall* was repealed, banks were free to consume innovative, derivative products," wrote Amar Bhidé, a professor at Columbia Business School. "CEOs appeared to turn a blind eye to reckless bets—not a bad policy, since they were richly rewarded for short-term profits."[9] Yet that behavior led some banks to a state where they became unable to sustain themselves as independent companies.

Recently, critics of the industry have argued that investment banks' penchant for risk-taking in the last decade was a function of their being public companies rather than private partnerships. They argue that these firms took on undue risk, knowing that, if things went badly, it would be the shareholders (not managers) who would be most affected. However, the employees of many firms, especially those that no longer exist independently, owned a large portion of their companies' stock. Bear Stearns's employees held roughly a third of the company's stock and lost over $5 billion when the business was sold to J.P. Morgan. Similarly, Lehman Brothers' employees owned about 30 percent of the firm's stock, which became worthless.[10]

INVESTMENT BANKING TODAY

The consolidation in the banking industry that ensued in 2008 allowed surviving firms to strengthen weaker areas of their businesses through acquisitions. J.P. Morgan gained highly regarded prime brokerage, as well as commodities, equity, and fixed-income trading businesses from its purchase of Bear Stearns. Barclays Bank, which had a relatively small investment-banking advisory division in the United States, purchased a large portion of Lehman Brothers' business. Bank of America,

---

*The Glass-Steagall Act of 1933 was a bill regulating the banking industry. In 1999, a key provision that prohibited banks whose primary focus was an investment business from receiving deposits, was repealed.

which had a somewhat unsuccessful investment-banking division, picked up Merrill Lynch's investment-banking advisory practice as well as its extensive network of investment brokers.

Although the number and the legal structures of the large investment banks have changed, the functions that these institutions serve remain the same. As J.P. Morgan CEO Jamie Dimon wrote in his March 2009, letter to shareholders, "The investment banking business, in many ways, will never be the same. Leverage will be lower and certain financial products will likely cease to exist. But the fundamental business will remain the same." Investment banks still advise companies on financial transactions, manage investments for clients, research and trade financial products, and invest their own capital. Although the opening quotation for this chapter may seem anachronistic, it is still true. Investment banks continue to play a key role in the U.S. economy, as they have for over a century, and financially reward those who succeed in the industry.

MOVING FORWARD

For a period of time, there will be fewer jobs in investment banking and lower compensation, at least in certain areas. Nevertheless, the industry will persist. Globally, banking jobs will increase, although less so in New York. "Partially that's because we are going to drive businesses to other parts of the world and partially it's because banking is a much more mature business in the U.S. than it is in the emerging markets," explains Jamie Dimon. The biggest change will be in the leverage that firms use in their own investing. In 2007, investment banks were leveraged 30 to 1, meaning that they were putting to use roughly thirty dollars of debt for every one dollar they had in equity. They did this to increase their returns and profitability. That will no longer be the case, and banks will likely have to comply with a stricter regulatory regime. In particular, the conversion of Goldman Sachs and Morgan Stanley into bank holding companies subjects them to more rigorous restrictions.

Banks will place a higher emphasis on risk management, eliminating some potential profit opportunities. Additionally, banks that took significant capital injections from the federal government, particularly Citigroup and Bank of America, may have to bear the brunt of higher government scrutiny and regulations. Although some of the investment strategies and products that were used to produce significant profits in the past will cease to exist, the disappearance of large competitors may afford the industry's survivors more opportunities for success in the future. After a series of losses, many investment banks returned to profitability more quickly than expected. The issue facing the banks today is whether they can return to the levels of money making that existed before the recession, without excessive leverage or posing risks to themselves and the broader financial system. Dimon believes it is possible. "If the whole industry has to use less leverage, then the products will simply get re-priced to bring the institutions back to a fair return. That's economic theory. Whether the returns in 2007 [at the peak] were real or not is a different question. At some other firms in the industry, a lot of the 'profits' in the 2007 timeframe were clearly not real."

HOW INVESTMENT BANKING WORKS

FOUR TYPES OF BANKS

Investment banks are a subset of the banking industry and have a special legal structure to execute their roles in the capital markets. There are four main types of banks: retail banks, commercial banks, investment banks, and universal banks. Retail banks are focused primarily on collecting deposits from individuals and organizations and making loans. Commercial banks are focused on serving the banking needs of corporations. For example, a commercial bank may offer a working-capital loan to fund the operation of a business. After World War II, 60 percent of lending in the United States was done by retail and commercial banks. By 2008, that was down to 20 percent. In large part, this shift was a result of the growth of money-market funds, bond funds, and securitization—all financial vehicles related to the investment-banking industry.[11] Universal banks engage in retail, commercial, and investment-banking practices.

THE ROLES OF INVESTMENT BANKS

Investment banks play critical roles in nearly every aspect of the economy. They are both the brokers and bankrollers of the business world and, recently, of the finances of everyday Americans. They are hired by companies and investors to buy and sell businesses, assets, stocks, and debts, as well as to simultaneously arrange the financing of these transactions. Imagine trying to sell a house with no real estate broker to advise you on price or attract buyers, and no financial institution to provide a potential buyer with a mortgage. Investment banks act as brokers for corporations: they help them to sell corporate divisions, to buy other companies, and to raise money by issuing equity (stock) or debt (bonds). They help local governments and nonprofits, such as universities and hospitals, borrow money for new infrastructure projects. These organizations generally use investment banks to raise money by issuing bonds, which the organizations pay back over time with revenues from profits or fundraising.

In the past few decades, investment banks have also played larger roles in the finances of millions of U.S. citizens. Student loans, home mortgages, and car loans, although issued by an array of financial institutions, were packaged by investment banks and sold off in pieces to investors. This process is known as securitization and occurs when an asset or group of assets is made into a security that can be traded on the market. For example, in the case of home loans, this involves packaging multiple mortgages together and then selling securities comprised of these loans to investors. The investors take the risk that the debtors will make their loan payments; in return, the investors receive the interest on those loans.

Investment banks also serve key functions for hedge funds. This role is referred to as prime brokerage. The banks are involved with everything from raising investor capital to clearing trades and finding sources of debt for those that use leverage. Many hedge funds depend on loans to leverage their investments and achieve large, above-market returns, and investment banks are often their conduits for these loans.

INVESTMENT BANKING SERVICES

Investment banks are comprised of several businesses related to the capital markets. Although the organizations are referred to as "investment banks," the investment-banking division is only one part of the firms' overall operations. This division serves corporations, governments, and private equity firms in major financial transactions: buying or selling companies, going public, and offering debt on the public market. The investment-banking division is a relatively stable operation, in that it is not financially leveraged or exposed to potential losses in the way that trading divisions are. It is a service business and, as long as deals are done, the bank is paid. Of course, when the economy goes into a recession, deal flow (the quantity of financial transactions being completed) drops, as does the number of potential clients.

Investment Banking Groups

The investment-banking division is segmented both by industry and product. Bankers at all levels are assigned to specific groups, to foster the development of expertise in that area. Industry groups include technology, media and telecom; defense and aerospace; healthcare; consumer products and retail; financial institutions; financial sponsors (private equity firms and other investors); and government. Product groups are based on the types of financial transactions that a bank would be hired to conduct: mergers and acquisitions, equity-capital markets (transactions related to stock), debt-capital markets, leveraged finance, credit risk management, and others. For any particular deal, people from the relevant industry and product groups are teamed up. At a bank, the culture within different groups varies, based on the people who are running things and the types of clients being served.

Attracting Clients

Investment banks attract clients by means of personal networks and effective presentations. That means "being in the flow of relevant information and being positioned to capitalize on and enhance existing individual relationships," says Chuck McMullan, an executive director at UBS Investment Bank. He explains, "Rarely does a banker identify a unique opportunity from afar, schedule a meeting with a new client, and generate a deal; although it can happen, you can't build a career that way."

In many instances, a company interested in investment-banking advisory services will host a "bake-off," at which it will invite a few banks to give presentations on why they are best suited for the purpose. As Chuck McMullan implies, being invited requires "being in the know" about possible deals, maintaining personal relationships in the industry, and having a strong reputation. Often, multiple firms will present to the potential client on the same day. The banks will assemble pitch books for these meetings, highlighting their previous experiences and detailing why they are well equipped to advise on a specific transaction. This competitive process can be pretty intense. A lot of detective work goes into these bake-offs, with bankers trying to figure out who their competitors are and using that knowledge to position themselves.

Banks are, to some extent, at the mercy of their clients' whims; on rare occasions that can mean an unusual selection process. "We were trying to get in as the sell-side banker for a large video-game company, going up against a couple of heavy weights with lots of experience in the sector," said an analyst at a boutique investment bank (the industry term for small investment banks focused on particular industries or regions of the country). "On one of the calls prior to the bake-off, the company's CEO told my firm's managing director that the company once made a decision on an advisor by letting two banks play the video game to win the business. He hinted that it might just come down to that again. Later that afternoon, we went out and bought an Xbox for the firm, and, for the next week, I spent an hour each day teaching the managing director how to play the game. In the end, we got to work on the deal without it going to that, but, still, it just goes to show that, what the client wants, the client usually gets."

The Buy Side and the Sell Side

Bankers can be hired by a client on the "buy side" or "sell side" of a transaction. A sell-side banker represents a company or private equity firm that is selling a business, and a buy-side banker works with a party that is making an acquisition. The need to be responsive to the client is the same in both roles, but the process is different in each. On the sell side, the focus is on valuing the company, positioning it for a sale through marketing materials and corporate memoranda (the formal documents sent to potential buyers), and then conducting the negotiated sale process. The sell-side bankers, in conjunction with the seller, put together documents that potential buyers will want to view in conducting their own due-diligence processes. The corporate memoranda contain information about the company's market and products, customer lists, competitors, contracts, growth prospects, and financial statements and projections. They are often lengthy (fifty to one hundred pages) and can be quite time consuming to assemble. These documents are placed in a digital data room, to which access is given to potential buyers. During the sales process, potential buyers often request information not contained in the data room, and it is the investment bank's responsibility to prepare such materials. For instance, a buyer interested in synergies with its own selling efforts might ask for historical sales by product or customer, and the bankers would have to work with the seller to compile that information.

On the buy side, the bank's role involves generating a list of potential acquisitions or analyzing a specific target business and determining the ideal financial structure for the purchase (for example, whether the buyer should pay in cash or use some debt). The bank also does an analysis of the value of the target business to help its client make an appropriate offer. The value of an offer price, as well as its timing and positioning, are critically important to the success of a deal. If a buyer bids too high, it can look foolish for overpaying; if it bids too low, it may lose the deal. In leveraged-finance deals, which generally involve a private equity firm, the buy-side investment bank may play a role in providing temporary capital commitments (such as acquisition facilities and bridge loans) for the debt portion of the acquisition. These commitments are later syndicated (sold off to others) in the leveraged-loan or high-yield capital markets.

Analysis and Models

Investment banking analysts and associates build the financial models that, among other things, may be designed to determine the proceeds from a sale, predict future operations, value companies, and assess transaction scenarios. Depending on the output required, such models can be incredibly complex. "When I was an analyst, we had a client who was interested in rolling up* assisted living/nursing homes," said Arash Farin about his time as an analyst at Goldman Sachs. "The client had an ambitious plan and needed hundreds of millions of dollars to make all these acquisitions. The client was putting up the equity, and our firm was potentially going to offer the debt. The model was designed to project future cash flows of the entire portfolio, based on as many details about each facility as possible, and there were dozens of properties we had to analyze. Putting the numbers together involved 65 MB of data—five spreadsheets linked together. The deal team included a managing director, a vice-president, an associate, and myself."

Arash Farin had inherited an early version of the nursing home model from someone who had been involved with the deal previously. When he could not make sense of how it was constructed, he had to "reverse engineer" the entire financial model to ensure that there were no errors, a process that consumed an entire weekend.

Fees

In nearly every case, an investment bank charges a fee that is a percentage of the transaction value of the deal on which it has worked. In the same way that a real estate agent is paid only when he or she sells a house (and the higher the price, the larger the commission), bankers make most of their money if and when deals close. If a bank is representing a seller, there is generally a sliding scale for the fees.

---

*When a business decides to purchase a number of companies and combine them into one entity, it is called a "roll up."

For example, if a bank is trying to sell a company for $100 million, it might receive 2 percent of the sale price for the first $75 million and 4 percent of every dollar paid above that level. On larger deals, the percentage would likely be lower. Some firms have minimum fees, and some firms are on retainer, meaning that they are continually paid to look at potential transactions for a corporation or private equity firm. Even in a retainer situation, the bank has an incentive to complete a deal because it receives a "success fee" when it works on a deal that actually closes. Large transactions can be tremendously lucrative for the bank. For instance, one $20 billion deal can bring in more than $200 million in fees.

SALES AND TRADING SERVICES

Like the investment-banking division, the sales and trading (S&T) division makes money when transactions occur. Yet rather than making tens of millions of dollars in fees from a single deal, the sales and trading division generates money from commission fees charged for the execution of transactions for clients (as well as from proprietary trading profits). Sales and trading clients are generally entities that purchase large amounts of public securities; they may be mutual funds, hedge funds, insurance companies, or corporations. The division engages in primary transactions (for example, new security issuances, such as IPOs or bond sales) and secondary transactions (trading securities on the public market). A primary or secondary trade is either proprietary (when the bank buys a security itself) or a flow trade (when the bank orchestrates a trade between two outside parties).

Primary transactions (debt and equity issuances) are relatively complex processes that involve multiple divisions within a firm. For example, if a university decides to issue bonds (debt) to build a new building, it will retain the services of an investment bank, which will put together a preliminary statement about the issuance. The bank will assemble a working group, with bond experts from the sales and trading side of the firm and the university's financial advisor. The group will create a sales-point memo and provide highlights of it to the sales and syndicate desk, which is responsible for issuing the securities to the market. The memo will include such information as what is securing the bond (whether there is a revenue source that will be used to pay back the debt), what is pledged as collateral (such as other securities or real estate), what the purpose of the debt is, and the credit rating of the university. The underwriting desk will enter information about the issuance into a trading system, to be able to disseminate information and take orders electronically. The sales department is then responsible for selling the debt to the market.

On debt and equity issuances, the bank will buy the security at a slightly lower price than it believes it can sell it for. This "spread" provides the bank with a profit cushion in case it is not able to sell all the security on the market. Secondary transactions involve trading securities on the market. Trades for clients, called market making, include buying a stock for a pension fund and orchestrating the sale of debt by a mutual fund to a hedge fund.

The sales and trading division is divided by investment areas: fixed income, currency, commodities (together referred to as FICC), equities, and derivatives. Within each of those areas are more specialized groups, such as municipal government debt (municipal bonds are called "munis") and European equities.

Investment banks use their access to inexpensive capital (borrowed money with low interest rates) and large balance sheets to engage in billions of dollars of transactions. Their ability to access capital at low rates is, in part, a function of the significant trading and lending that occurs between the firms. This allows trading to be incredibly profitable, but it also makes the banks heavily dependent on one another's ability to meet their obligations. This became apparent when the collapse of Lehman Brothers nearly pulled down the investment-banking system.

Profit and Loss in Sales and Trading

The proprietary trading groups can be important profit centers for banks. The strategies they utilize differ and are highly confidential, but the objective is to use money borrowed cheaply by the firm and make trades that garner returns higher than the cost of the borrowed money.

In many ways, these groups operate like hedge funds and employ many of the strategies to be discussed in Chapter 4. For example, a proprietary trading group might engage in a multi-layered "carry trade," in which it shorts yen and lends money in dollars. Since the interest rate the bank pays on the borrowed yen is much lower than interest rates it collects on the loan in the United States, the trader is able to profit from the difference (assuming the currency exchange rate does not move significantly).* These groups also employ algorithmic programs to capture small profit opportunities that arise as a result of pricing discrepancies across global markets.

Sales and trading divisions utilize a great deal of advanced computer technology to execute many of their trading functions. Unlike investment-banking divisions, which rely largely on Excel and Power-Point programs that have been around for decades, S&T divisions invest millions of dollars in sophisticated computer and electronic trading systems. These tools are used to effectively route trades orders (to buy and sell at optimal prices), identify and capitalize on inefficiencies in the market, and avoid disclosure of large buy or sell orders. Secrecy in large trades is important to prevent people from profiting through pre-buying or selling just before a large order. For instance, if Fidelity wants to buy a million shares of stock in a company, it does not want prior knowledge of its large order to increase the stock price as it is making the purchase.

Sales people and traders not only sell and trade traditional assets, they also create securities called structured financial products. Clients' financial needs often cannot be met by traditional securities, so they turn to investment banks to help them structure new instruments. For example, airlines' operating expenses are highly influenced by the cost of oil, which fuels airplanes. In order to mitigate massive fluctuations in operating budgets, the airlines work with investment banks to trade oil derivatives. A derivative is a financial contract based on the value of something else, such as oil. The oil derivatives that airlines buy

---

*As long as the pricing of a debt instrument remains stable, if the interest the debt produces exceeds the cost of borrowing for the investor, a positive "carry" is generated.

through banks permit the airlines to buy oil at prearranged prices. Owning a derivative can cost an airline money if oil prices drop, but it also protects it from being in a dire position if oil prices skyrocket. Similarly, companies that generate significant portions of their revenue abroad can hedge their exposure to fluctuations in foreign currency with derivatives, in order to create more operational stability.

Within sales and trading there are two types of transactions: cash and synthetic. Cash transactions involve a security available on the public market, in which one party pays another for that asset. Synthetic transactions involve customized financial products and contracts, like the derivatives discussed above. The cash trading business is mostly commoditized across the banks—meaning that there is very little difference in the service or product offered—so the bigger profit opportunities exist in synthetic trading.

It was, in part, because of synthetic transactions that the sales and trading divisions across Wall Street were making so much money in the early 2000s. However, in doing so they were taking huge risks. In addition to creating structured products, such as oil derivatives for the airlines, the banks were also packaging various forms of debt—consumer mortgages and car loans, commercial real estate loans as well as high-yield leveraged buyout loans—and selling them to investors. Segments of the consumer loan universe, namely mortgage-backed securities (MBSs), received high ratings from the credit agencies and, consequently, could be sold off to an array of investors who were looking for financial products with little perceived risk and solid returns. In order to create these packaged securities, the banks had to purchase the underlying debt, so at all times they owned billions of dollars of these loans.

The investment banks recognized that these products entailed risk and wanted to have a hedge on their exposure. To protect themselves, some banks sought insurance to protect against losses from defaults on the loans. That insurance was called "credit default swaps," and one of the largest providers was AIG. The banks purchased these instruments, which paid out only if there was a default on the debt being insured. AIG presumably assumed that, although some loans might go into default, there was no reason that a huge portion of loans would simultaneously do so. Yet, in 2008, the massive deterioration in real estate–related securities and the market dislocation caused by Lehman's bankruptcy left AIG owing tens of billions of dollars to credit-default-swap customers, namely large investment banks. AIG had insufficient cash to pay these claims and, without massive bailouts from the U.S. government, the firm would have been forced into bankruptcy. Had that happened, the investment banks that held credit default swaps would have experienced blows to their solvency. The bailout of AIG was, in part, a stability measure for the investment banking business, which had hedged its exposure against the potentially risky loans it made. Despite the credit default swaps, the deterioration in debt-related financial products still dramatically impaired the stability of the banks. Citigroup and Merrill Lynch, two banks with particularly large portfolios of collateralized debt obligations, experienced some of the most severe losses.

Among the ensuing wreckage on Wall Street was the elimination of thousands of sales and trading jobs. In some cases, banks disbanded entire trading groups (such as mortgage-backed securities) from which the banks no longer believed they could profit. However, sales and trading, on the whole, remains a key aspect of the investment-banking business.

ASSET-MANAGEMENT SERVICES

The responsibilities of the asset-management division usually include operating some alternative asset groups (internal private equity and hedge funds), managing investments for others, and offering services for investment firms, such as hedge funds. Some banks also own parts of mutual fund companies and have ownership stakes in other investment-related businesses.

The primary function of the asset-management (or wealth-management) division is advising individuals and institutional clients on how to invest their money. Some firms have retail-type investment-management services, such as Wells Fargo Advisors and Bank of America Investment Services, which do not require large account minimums. Other asset-management groups focus on individuals with high net worths. These firms tend to provide their clients with more services and a larger array of investment opportunities than do retail investment advisors. These opportunities include private equity, real estate, hedge funds, as well as selective mutual funds.

Working in the asset-management division involves assessing the value of different investment vehicles as well as maintaining existing client relationships and fostering new ones. The asset-management division generally does not pick individual stocks, bonds, or other financial assets, but selects managers and funds that it believes will produce strong returns. Because high–net worth clients tend to be relatively sophisticated investors, they often require highly personalized investment strategies. That higher level of service is justified for the banks, because wealthy individual clients can yield millions of dollars in management fees. In the past, asset-management clients were also potential investors in the banks' own investment funds. However, concerns about conflict of interest decreased this practice.

Internal Investment Funds

Many investment banks have groups that control a pool of capital to make private equity investments, run a fund-of-funds (investing with managers outside the bank), and/or operate a hedge fund. In most cases, the capital these groups invest comes from the firm's money, its employees, and outside investors. The investment bank takes a cut of the profits. As a result, employees who run incredibly successful internal funds often leave to start their own investment companies.

Although these internal funds can be very profitable, the experience of Bear Stearns's two failed hedge funds may cause some banks to hesitate before setting up highly leveraged investment entities. Bear Stearns itself did not hold a large share of either fund, but investors forced the firm to make an investment of over a billion dollars. This payment helped to stabilize things by paying some of the costs of the borrowed money the fund used. Nevertheless, it probably was one of the things that led to the deterioration in the market's confidence in the bank.

Fees

Like most investment advisors, banks charge management fees for all of a client's "assets under management." Some banks also have incentive fees, meaning they receive more money if their investment strategies yield strong results. The internal funds that the banks operate charge fees comparable to their "independent" peers, generally both a management fee and a portion of profits generated. The fee structures of venture capital, private equity, and hedge funds will be discussed in greater detail in subsequent chapters.

RESEARCH SERVICES

The research division of a bank informs the firm's investment staff and clients about the values, trends, and key issues affecting companies, industries, and global markets. Banks hope that the ideas their research departments offer will drive trading volume from clients, particularly institutional investors. Analysts are assigned to cover specific sectors and become experts in these topics. They listen to all earnings calls for the companies they cover and question senior officers from those firms. The reports they compile vary in length and depth, but often include information about stock trends, financial metrics, and valuation analysis. The valuation modeling helps the analysts to determine whether a stock is over- or under-priced. The research analysts are the ones on Wall Street who issue "buy," "sell," and "hold" recommendations regarding stocks. (They are like Jim Cramer on CNBC's show *Mad Money,* but with more analysis and less showmanship.) Given the thoroughness of most research departments, releases of reports can immediately impact stock prices.

Research is not limited to public equities; some analysts are focused on industries, commodities, and other asset classes. The members of the research department think like investors, but do not actually commit capital.

Although research divisions are meant to provide independent analysis of public securities, their neutrality has been compromised in the past. In the lead up to the tech bubble, research departments allegedly were in collusion with other parts of their banks, which encouraged analysts to favorably evaluate companies from which the banks sought to win business. Lawsuits ensued, and there are now greater controls that attempt to limit the impact of external forces on a research department's analyses.

"BOUTIQUE" BANKS

The increased size and breadth of investment banks created an opportunity for the development of smaller, more focused banks in the mid-to-late 1990s. These firms, called boutique banks, tend to focus on investment-banking advisory services, often in a particular sector (such as technology or healthcare) or a region of the country (such as the Silicon Valley or the Southeast).

Most boutique banks originated when partners at bulge-bracket banks (the industry term for large, multiservice investment banks) decided to start their own businesses. For example, before starting Greenhill & Co., one of the largest boutique banks, Robert Greenhill was the CEO of Smith Barney and a former head of investment banking at Morgan Stanley. Similarly, Kenneth Moelis left his position as president of UBS Investment Bank to start the investment-banking advisory firm Moelis & Company. "We are in a period of time when many of these smaller boutiques have been able to do reasonably well," says Bill Shutzer, who was a managing director at Lehman Brothers before joining Evercore Partners. "They recruit senior people from large firms, who are tired of the politics or bureaucracy of a bigger firm or don't want to work quite as hard. There are plenty of reasons why someone would want to join or help start a boutique. I think there will be more of them in today's world." Senior bankers leave bulge-bracket firms with large rolodexes and expertise in specific industries or deal types. They are able to secure new work through the reputations they have built during their careers. The public condemnation that was hurled at bankers from large firms in late 2008, and the increased government scrutiny and restrictions placed on bulge-bracket banks, contributed to many senior bankers pursuing this route. Boutique investment banks usually provide only advisory services on deals and do not have roles in selling the debt from such deals on the public markets.

PART 2

INSIDE AN INVESTMENT BANK

ORGANIZATIONAL CULTURE AND LIFESTYLE

Working in investment banking is not always glamorous. One Goldman Sachs banker described the effects of the grueling nature of the work. He found an associate "lying in the fetal position on a New York City sidewalk" in front of their apartment building, dressed in a now-filthy, thousand-dollar suit. The associate had worked "48 hours straight and finding that he had left his keys at his desk, simply passed out in front of the building," too exhausted to return to the office to get his keys. Although nearly everyone at an investment bank works hard, the lifestyle varies between the divisions. Investment bankers, who work in a service capacity, tend to work the longest hours—often eighty to a hundred hours per week. This entails working past midnight every night during the week and putting in full days on the weekends. Even at the vice-presidential level, the work-life balance can be uneven. Vice presidents may work six or seven days per week, for a total of seventy or more hours, and travel frequently. For those who do not love the deal process, this tends to be unsustainable. In addition, one needs to be available to clients and often operate on their schedules. "The least enjoyable aspect was not the number of hours I had to work, but the need to constantly be on call with limited flexibility," explains Suzanne Nora Johnson, former vice chairman of Goldman Sachs.

Banking is a business with lavish perks, but they often come at a lifestyle cost. "The banking group that I worked in had a trip out to Alta [a ski resort in Utah]," recalled one banking analyst. "The cost was proportional to your level within the firm, so analysts only had to pay fifty dollars for this lavish weekend. However, even though it was meant as a firm-sponsored event to relax, it was far from work free. Analysts would be in the middle of ski runs and get urgent BlackBerry messages that they were 'needed ASAP at the base lodge.' What was needed was never critical or something that the VPs could not have done themselves, but in banking, when possible, higher ups always delegate unexciting tasks to the analysts." Many of the most lavish banking perks were cut or scaled back amidst the government bailouts and public scrutiny.

Employees in sales and trading less commonly have to work weekends and all night, but their days start early—around 6 A.M. for many traders. Work time is intense, particularly during the hours that relevant public markets are open. Traders have their lunches delivered to them so that they do not have to leave the multiple monitors on their desks, which show financial news and the prices of whatever they trade.

Traders tend to embody a kill-or-be-killed mentality, even at the most junior levels. "When I started working in sales and trading, the head of the division came to speak with all the new summer interns," recalls one banker. "In his remarks on that first day of work, he said, 'Don't even think about calling in sick. If I hear that one of you called in sick, consider yourself fired. If you can't play hurt, don't play at all.' He was no less intense in describing the work we would do in the office. 'When you come into the office in the morning, you should read every article in every business publication—*The Wall Street Journal, Financial Times,* etc. If I ask you what's on page three of the *Journal* I expect you to be able to name three or four of the articles on that page.'"

The principal investment groups at banks (the internal hedge funds and private equity groups) put in hours that generally fall somewhere between those of the traders and the bankers. Wealth management involves perhaps the tamest work lifestyle of the major areas within a bank, but there are night and weekend events that cater to institutions and wealthy individual clients.

The nonstop lifestyle of many banking jobs is not just a function of the associates' work schedules but also of an active social life. Many find that with the combination of intense work and partying, it is sleep that gives way. An analyst at Citigroup recalls:

> On a Thursday night, I went to a holiday party hosted by the head of my trading group. I ended up staying out partying until 4 A.M. at which time I had an important game time decision: go back to my apartment in Hoboken [New Jersey] to catch an hour of sleep or go

straight to the office. Though going straight back to work seemed unappealing, I knew there was a high likelihood that if I went home I would oversleep and get yelled at for being late. I got to the office at 4:30 A.M. and slept with my head on the keyboard until 5:30 A.M. when I heard "Anteneh, is that you?" I awoke, startled to find the head of trading standing next to me. "What are you doing here?" I decided honesty was the best policy on this one and explained my logic about preferring to catch a nap in the office rather than potentially being late. He laughed, said I made the right call and even offered me the couch in his office for the next time I found myself sleeping at the firm.

Needless to say, the investment-banking lifestyle does not leave a lot of time for other pursuits. However, it is possible to fit in public service, if that is a priority. "For the first couple of years it is difficult to spend a lot of time doing service, but at Goldman there were a variety of service projects offered that could be fit into the parameters of your schedule," says Suzanne Nora Johnson. "Early in my time at Goldman, I was a member of a team that would spend one morning every other week with a class at a New York City public school in East New York. Being able to participate meant that you had to push yourself to get your work done and be able to devote that amount of time to service."

CHARACTERISTICS FOR SUCCESS

Succeeding in any division of an investment bank requires intelligence, strong communication skills, the ability to think through a set of principles or concepts, and the wherewithal to see different perspectives on the same market or asset. The most successful people are extraordinarily client focused, resourceful, driven, and collegial. In some areas, especially in investment banking and wealth management—in which people work in teams—collegiality is particularly important. At Goldman Sachs, among other metrics, a significant part of an employee's evaluation is how well he or she works with others. "We have a 365-degree review system, whereby anyone who has interacted with you in the workplace reviews you," explains Suzanne Nora Johnson, former vice chairman of the firm. "People are evaluated by those both above and below, as well as their peers within the organization. With this system you can have insight on whether people are good at managing up and down. However, having a team focus does not mean that mediocrity is tolerated or absorbed by team members."

There are differences between the types of people who succeed in various divisions. Advisory work requires persistence and endurance. A significant portion of one's success comes from being able to maintain a positive attitude and pleasant demeanor, even after one has been at the office late into the night and through the weekend for a couple of weeks in a row. Sales people enjoy the selling process, have a deep knowledge of finance, and can present complex investment instruments in ways that are easy to understand. Traders are competitive people who tolerate risk and thrive in high-intensity, chaotic environments.

The intensity of the work also requires employees to figure out how to live with imperfection. "For people new to the industry, the ability to work through fear of your own ignorance and resign yourself to the occasional constructive failure is also essential," said Chuck Mc-Mullan of UBS. "Fear of not being perfect can freeze some very smart people. In banking, getting to a fast B-plus is generally remembered more positively than getting to a slow A-plus. To some people, that is hard to adapt to."

Who enjoys banking? "Very smart people, who see that the outlet for their talent is working with, learning from, and contributing to deal teams comprised of other smart, ambitious people," say Arash Farin, who has worked at Goldman Sachs, Blackstone, and Lehman Brothers. "Many of them are deal junkies and enjoy coming up with new or innovative ideas and pitching them to their clients. They love finance and are quantitative. They have a thirst for deal making and an interest in seeing it through to fruition. They are highly ambitious and stop at nothing to be successful."

PROMOTION AND MOBILITY

The most important skill sets change as one becomes more senior. "At the analyst and associate level, bankers are production units. They are graded on their ability to produce accurately, not necessarily their ability to think. As you get higher up, you no longer produce, you become a captain," explains Jeff Bloomberg, a principal at Gordon Brothers and a former senior managing director at Bear Stearns. At the senior level, bankers are responsible for developing and then maintaining client relationships, strategic thinking, and product development. This requires a reasonable amount of social interaction with one's clients to help create lasting bonds. As a result, notes Bloomberg, "many people who ultimately would be good managing directors wash out or have a difficult start, because they are ill-equipped for the entry position where production skills are of paramount importance."

Traditionally, a large portion of the industry's leaders have come from investment-banking divisions. Recently, however, traders have taken many top jobs. Suzanne Nora Johnson explains, "Wherever the money is being made in a firm, the people leading those divisions will ascend in rank. At Goldman Sachs, there is a long history of alternating leadership between the advisory and trading sides of the business." Bill Shutzer, senior managing director of Evercore Partners, elaborates: "Right now it would be hard to say the sales and trading side of most firms wouldn't be the key area. Many of the investment banks are large and have so many assets. Making a return on those assets, as opposed to doing a financial advisory assignment, is the more lucrative place to be at any of these big investment banks."

Not all industry leaders began their careers at large investment banks. Right out of business school, Jamie Dimon passed on job offers from top banks and instead chose to work for Sandy Weill at American Express. "I had this unique opportunity to go be Sandy Weill's assistant. The position was offering a lot less money [than the investment banks], but I was going to have an inside look at how a big company works, with a boss who I believed was a pretty exciting guy. I thought that 'worst comes to worst, I can always come back to Wall Street; this is a chance to do something unique.' And I never looked back." Weill and Dimon worked together for sixteen years and built Citigroup through a series of mergers and acquisitions.

Business school is not a prerequisite to promotion, but can be a valuable experience. Alan Schwartz, who worked across divisions at Bear Stearns before rising to the position of CEO, says that he now thinks more highly of business school. "Undergraduates are exposed to a narrow focus. . . . [In business school] people get a chance to round out their business knowledge and skills. I think they then have a much better opportunity of growing in an organization, rather than potentially hitting the top of a silo and not having the skills to go across." However, he does not think that an MBA is a requirement if someone is at an entrepreneurial organization that places an emphasis on training and career flexibility. Other degrees can also be advantageous in investment banking. JDs, PhDs, and analytical masters degrees lack the business breadth of an MBA, but can provide different sets of skills that allow people to thrive in investment banking.

Investment banking provides institutional support and guidance, but it is a not an industry that holds an employee's hand. Learning the ropes is as much about watching successful individuals in the firm as it is about being told what to do by mentors. "I think that there are very few people who go out of their way to help you keep your eyes open," says Alan Schwartz, the former CEO of Bear Stearns. "On the other hand, there are people with a wealth of knowledge and experience. Of the mentoring I received, it was 25 percent what people told me directly and 75 percent what I absorbed from watching them. I think that people who look for mentoring to be handed to them on a plate are probably going to be disappointed."

The continued specialization of areas within investment banking is both good and bad in terms of flexibility within the firm. On the one hand, people can be pigeonholed earlier in a specific area, such as trading municipal bonds. However, as banks continue to develop new financial products and services, they will continue to seek people in existing areas to work in and run the new businesses.

One of the constraining factors with lateral mobility is compensation. It is usually easier to move early in one's career than to move midway through. "Historically, lateral mobility is highest in years two through six," says Suzanne Nora Johnson. "At this stage you have some experience, but you're not too costly to hire relative to someone with more experience. If people are moving laterally when they are older, the perception is that hiring them is riskier and more expensive, and that they will be more difficult to retain."

Vertical and diagonal mobility, however, is common at the senior level when people are promoted into roles with increasing responsibility. The head of a trading desk might gain responsibility for a firm's entire trading operation or join the firm's management committee. However, at this level, lateral mobility is rare. For example, a senior trader focused on corporate debt is unlikely to become a mergers-and-acquisitions investment banker.

There is a natural progression of traders who start their own hedge funds and of bankers who join private equity shops and boutique M&A advisory firms. "Banking prepares you well to pursue other opportunities," adds Suzanne Nora Johnson. "One of the things that the world is most in need of is people who can synthesize well. Banking teaches this, as well as the ability to see different points of view and an understanding of capital." She adds that a number of partners at Goldman Sachs have gone into public service, including Robert Rubin and Hank Paulson, both former secretaries of the Treasury, and Jon Corzine, the former governor of New Jersey. Other firms also claim many alumni who became active in public service and the not-for-profit sector. For example, George Schultz, a former secretary of state, worked at J.P. Morgan, and university president Erskine Bowles worked at Morgan Stanley.

COMPENSATION

The high compensation attracts many people to investment banking. In good times, first-year investment-banking analysts can earn between $125,000 and $150,000, with significant increases year after year. At the vice presidential level, compensation can reach $400,000 to $600,000. Prior to the 2008 downturn, these numbers had been steadily increasing for a few years. Then, suddenly, people who were expecting more of the same ended up unemployed or with significant reductions in earnings. The vast majority of compensation comes in the form of annual bonuses (rather than large base salaries), so it is relatively easy for firms to trim compensation. The economic downturn and the resulting pay cuts made a huge number of people who worked at investment banks very unhappy. "They should be pleased to still have their jobs, but the issue is that this year they are making significantly less money than they expected and than people did the year before," said a trading associate about his colleagues in 2008. "There are a lot of people who would rather be working in a nonprofit or feeling like they were doing something that was changing the world. The huge compensation had been keeping them happy, but, all of a sudden, with that gone, they are coming to terms with the fact that they really do not enjoy the job itself."

Even Goldman Sachs, one of the banks in the best position throughout the decline in the financial sector, dramatically cut its employee compensation. In 2008, the firm paid $10.9 billion in compensation and benefits, compared with $20.2 billion in 2007.[12] The decrease came through a combination of layoffs and smaller bonuses.[13]

The payment of bonuses to executives at the insurance company AIG in 2008 sparked massive public outrage at the pay levels within firms receiving government money. This led members of Congress to draft a bill taxing compensation over $250,000 at 90 percent for employees of firms that received large amounts of federal bailout money. This bill was not enacted into law, but it certainly scared many in the industry. Although regulation of compensation may still be effected, the industry is likely to find new ways to compensate its most successful participants.

Before the investment-banking crash, Alan Schwartz, the former CEO at Bear Stearns, warned people about entering investment banking solely for the money. "Don't even think about trying to base your decision of what you want to do, based on where the money is being made," he said. "If anybody had said thirty-something years ago when I was getting out of school that going to a brokerage firm would be an area where you could make a lot of money (a lot of money in the context of what people are thinking about today), you never would have dreamed it versus getting a top corporate job or top consulting job, but changes occurred." He explained that while people should decide whether they want to be in an industry where profit motive ranks high versus academia or the social sector, picking an industry within the business world because of compensation does not make sense.

THE BALANCE OF THE SEXES

Although Wall Street was once heavily male dominated, women now have fairly equal access to top firms at the entry level. Most banks have been relatively effective in recruiting women, and there are institutional programs to boost the number of female recruits. That being said, the industry's leaders are still mostly men. Suzanne Nora Johnson, one of the most prominent female bankers, notes that "the numbers are still skewed towards men on Wall Street. Banking has not reached the gender balance of professional schools or even other service professions. However, I think we have made some progress over the past two decades, particularly at the analyst level."

HIRING PRACTICES

When hiring, banks look for many of the same characteristics as do other professional service firms: high achievement, strong academic performance, and a record of leadership. However, most important is a true excitement for the type of work and the demonstration of a personal drive to responsibly and diligently execute time-sensitive tasks. Regardless of the compensation, people who do not enjoy investments or deal-making burn out very quickly. Banks assess a candidate's true interest through interviews. "A good [interviewee] story starts with why you want the job and how you are a differentiated candidate," explains Chuck McMullan of UBS. "Knowledge of what an investment bank or broker does, and what investment banking is, are also important. With so much information available, a demonstrable effort to understand finance ideas and topics also counts more and more. But, these days, competitive candidates are all smart, informed, and hard working, so getting the job—like succeeding at the job—requires an element of personal salesmanship." Banks often seek to test candidates' mental toughness and financial acumen during the interview process. Interviewees may be asked technical questions, such as "Why would the chairman of the Federal Reserve consider changing interest rates?" or investment questions, such as "What stock would you be most excited to buy tomorrow?" Interviewees are not expected to answer every question correctly, but their ability to deal with pressure and think on their feet is evaluated.

Smart college athletes are particularly prized by investment banks. In fact, former Morgan Stanley banker Ron Mitchell created a company, Alumni Athlete Network, that focuses exclusively on placing athletes in investment banks and corporations. Athletes are naturally competitive and are used to getting up early, training hard, and knowing how to take criticism. Investment banking requires great mental endurance, and sales and trading has the environment of a nonstop, twelve-hour athletic competition, in that it demands that players digest lots of information and respond to requests from all directions. The top twenty-five colleges tend to be major feeders for investment banking, but firms are open to candidates from a wide array of schools.

PART 3

INSIGHTS FROM INDUSTRY LEADERS

JAMIE DIMON, CEO OF JPMORGAN CHASE & CO.

Jamie Dimon is in the rare position of having led a major investment bank through the financial crisis and come out of the turmoil stronger than ever. Over the last two years his firm, J.P. Morgan, has acquired major competitors and gained share in key markets.

In the last year, a number of pundits have talked about the dangers of having banks "too big to fail." Through the acquisitions of Bear Stearns and Washington Mutual, J.P. Morgan has become even larger than it was at the beginning of the economic crisis. Does the size of firms like yours pose future dangers to the financial system or is the "too big" criticism a red herring?

It is mostly a red herring because a significant portion of the size of these organizations is related to the size of their counterparties, their credit, and their exposures. You can't be in our business, have enormous credit exposure to a thousand corporations, institutions, and governments around the world, and not have that scale. The need for increasing programming and data centers, among other things, requires us to get bigger. There may be parts of big banks that don't require that scale for execution, but for the most part the needs of the services provided drives the economies of scale.

The non-red-herring part is that if banks are too big to fail, such that the government has to subsidize them to prevent a failure, then there is a societal question: "How much can the government lose if one of these things needs to be taken over?" The right answer to that question is that the government builds resolution mechanisms. Those mechanisms would allow the company to fail, for it to then be taken over, managed, and then dismantled the way the FDIC does with big U.S. [retail] banks. It is a little more complicated in the case of investment banks because the business is more complex and they are global, but a resolution mechanism is still possible. As a citizen, you don't want to stop a company from failing. What you really want to have is a resolution mechanism that allows the banks to fail, but in a way that does not bring down the financial system of your country.

You have said that taking TARP funds was not necessary for your firm, but that it was the right thing to do for the U.S. financial system. On an ongoing basis, are there decisions J.P. Morgan makes that prioritize the system over short-term profits or is the only constraint the regulations you are required to abide by?
One of the great misconceptions about business is that everything you do is for profit. A lot of times you do things that are good for the employees, good for the system, and good for the client. You have to build the data centers, the products, and the services. Profit is an outcome of doing a great job for customers and earning a fair profit on it. What you earn as a profit in a quarter has to do with actions you have taken over the last five years. It's no different across businesses. It's not just "this is profit and everything else comes second." You always try to build the right type of company. When it came to Bear Stearns or TARP you couldn't have done something that was completely negative to shareholders. With Bear Stearns, we did it because we were asked and we believed it would help the system, but we had to do it in a way that made sense for shareholders.

What do you think it will take for investment banking, as an industry, to regain its prestige?

I think almost everything has lost its prestige, which I believe is a bad thing. There is also a paradox. If you ask people "do you trust lawyers?" they say "no," but if you ask "do you trust *your* lawyer?" they say "yes." It may just be some sort of group-think that gets created by the media and other factors. Most of the customers that do business with us, like us. But "banks" collectively are viewed with distrust right now. It is going to take a while to get out. I believe it's true that some financial companies did terrible things and helped damage the system, but not all of them. They all got painted with the same brush and I think that's unfair.

You seem to offer much more disclosure on J.P. Morgan's operations than some of your peers. Do you think the industry overall should be more transparent to the public?

While companies all have different strategies, I believe that being transparent is a good thing for all of them. It's a good thing both for shareholders, who want to know all about the company, and for the people inside the company. I have always been afraid that if you always put a spin on how well you are doing, when you are not doing well, you teach the people inside the company that they're doing well even when they are not. For me, honesty is the best policy. Everyone knows where you are, where you are going. Ultimately it makes you do a better job. Over a many-year period you do a better job, even if you point out your own warts now and then. I am in the Warren Buffett school on that.

What is your view on the government actions in the banking sector over the last two years, and its position in the financial sector today? Do the banks with significant government ownership have any competitive advantages?

I think that the actions that Paulson, Geithner, and Bernanke took really did help the system. We will never know for sure, but they likely prevented things from getting a lot worse. That does not mean that they bailed out every bank. A lot of banks would have done fine regardless of their actions, but even the ones who were doing fine were better off as a result of the government intervention, as is every business and every individual.

Now, of course, the government has a controlling stake in a lot of these banks. It remains to be seen how they will act with those. They should let companies like AIG and Citi do what is in their own best interest in order to get as healthy as they can as quick as they can. I hope that political influence does not impede that from happening. It would be bad for the system, bad for the customers of those companies, and bad for the employees.

SUZANNE NORA JOHNSON, FORMER VICE CHAIRMAN OF GOLDMAN SACHS

Suzanne Nora Johnson never aspired to work in investment banking. Upon graduating from USC she enrolled in Harvard Law and later clerked for a circuit court of appeals. After working at a law firm for a few years she applied to a World Bank program. Despite her legal training, the World Bank responded that she needed financial experience before she could apply. She joined Goldman Sachs and ended up having a career that spanned two decades. During her time at the firm she was responsible for the Latin American Business, Healthcare Investment Banking, the Global Research Division, and the Global Markets Institute.

Law school is a somewhat unusual background for a career in finance. What drove you to pursue that route?
From the work I did in the community, while an undergraduate at the University of Southern California, I realized that economic independence and access to capital was key to pulling people out of poverty. I did not know that I wanted to pursue a career in finance but I had the sense that developing a financial skill set was important to be able to make a positive social impact. At that time, law school provided a broad experience in understanding the intersection of markets and the legal system. I also developed a method of analytical thinking that has proven very useful.

While working in the legal field, I applied to the Young Professionals Program at the World Bank, which told me that it would not even consider my application until I had two years of finance experience at an investment or commercial bank. Since I was eager to participate in the World Bank program, I decided to find a bank to gain the requisite experience. I had three criteria in selecting the firms to which I applied. First, the institution had to be ethical. Second, it had to be intellectually robust and respected by clients. Third, I had to be confident that the bank would survive for at least two years (the time at which I would be reapplying to the World Bank program). I applied to three firms and ended up at Goldman Sachs. I started in the firm's private finance division in investment banking, where I had the opportunity to work on projects ranging from infrastructure to small business to venture capital and private equity. Because of the small size and project range of the group, I developed experience in investment banking very quickly. I was exposed to a broad array of financing vehicles, which allowed me to constantly be learning new things.

Did you find investment banking to be a fulfilling profession?
It was very fulfilling to bring capital providers together with companies that were growing and doing good things, creating jobs, and new products. I helped start Goldman's Latin American Business and was able to provide companies on the continent with access to capital that enabled them to grow. Similarly, it was an extraordinary feeling to be able to provide capital for biotech companies to assist them in becoming sustainable economic forces when they were at a critical stage in the industry's development.

CHAPTER TWO

THE SHEPHERDS AND BUILDERS OF BUSINESS

VENTURE CAPITAL AND

ENTREPRENEURSHIP

Venture capital is one of the greatest businesses in the world but, like everything in life, it is high risk-high return. You do take high beta bets; you do lose companies; you do have to fire management teams. If you don't have your feet on the ground, have really good partners and a good stomach, it is not the business for you.

—Jeff Hurst, cofounder of Commonwealth Capital Ventures

My definition of an entrepreneur is one who steals office supplies from home and brings them to work. It is just a different mindset. There are elementary school teachers who bring crayons into class from home; that is the entrepreneurial mindset. These guys at Fortune 500 companies who you read about in the paper taking all of these perks; that is the opposite of being entrepreneurial.

—Auren Hoffman, entrepreneur

A HISTORY AND DESCRIPTION OF
VENTURE CAPITAL AND ENTREPRENEURSHIP

Susan walks down what feels like the 200th row of booths at the annual Software Industry Conference. Although her firm finds many of the emerging businesses in which it invests through the extensive network of entrepreneurs it has worked with, as an associate she is responsible for doing her own sourcing. Thousands of businesses are started each year, and only a few become great successes. While having an extensive network is great, Susan is well aware that many of America's largest corporations—such as Oracle, Apple, and Microsoft—were created by unproven, first-time entrepreneurs.

Back in her office, business plans and technology trade journals are piling up. Every day, Susan[1] looks at ten or more proposals from people who are seeking venture investment and meets with at least one entrepreneur whose business proposal seems promising. Although she loves the hunt for new businesses, the trips always set her back at work and result in long days at the office after she returns. Nevertheless, Susan recognizes that "a lot of work" for her pales in comparison with the schedules of her friends who work on Wall Street.

Susan made a tradeoff by going into the venture business, forgoing higher initial compensation and the fun of working in the center of a city (her firm's office is located in a tech-heavy suburb of Boston) to engage in one of the financial industry's more "Lone-Ranger" fields. Susan loves the thought of living the lifestyle of the partners at her firm. Most of the senior people work reasonable hours and divide their time between reviewing new business opportunities and collaborating with the managements of their portfolio companies. At the associate level, the process of finding and evaluating new companies for the firm, though exciting, lacks the camaraderie enjoyed by her friends who work in other fields of business. Susan also misses the excitement of building her own company (she started a mobile ringtone business the year after she graduated from college, which helped her get this job). However, she enjoys the ability to learn about and be involved with businesses across a number of different industries, rather than being limited to a narrow space as an entrepreneur on the front lines of an emerging technology. More importantly, the venture business gives Susan the opportunity to play a role in providing capital and helping to advise a host of companies that have the potential to create jobs and new products that will reach millions of people.

WE ORIGINALLY planned to have separate chapters on venture capital and entrepreneurship. However, during the research and interviewing processes, it became clear that the two business areas have a symbiotic relationship and that the careers of many people involve working and interacting within both fields. Entrepreneurship, in the context of business, is the process of taking a new product or idea for a company and building it into a business. Venture capitalists seek to find entrepreneurs with business plans and young companies that have the capacity for significant growth that need capital in order to start or expand. A venture-capital firm invests in a company in return for equity (partial ownership of the business). The venture capitalist then works with the firm's management to develop the company and, after a number of years (if the business does well), to assist in the sale of the business to a corporation or help take the company public.

ENTREPRENEURSHIP

Modern entrepreneurship has many forms, including founding a nonprofit organization, starting a new division of a large company, and developing an idea into a multibillion-dollar business. Not all entrepreneurs need venture capital to build their organizations, but venture funding has contributed to the development of many of the largest corporations in the United States, including Microsoft, Google, Apple, Sun Microsystems, Starbucks, Amazon, and eBay.

Although venture capital is an enabler of new businesses, the U.S. obsession with entrepreneurship is the catalyst for the development of new companies. Thousands of businesses are started every year in the United States, and, with the exception of those who have inherited wealth, nearly every new American billionaire is an entrepreneur. The investment firms that Julian Robertson and Henry Kravis started do not produce products, but they too were entrepreneurial ventures. Starting their own firms and controlling large portions of their businesses' profits is what enabled these two men to become extremely wealthy by managing money.

Of course, entrepreneurs who attain great financial success are the exceptions, not the rule. More than 10 percent of Americans are self-employed, and tens of thousands of businesses are started each year. However, three-fourths of all new businesses have no employees, and less than one-third of new companies are still in business ten years after they are incorporated.[2] Beating the odds requires a strong value proposition for customers (offering them something they cannot already get or a better or cheaper version than competitors), a strong team to execute the business plan, and, often, some luck.

For example, Noah Glass had an idea for a service by which people could preorder coffee or food through their cell phones. The service was innovative and had a strong potential market in Manhattan, where lines at popular coffee shops and fast-food places during peak times are often massive. However, the company, GoMobo, did not take off at first and it received little publicity. "I had spent two months sending out press kits that I had meticulously worked on, but people, at least those who would even take my calls, kept saying that GoMobo was not a story until we were in a thousand stores," recalls Glass. He decided that he had to go "grass roots" in order to garner new customers. He and three of his employees donned large sandwich boards and handed out flyers on Wall Street advertising the service. With that act of entrepreneurial scrappiness, GoMobo caught a break. "One of the four us— I like to think it was me—happened to hand a flyer to a tech writer for the *Wall Street Journal*," relates Glass. The writer liked the concept and wrote an article about the service. Having seen the piece, Dow Jones and CBS Radio called to gather information for their own stories. Venture investment gave GoMobo the ability to get off the ground, but it took hard work to make the business a success.

For every great entrepreneurial story like this, there are hundreds of others in which good business ideas never got off the ground. Venture-capital–backed companies have better success records than the general pool of startups, but many do not develop into large and profitable businesses.

There is no way to comprehensively explain the mechanics of entrepreneurship, as no two businesses evolve in exactly the same way. However, understanding venture capital provides insight into the stages a new business goes through and knowledge about one of its most important potential sources of funding.

THE HISTORY OF VENTURE CAPITAL

The genesis of modern venture capital, commonly referred to as "VC," occurred after World War II, but the basic idea originated much farther back in history. In fact, Christopher Columbus's voyage to the Americas was enabled by a venture-capital investment. Columbus was an entrepreneur who believed that, by pioneering a new route to the Indies, he could generate significant economic value. He needed the financial support of someone with a lot of money to procure a ship and crew to sail the new route he envisioned. After being rejected by the Portuguese and the British, Columbus turned to the Spanish monarchs Ferdinand II and Isabella, who became his financial backers. As with some businesses, Columbus's venture did not work out as he planned; nevertheless, the monarchs realized a significant financial return on their investment.[3]

After World War II, a group of East Coast business and civic leaders was concerned about the effect of New Deal reforms and the ability of the U.S. financial system to recover from the Great Depression. This group believed that World War II investments in technology had the potential to be the seeds for a host of new American businesses that could drive growth in the overall economy. At the time, there was a lack of institutions with money dedicated to making investments in new businesses.[4] In 1946, members of that group helped create American Research and Development, the first modern, non-family venture-capital firm. Previously, wealthy families such as the Rockefellers had created their own venture-investment vehicles, but American Research and Development was the first venture fund that had to raise its own capital from outside investors.[5]

Although having the money to invest is critical to venture capital, so is finding new ventures that are worth funding. In the aftermath of World War II, there were a few major catalysts for innovation. One was the vast number of scientists emigrating from Europe to escape persecution; these people had ideas, talents, and ambitions that flourished in America. The second was the Servicemen's Readjustment Act of 1944, commonly known as the "GI bill."[6] It provided money for young American veterans returning from war to pursue college educations and advanced training. The combination of talented scientists and veterans trained in technical fields allowed new businesses to flourish and venture firms to grow. Additionally, U.S. bankruptcy laws make failure less of a deterrent than it is in other countries. (In the United States, an entrepreneur has less personal liability if his or her business fails.) This encourages more people to take the entrepreneurial leap and allows those who fail to get up and try again.[7]

Venture capital's growing prominence in finance did not ensure continued success. Like nearly all sectors of business, it is subject to economic cycles. The U.S. economic decline in the mid-1970s caused many startups to go out of business, making investments worthless and forcing a number of venture firms to close. Nevertheless, for those that weathered the difficult years, the 1970s proved to be a time of significant opportunity. Successful venture firms racked up investment returns of 25 to 35 percent, compounded annually.[8] These returns were facilitated by two factors: a decrease in the capital gains tax in 1978 and an increase in the prices paid for small technology companies.

When a company is acquired, the purchase price is negotiated, but is roughly based on a multiple of the company's revenues or earnings. For example, if a business with $10 million in profit is purchased for $100 million, the buyer would have paid an earnings multiple of ten times. The multiple paid to acquire a company varies over time; in the late 1970s, it was on the rise. The tax changes and increasing multiples contributed to a quadrupling of money invested by venture-capital firms. From 1975 to 1980, investment by such firms grew from $250 million to $1 billion.[9] In the 1970s, new technology, a key driver of the venture business, started to pick up significantly with the advent of the personal computer. The PC spawned an accelerating use of technology in the workplace, which created an opportunity for a new wave of innovation and more opportunities for venture capital firms to invest.

During the 1980s, most venture firms were located in either Boston or the Silicon Valley and predominantly funded entrepreneurs in their own geographic areas. A few firms took a more international approach—most notably TA Associates and General Atlantic Partners.[10] The European markets, in which they invested, had limited venture capital, and the U.S. firms sought to take advantage of changes, such as the creation of new French technologies that could compete in the United States. The venture-capital market in Europe was small at the time because the prevailing view was that large corporations, not entrepreneurs, would be the sources of new products and services (a view that proved to be somewhat self-reinforcing). Today, many top U.S. firms have offices in London, India, Israel, and China, although Boston and San Francisco remain the biggest centers for the industry.

In the 1980s, venture capital was proving successful but was still flying under the radar of public consciousness. That made it more difficult to find entrepreneurs to fund. Bruce Evans, a managing director at the firm now called Summit Partners, recalls, "Our name at the beginning was Summit Ventures, and when we would call entrepreneurs, their assistants invariably would say, 'Summit Adventures? What are you, a travel agency?' We had to explain the concept of venture capital to many people in ways that you don't any longer have to do." When Summit raised its first fund of $160 million in the 1980s, it was thought to be the largest first fund that had ever been raised, making it a big fish in what was a small pond. At that time, there were only 2,000 to 3,000 venture-capital professionals in the United States. However, that number grew, and, in 1995, the initial public offering of Netscape marked the beginning of the Internet boom and a five-year period of exponential growth for venture funds.[11]

Prior to the rapid Internet value expansion, the venture industry was investing roughly $20 billion per year. The market was limited because there were only so many new businesses that had strong potential for growth. In the mid-1990s, the success of venture-backed technology companies caused a massive expansion of the amount of money being raised for venture investments. This was aided by two factors. First, with increasing access to information, people could very quickly read about the high returns that certain firms were making. Second, there was more money that could be invested than ever before, particularly from pension funds. "What drove the bubble was people saying 'Wow, the venture returns are so great; I should have some money working there,'" notes Jeff Hurst, cofounder of Commonwealth Capital Ventures. "In the late '90s, new venture funds were raised by buyout firms, hedge funds, corporations, and even real estate guys who thought they could be in the venture business." [12]

At the market's peak in 2000, the multiples paid for high-tech businesses went through the roof, and so did the stock prices of public technology companies. People began to believe that the traditional methods for valuing new technology stocks were obsolete in the Internet age and that companies focused on the Internet had huge potential. Investors of all types poured money into new technology companies, in the form of private investments and purchases of stock in businesses that had gone public. "The additional funds invested created a lot of new competition; it put a lot of money in the hands, in some cases, of less-experienced people, and it drove up valuations," ex-

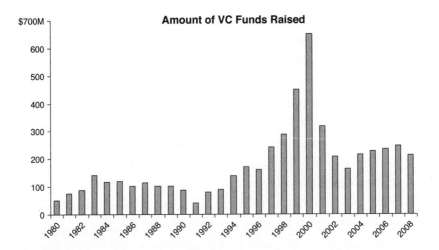

Source: Thomson, Venture Capital Association

plains Craig Foley, the former head of Chancellor Capital Management. "A lot of venture-capital firms were doing quick flips in a year or two and they began to believe that was sustainable. It used to be that you had to have a profitable company before you could take it public. And then it became possible to take companies public that were losing money. That could not and did not last."

When the tide went out, those who had thrown fundamental analysis to the wind and had been "swimming without bathing suits" were fully exposed. It was not a pretty sight. In March 2000, the NASDAQ, the public market on which most public Internet companies were traded, began a precipitous decline. With the NASDAQ's drop came the end of an era of inflated expectations about venture capital. In that process, a lot of invested capital became worthless as unprofitable companies went bankrupt, including well-advertised businesses, such as eToys.com and Pets.com, and thousands of others that no one had ever heard of (but on which investors had bet tens of millions of dollars). For example, in 1997, the startup eToys.com was formed with the aspiration of becoming the leader in online toy sales. Some well-respected venture-capital firms believed in the concept and invested millions of dollars. Two years later, the company went public. Prior to the mid-1990s, companies that went public tended to be large and profitable. Those profits and free cash flows were key inputs in valuing the businesses. However, like many other Internet-based companies in the late 1990s, when eToys.com sold shares on the NASDAQ stock exchange, the company was losing millions of dollars. Nevertheless, investors were so confident that the company would become a huge success that, in its first day of trading, the stock nearly quadrupled. At its peak, this Internet-based company, which was losing money, was valued at $8 billion. When the NASDAQ started to decline, investors began to fear that eToys.com might not be worth even a fraction of that amount and started selling their shares, which pushed the stock way down. By 2001, the business was still losing money, could not raise additional capital from the public market or venture firms, and declared bankruptcy.

As an industry, venture capital has performed quite well compared with the stock market. According to Thomson Reuters' performance index, all classes of venture investment—early stage, balanced, and later stage—have produced annual returns greater than 14 percent over the last two decades. It is important to note that the ten- and twenty-year returns are heavily influenced by successes in 1999 and 2000, at the peak of the tech bubble. Very soon, the ten-year returns will look less rosy, as blockbuster return years fall outside the period. Additionally, there is significant variation between firms, with top performers buoying the rest. A large number of firms have lost significant portions of their investors' money, while others have multiplied it many times. Most remarkably, Matrix Partners produced annualized returns of 516 percent on a fund raised in 1997 and 223 percent on its 1995 fund. Kleiner Perkins and Sequoia Capital also had back-to-back funds with annualized returns of greater than 100 percent.[13]

To function, venture capital needs three ingredients: investors in VC funds, entrepreneurs, and receptiveness among corporations and/or the public market to buy or invest in new companies. After 2001, it became more challenging to find great entrepreneurs. "After the Internet bubble blew up, fewer really capable people became entrepreneurs," Hurst explains. "They hid out in big companies because they were less willing to take risks. When the economy is stable, entrepreneurs become more willing to jump out of safe environments."

During the recent economic growth years (2004 to 2007), existing venture-capital firms expanded their operations. Many increased the size of their funds, while others expanded geographically or into new invest-

THOMSON REUTERS' PERFORMANCE INDEX*

	Years				
Return to investors (%)	1	3	5	10	20
Venture Capital	−20.9	4.2	6.4	15.5	17.0
Early/Seed	−20.6	1.7	3.7	36.0	21.8
Balanced VC	−26.9	4.6	8.4	13.5	14.5
Later Stage	−6.8	9.5	8.7	7.5	14.5
NASDAQ	−38.1	−10.3	−4.6	−3.2	7.3
S&P 500	−36.1	−10.0	−4.0	−3.0	6.1

*Returns are net to investor after management fees and carried interest. Data is through 2008.

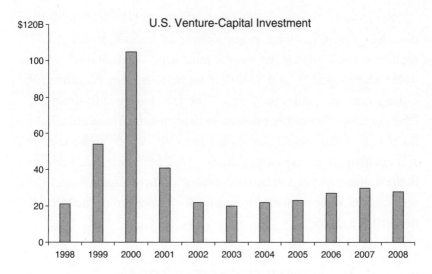

Source: Thomson, Venture Capital Association

ment areas. TA Associates and Summit Partners expanded by completing bigger deals, investing in larger businesses, and even doing leveraged
buyouts. The international markets for venture capital continue to expand, which creates new employment and investment opportunities
across the globe. "The emergence of the European market has meant significant growth in the venture business in London," notes Megan Clark,
who ran a venture fund for the Australian investment firm NM Rothschild. "The Australian market is now the fourth largest in terms of dollars available for investment through pension funds. Additionally, the
Asian markets are still emerging and becoming some of the fastest growing in the world. The U.S. is still the best training ground, but the playground has gotten bigger, it's now a global playground."

The 2008–2009 recession took a toll on the venture business, but
the effect was not as dramatic as in 2001 and 2002, when technology
companies were disproportionately clobbered in the downturn. Still,
between 2008 and the first half of 2009 the number of venture capitalists decreased by 15 percent.[14] As venture firms with exposure to a high
number of unsuccessful companies failed to find new investors for
subsequent funds, the amount invested by venture-capital firms fell to
roughly one-fifth of what it had been in 2000.[15]

Nevertheless, venture capitalists continue to take pride in the fact that their investments are major drivers of innovation for the U.S. economy. The United States has the most active venture market in the world and (arguably, as a result) is home to a large portion of the world's new companies each year. "The U.S. has an infrastructure, a DNA, to allow the venture business to happen here. The venture industry is one of the biggest pumps for innovation, jobs, value creation, and wealth generation that this country has," Jeff Hurst says. According to the findings of a report by the National Venture Capital Association, ventured-backed companies accounted for 18 percent of the U.S. GDP from 1970 to 2005.[16]

VENTURE CAPITAL TODAY

Venture capital continually seeks to be at the forefront of innovations in science and technology. At the moment, two of the hottest VC areas are nanotechnology and renewable energy. Large established firms have raised funds dedicated to these fields, and new firms specializing in one area have been created. The Obama administration's initiatives to increase government spending in health and alternative energy should provide the impetus for new entrepreneurs and the resources for existing VC-backed companies to grow.

In the last decade, another type of venture investing has emerged: social venture. In social venture, the venture-capital model (providing funding and advice to entrepreneurs) is applied in the nonprofit sector. For example, Acumen Fund, a New York–based nonprofit, raises money and then invests with businesses focused on providing low-cost critical goods and services—like water, health, energy, and housing—to help the world's poor. The organization makes equity investments in these companies with the expectation that they will produce financial returns. However, rather than distributing profits to investors, Acumen uses the returns to fund other companies. Although Acumen and peer organizations such as Grameen Bank and Kiva manage only a small amount of money compared with their for-profit counterparts, they still have made significant impacts.

Despite new fields and innovation, challenges remain. Trouble-some economic times limit many firms' ability to exit their investments and, thereby, make profits. It is more difficult to have an initial public offering for a business in a weak stock market, both because there are fewer buyers and because expected company valuations are lower. There also are fewer potential industry buyers. Firms can be patient to some extent, but the longer they wait to exit, the lower their investment returns will be (because returns are generally viewed on an annualized basis). To address the challenge of limited exit opportunities, veteran venture capitalist Tim Draper is helping to fund an exchange on which institutional investors and wealthy individuals can buy shares in start-up companies. To participate on the exchange, companies need to have at least $20 million in revenue. In an interview, Draper explained that "it's an opportunity for an entrepreneur to get a little bit of liquidity and . . . for venture capitalists to either show that these companies have some real value to them or to sell some." Although this is not the first exchange for investments in private companies, the involvement of the VC community may give this significant credibility.[17]

Unlike leveraged buyouts, venture capital does not require debt to make the initial investment. Yet being able to sell growing businesses is still critical, and negotiating mutually acceptable acquisition prices with entrepreneurs is more challenging in down markets. Entrepreneurs are like people who own homes in that they value their ownership based on recent prices for similar assets. Unfortunately for sellers, when markets dive, previous purchase prices are meaningless. For example, in the California real estate market, everyone was looking at the house down the street that just sold and thinking, "my house is as good as that one, so I should get at least as much money," explains Craig Foley. The problem, he notes, is that when the market goes south, buyers are not willing to pay the same prices that people did during the peak. "The same thing happens in the venture area. Every entrepreneur is looking at the last company that did a round of financing." When a VC firm offers a price that reflects the lower valuations of a normal market, "the entrepreneur says, 'you guys are trying to screw me; there is no risk in this company; look at how company X was valued six months ago.'" As a result, fewer VC investments are made in bad times.

Some seed-stage investors, often called "super-angels," seek to take advantage of the conservatism of many large funds by investing in more businesses. Although their funds are smaller than those of the more prominent firms, many startups do not need huge amounts of capital. "Ten years ago, it would cost $5 million to launch a startup," reported *Business Week.* Today, "thanks to plummeting technology costs," companies in some industries can launch products for less than $1 million.[18]

Venture firms also tend to be more cautious in funding new start-ups or providing additional capital to portfolio companies, because economic turmoil creates big challenges for entrepreneurs who are trying to win new customers and grow their businesses. Because potential entrepreneurs are less likely to leave secure jobs and start new ventures in a bleak economy, the pipeline of new VC investment opportunities is narrowed.

MOVING FORWARD

The recent recession's combined effects of decreased exit opportunities for portfolio companies and fewer entrepreneurs willing and able to start great new companies will likely lead to a contraction in the number of VC firms and the amount of money invested in the asset class overall. Nevertheless, despite the recent turbulence, the venture-capital business will persist and continue to play a key role in the growth of new enterprises. The industry's value proposition is clear: to deploy capital in order to help new and growing businesses expand and flourish. This is easier said than done (especially in tough economic times), but venture capitalists and the entrepreneurs they fund are major forces for global innovation and economic expansion.

HOW VENTURE CAPITAL WORKS

Venture-capital firms raise money for their funds from institutional investors, such as universities, foundation endowments, and pension funds, as well as from wealthy individuals and the VC firms' employees. The investors commit money to a specific fund and forgo liquidity (the ability to withdraw an investment) for a set period of time, usually between five and ten years. The investors are referred to as limited partners (LPs). They have less liability than the partners of the venture firm (the general partners, or GPs) because they have no involvement in specific investment decisions.

The venture investment process is a cycle in which venture-capital firms serve as intermediaries between limited partners and businesses that need capital in order to grow. The diagram that follows illustrates the relationship between the three main parties.

Like other alternative asset managers, such as private equity and hedge funds, a VC firm generally charges a 2 percent annual management fee on all the capital invested with it and takes 20 percent of the profits it generates (this fee structure is described in more depth in Chapter 3).

FINDING INVESTMENT OPPORTUNITIES

Venture capitalists look for investment opportunities primarily through the networks that their firm and its partners have built over the years.

VENTURE CAPITAL INVESTMENT CYCLE

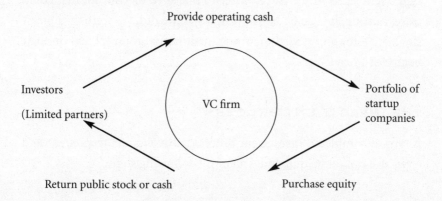

They look at entrepreneurs whom they have successfully backed in the past as well as at people who those entrepreneurs recommend. They also spend time at trade shows, read industry publications, and talk with business contacts. Being proactive in "deal sourcing" is critical to finding great, early-stage investment opportunities. Most venture firms look at a very large number of potential investments but commit money only to a small percentage of them. "If you look at something that comes across your desk, you are looking at something that everyone else is looking at too," explains Megan Clark, who made corporate venture investments for BHP Billiton and was the head of an early-stage venture fund at NM Rothschild. "Having an understanding of what's going on in sectors and a thesis about where the best investment returns are going to come from is also important."

"The first retail investment I ever made was in Costco," recalls Craig Foley. The investment did very well, and I developed a friendship with Jeff Brotman, who was the founder of the business. We had a really good experience investing together. As a result, when he decided to make a large personal investment in a tiny Seattle coffee company called Starbucks, he called me. He said 'I know you looked at this company a year ago and turned it down, but I want you to do me a personal favor and look again.'"

Despite Foley's initial hesitance, this call was the most profitable one he ever received. "We spent a lot of time on the diligence. We were skeptical whether the model would work well outside Seattle. We thought maybe there were some reasons why that particular climate and that particular population had become enamored with the concept. We needed to convince ourselves that it was a concept that could travel outside the Pacific Northwest, which we did. We were the biggest single investor and we led their first institutional round. I was on their board for fifteen years."

THE INVESTMENT PROCESS

A typical completed investment process between an entrepreneur and a venture capital firm includes all of the following steps:

- *Referral:* The entrepreneur is referred to the VC firm by someone the firm has previously worked with (VC firms vary on how seriously they consider unsolicited proposals).
- *Business plan:* The VC firm requests a business plan from the entrepreneur and reviews the document.
- *First meeting:* If a venture capitalist is interested in the plan, they meet with the entrepreneur.
- *Some due diligence:* The VC firm begins to investigate the potential market and business opportunity.
- *Second meeting:* The VC firm seeks to learn more about the proposed company or idea.
- *More due diligence:* The VC firm investigates the entrepreneur and the proposed plan more thoroughly.
- *Introduction to partners:* The partners of the VC firm, who make the ultimate investment decision, meet the entrepreneur.
- *Due diligence is completed:* The VC firm decides that it is comfortable with the market opportunity and the ability of the startup company to grow and succeed.
- *Term sheet:* A document is prepared that outlines the terms of the financial agreement, explaining, for instance, how much of the company the VC firm will own in exchange for the money it invests.
- *Agreement finalized:* The attorneys of the VC firm and the entrepreneur finalize the agreement.
- *Deposit slip:* The investment is formally made in the startup company.

It is not easy to calculate the worth of a company with no or little revenue. However, venture capitalists must assess value in order to determine what percent of a company they will own in return for the capital they are investing. Typically, there is a symbiotic relationship in the negotiations. The VCs know that this won't be the last deal they do, and entrepreneurs don't want to negotiate so hard that the VCs walk away. That being said, venture capitalists are experienced deal makers and often structure their investments to maximize their control of a company and the likelihood of achieving a positive return on their investment. For example, a VC firm may structure its investment as convertible preferred stock, which guarantees that it will get its money back before the entrepreneur receives any profit. It might also stipulate annual per share dividends, which the board can choose to pay or defer each year. A liquidation-preference provision gives the VC firm a claim on the money it has invested plus 10 percent per annum, compounded, if the company is sold, merged, or liquidated. The most important element of the negotiation, however, is usually the valuation.

The basic equation that venture firms use is:

$$\text{\% OF EQUITY ACQUIRED} = \frac{\text{CASH INVESTED}}{\text{(NEGOTIATED PRE-MONEY VALUE} + \text{CASH INVESTED)}}$$

The terms that venture capitalists use to describe investments in companies at different stages of their development also describe the progression that entrepreneurs go through as they build companies. They are:

- *Seed investment:* The initial capital invested in an entrepreneurial endeavor. At this point the idea or company is in its "seed stage" and has little or no revenue. One type of investor at this stage is the "angel investor," who provides money before the idea has been fully acted on. Angels are rarely involved in the operations or management of the companies in which they invest.

- *Early stage, or Series A:* The new company has begun operations but is still at a very early stage in terms of product development and sales. Series A refers to the preferred stock in the company that investors receive for contributing capital during this phase.

- *Later stage or Series B:* Investments are made at this point to provide the company with capital to grow. Later-stage companies have reached significant size, but often still have deficit spending (which means that they are spending more money than they are generating) when this investment is made.

- *Growth stage:* This type of investment is generally made in a mid-size company that is trying to raise capital with which to expand its operations.
- *Strategic/industry acquisition:* This means that a company is purchased by another business. This is the most common way in which a venture firm successfully exits a portfolio business and realizes a profit on its investment. An alternate exit is an IPO.
- *Initial public offering (IPO):* In a public offering, a company sells a portion of its equity (ownership) on a public stock market.

THE INVESTMENT STRATEGY

Different firms have various strategies for achieving the success rates they expect from the businesses they fund. Many firms limit the types of companies they are interested in funding, by sector (for example, software, life science, consumer products), by geography (e.g., the Silicon Valley, the Southeast, the Northeast), and/or by investment stage (such as early stage or later stage). An early-stage investor seeks to be one of the first institutional investors in a young company (or, better yet, the first). "The deals we invest in have to have a potential for ten-to-fifteen times growth, because we know that many of the companies in which we invest will not bear fruit," says Kip Frey, a partner at Intersouth Partners, an early-stage firm. "We don't enter a deal with a specific end point in mind; we try to make the company as valuable as possible and let the market determine the right time for an exit."

The economics of venture capital are such that one can succeed with a few big hits or with a more consistent approach. If a firm invests $10 million in ten different companies ($100 million total), and nine of those investments yield nothing, but one investment pays $300 million, the fund has generated a three times return on its capital. That is the same return as if all ten companies had tripled in value. A firm can get to a 30 percent or higher annual return with either approach.[*]

---

[*]*Annualized returns are computed by taking the total percent change in money invested and adjusting for the total period of time.*

THE FOUR KEY QUESTIONS IN EVALUATING A VENTURE
INVESTMENT ARE:

1. IS THE ENTREPRENEUR SOLVING A REAL PROBLEM?
2. IS THE PROBLEM THAT IS BEING SOLVED A BIG ONE?
   (THE VC DOESN'T WANT TO BE 100 PERCENT OF A $2
   MILLION MARKET.)
3. WILL THE PROPOSED VENTURE SOLVE THE PROBLEM
   IN A DEFENDABLE WAY? (CAN IT MAINTAIN ITS MARGIN
   BECAUSE IT HAS GREAT INTELLECTUAL PROPERTY,
   SUCH AS A PATENT OR BECAUSE THE ENTREPRENEUR
   HAS INVENTED SOMETHING THAT NOBODY ELSE CAN
   DO?)
4. IS THE MANAGEMENT TEAM ONE THAT THE VC THINKS
   IT CAN BUILD ON?[19]

Greylock, a firm that has maintained a high hit rate and had some mega-successes, tends to have a very relationship-oriented approach. When it funds an entrepreneur, it commits to that entrepreneur. "A lot of the projects that Greylock funds are repeat fundings of entrepreneurs it has invested in before. It would never fund two companies in the same space, because that would be betraying one of the entrepreneurs in the family," explains Sam Clemens, a former associate at the firm.

Intel Capital takes a different approach. Because Intel is a public company, Intel Capital cannot hold more than 19.9 percent of any company.* When ownership is limited, the investor has to put money to work in more places in order to increase profits. Corporations that

*If a company owns 20 percent or more of another business, it must include the business on its financial statements. As a result, most corporate venture groups cap their investments at 19.9 percent.

take this approach usually do not create limitations on investing in multiple companies with similar business models.

The assessment of the difficulty of young or first-time entrepreneurs obtaining VC funding depends on who you ask. "Between 1997 and 2000 it was easier for a twenty year old with a technology or web idea to get funding than today because back then very credible firms were backing young entrepreneurs with millions of dollars. Since the crash, most venture capital firms are very wary of providing capital to new entrepreneurs and those that are risk-taking expect more for their investment, often 25 percent ownership of the company in exchange for seed capital," explains Noah Glass, the CEO of GoMobo and one of *Business Week*'s top young entrepreneurs. In contrast, Auren Hoffman, a more experienced entrepreneur who sold his first tech company in the mid-1990s, feels that it has never been easier to get funding, especially if you are young. "I don't think Facebook.com would have gotten the funding it received [a few years ago had the company been started in the late 1990s]. There is this rumor that there were all these twenty year olds who got funded during the late 1990s. That's not true. Many more twenty-two-year-olds get funded now then they did back then."

Regardless of whether Glass's or Hoffman's assessment is more accurate, the success of companies like Facebook and YouTube have shown that young people can hit it big with new Internet businesses. Venture firms, even the oldest and most reputable, seem to understand this and are willing to, at least, consider funding untested entrepreneurs with good ideas. In the end, for venture capital, it's all about investing and helping to grow business that someone else will want to buy for a lot of money.

However, VC firms are mindful that, statistically, successful repeat entrepreneurs (often referred to as serial entrepreneurs) have a higher likelihood of producing positive outcomes in their next ventures. A 2008 Harvard Business School study found that entrepreneurs who had started companies that went public had a 30 percent chance of succeeding in their next ventures. In contrast, first-time entrepreneurs had an 18 percent chance of success, and entrepreneurs who had previously failed had a 20 percent success rate.[20] It is, therefore, not a surprise that many top VC firms actively seek to maintain strong relationships with the successful entrepreneurs they fund.

Subsequent Funding

Venture-capital firms do not initially release all the money they might be willing to commit to a business; a large portion of the capital is reserved for subsequent funding. Between the initial investment in a business and its IPO or acquisition (if the investment is successful), there are often multiple rounds of financing, to provide the startup business with cash to grow (for example, to expand or to acquire another company). A VC firm often stipulates in the initial investment contract that it has the right to maintain its percent of ownership by contributing more capital if the startup business seeks to raise additional money.

Many firms participate in every subsequent funding round so that they can maintain the same percent of ownership when other investors join the mix. "If initially we own 25 percent of a company, we try to stay close to that level, *pro rata*," says Kip Frey of Intersouth Partners. Maintaining ownership *pro rata* means that the firm seeks to proportionally own the same amount of the businesses in which it invests even as they expand. For example, if Intersouth were to invest $1 million to own 25 percent of a company, and the company sought to raise another $10 million a few years later, Intersouth would invest an additional $2.5 million in order to maintain a 25-percent ownership of the business.

HELPING A BUSINESS TO SUCCEED

Raising money from new investors in subsequent funding rounds is seen as a validation of the company's development and can add new resources. Having more venture firms involved means a bigger network for the business to draw on and more smart people around the table helping the entrepreneur to make decisions. Venture-capital firms actively seek to use their large networks to assist the businesses in which they invest. This includes helping to recruit new executives and negotiating deals with production and service providers. Venture firms compete with other venture firms, but they also cooperate to help build businesses in which they are mutually involved.

Partners from the firms that invest will jointly sit on the board. The boards of public companies are made up of business and civic leaders who are charged with looking out for the interests of stockholders. Private companies, however, particularly venture-backed startups, have boards that are made up of those who have invested in the companies. A board usually consists of five to seven people who are primarily focused on managing their investments by increasing the profits of the business.

Jeff Hurst, a cofounder of Commonwealth Capital Ventures explains the responsibilities of serving on a board of an early stage company:

> When you get involved in very young companies, you are rolling up your sleeves and partnering with the management to build the business in a lot of different areas. In some instances, you need a law firm, a bank, or a real estate guy. The VC helps with that because we do that type of thing all the time. We know who the best guys are. A lot of the entrepreneurs are not experienced in business so they don't know how much to spend on something or how many people they should hire. The VC helps them tweak their business plan and then you spend a lot of time with them on strategy—how to bring the new product to market, hiring people and building the team. What is the type of person I need? How many do I need? When do I need them? You help them build the board. You need independent directors. What should their capabilities be? You are helping management build the company from the ground up and you do that on a daily basis. As the company gets bigger you get involved in human resource decisions and compensation plans and you have an audit committee and compensation committee on the board.

THE EXIT

The "exit" from the investment is where VCs make most of their profit. This can be by means of either an offering of the company's stock on a public stock market or the acquisition of the company by another business.

Recently, acquisitions have accounted for the majority of successful VC exits. The Sarbanes-Oxley Act of 2002, which was passed in the wake of the Enron and WorldCom accounting scandals, has made it more costly to operate a public company. The act stipulates that all public companies must follow a host of procedures, which add significant expense to the overhead of a small business. "Since Sarbanes-Oxley, it may not make sense for a company to go public with less than $100 million in revenue, simply because the costs of being public can amount to one percent or more of revenue. Right away, that raises the bar higher than a lot of VC-funded companies will be when looking for an exit," explains Sam Clemens, formerly of Greylock Partners. "Usually there is a moment in time [before IPO-level revenue] when the likelihood of growth is high enough that someone will acquire the company at a price that accounts for that potential," adds Kip Frey. "When a company has real revenues, you start to talk to investment bankers who assist in the selling process."

However, even when businesses have sufficient revenue to go public, the management team may be resistant to doing so. Craig Foley notes that there are management groups that "are great at managing private companies but don't want to be in the public eye. Particularly today," he says, "the demands of being a public company (including Sarbanes-Oxley compliance, public relations, and investor relations) are a tremendous burden. That will divert a lot of management time from running the business."

Of course, not all ventured-backed portfolio businesses make it to a profitable exit. "The least enjoyable aspect of venture investing is when a business you invested in begins to fail; you cannot shrink from that investment. You have to do your best to try to save whatever you can of your investment for your investors," notes Bruce Evans of Summit Partners. "Usually the least enjoyable part of the job is when you have to work with those companies that, in retrospect, were the beneficiaries of a stupid investment decision."

AN EXAMPLE VENTURE INVESTMENT

Commonwealth Capital's investment in the MacGregor Group, a software business, is an example of a typical venture investment cycle. MacGregor builds trade-order management systems for money-management firms to use in previewing hypothetical financial transactions and executing orders. In 1999, Jeff Hurst met the two founders, who were young rocket scientists at MIT. They had built some one-off proprietary systems for Wall Street firms and had decided that wealth management was a rapidly growing industry. Their business had a small number of customers and was making a few million in revenue. "They had a vision of growing the business, and I bought into that because the use of technology on Wall Street was accelerating," says Hurst. Commonwealth invested some money in the business in exchange for partial ownership. Given its confidence in the company, Commonwealth invested additional capital a short while later, in order to allow the MacGregor Group to buy one of its competitors. Commonwealth's investment partners in this deal were Bain Capital and the Audax Group, which also provided the MacGregor Group with cash in exchange for partial ownership. "Over a period of about four and a half years, we took a profitable company, advised it to spend heavily into the red, helped it increase its employee count from fifteen to two hundred while rebuilding the entire management team (keeping the two founders); we assisted its acquisition of a competitor, put some of its services on the Internet, and worked to build the board," Hurst reports. Five years after Commonwealth's investment, the MacGregor Group was sold to ITG, a public company, for over $250 million.

ORGANIZATIONAL STRUCTURE

Most venture-capital firms are composed of some combination of associates, vice presidents, principals, and partners. The structures of firms vary with their sizes. Kip Frey, a partner at Intersouth Partners, explains that in small- to medium-sized firms, such as his, "There are partners, who sometimes are called principals, and there are people who are not partners—associates, interns, et cetera. Partners make the investment decisions, share in the upside of the financial gains to a large extent, and take the board seats on the companies in which the firm decides to invest. Associates do the background research on companies and occasionally accompany partners to board meetings, just to watch. They are essentially apprentices." Although many jobs in finance involve hands-on learning while working closely with more senior members of a firm, venture-capital firms are probably the most apprenticeship dependent.

Traditional, early-stage, venture-capital firms tend to be small. As a result, associates end up having many of the same roles as partners. In general, the three responsibilities are:[21]

1. Looking for interesting companies, which includes spending time with entrepreneurs, visiting trade shows, and reading the trade press;
2. Evaluating projects that come into the firm—both those that the associate finds and ones that others bring in; and
3. Helping to manage companies that are in the portfolio.

PART 2

INSIDE A VENTURE-CAPITAL FIRM

ORGANIZATIONAL CULTURE AND LIFESTYLE

The lack of formal structure in many firms reflects the more independent nature of the venture process. Finding small companies that have potential can mean lonely trips to trade shows and long flights to visit small businesses. "The venture business is more of a Lone Ranger business, where you are making decisions with less information; you are more often negotiating directly with the entrepreneur who runs the business," explains Bruce Evans. "Consequently, your sales skills are more on display, the bets you make are smaller, but the upside you might generate is larger as a multiple of your money. It takes more of a salesman type in the venture business."

Even in the office, the venture lifestyle can feel isolated. "I tell everyone that we hire, you may not see me for three weeks. If you can't get up in the morning and figure out something really exciting to do on your own, you are in the wrong place," says Jeff Hurst. At most firms, there is no HR department and no company social activities. The few associates will likely be more than ten years younger than the next-youngest person in the office. "You are basically working with a

bunch of old guys who have their own offices and who may meet together only once or twice a week," reports one associate.

In firms that make later-stage investments, convincing CEOs that
they would benefit from your investment is a key step that follows
finding interesting businesses. Earlier-stage companies usually need
capital and, therefore, require less of a sales process. Sam Clemens says,
"I would check out fifty opportunities per week—through phone calls,
checking out the websites, and doing background research. I would listen to a formal pitch from five companies per week. The conversion to
actually funding something was probably one in a hundred or two
hundred. Every single day, I had breakfast, lunch, and sometimes dinner with people I thought could be helpful in finding investment opportunities. That is fun at first, but it gets old quickly."

CHARACTERISTICS FOR SUCCESS

Most VC firms seek independent people: employees who thrive in a
work environment in which they have to learn things themselves and
create their own schedules. "If you are the kind of person who wrote a
thesis by setting up a timeline with goals and markers along the way,
you will do well," says Sam Clemens. "If you waited until the last week
to write the entire paper, you will be crushed in the venture business.
Since you are sourcing deals, analyzing businesses, and helping portfolio companies, you can't just cram work in at the last minute. You have
to be self-directed."

Associates are on the front lines, finding the deals that the firm
pursues. That involvement is one of the key things that differentiates
venture firms from other investment professions. At consulting firms
and banks, the partners find the clients. At hedge funds, the investments (for the most part) are publicly traded companies; and at private equity firms, deals are either brought to the firm by investment
banks or sourced by the partners. The wherewithal to find and qualify
good investment opportunities is what distinguishes really good VC
associates. It requires:

1. Seeing trends in technology spaces;

2. Proactively searching for opportunities;

3. Having the confidence to cold call or engage an entrepreneur with little introduction and to gain the entrepreneur's trust;

4. Being able to judge people's talents and evaluate whether they will be able to successfully do things they have never done before; and

5. Communicating to partners why a business or person is worth risking capital on.

Technical aptitude and investment sense are also key characteristics. The ability to understand financial statements, new industries, and technologies and then synthesize and communicate that information to partners is critical. Venture firms want people who are perceptive from an investment point of view and savvy about business decisions. They need to develop noses for good deals, recognizing when to spend time on a particular opportunity and when to move on to something else. "The deal sense is the [trait] that is the hardest to see up front [in people] but that is best developed in the apprenticeship model that most firms in our business use," notes Bruce Evans.

Venture is not a job for people with big egos. "If in banking you kill the deal, in venture you marry it," joked one venture capitalist. When an investment is made, the VC is tied to the entrepreneur and the firm becomes an agent to help achieve the portfolio company's full potential. To close a venture deal, a VC must convince an entrepreneur that the VC understands the entrepreneurship process and can help the firm. That can mean being understated in one's lifestyle. As an insider put it, "If you are trying to invest with an entrepreneur who is risking her life savings and forgoing a salary to start a business, you are not going to gain much trust by showing up for a meeting in a Ferrari." There are venture people who own private airplanes and make million-dollar charitable contributions but choose to drive a Honda. As a VC insider remarked, "This is a business for people who like building things, not just making money." Venture capitalists can become extremely wealthy (a handful, such as John Doerr and Michael Moritz, are billionaires), but an exclusive focus on wealth creation is not the ethos of the business. Being humble and building relationships with entrepreneurs is important for long-term success in the industry.

PROMOTION AND MOBILITY

In the venture business, firms need to be directionally correct, but they can survive on approximations in terms of what they think will happen from year to year. Venture partners generally (especially in early-stage investments) have to make investments based on their confidence in new ideas and the people who will execute them. As a result, "VC is one of the last apprentice businesses in the world. It could take you five or ten years to become a general partner," says Hurst.

Some of the most successful VC firms do not have partner tracks for associates. At the same time, the lack of a formal training process and promotion schedule can create flexibility as to when someone becomes a partner. "If somebody is really good, and they have been in an associate level role long enough so that they know the business, it will become obvious that they need to become a partner. If we don't make them a partner, they will go to another firm and become a partner. It is not really dependent on a slot being open. If we have an additional partner, we will just [seek more money] the next time we raise a fund," says Frey.

On the other hand, top VC firms are able to recruit highly successful former CEOs as partners. Because so much of the venture business is based on sourcing and investment instinct, these people bring a lot more to the table than most associates, who have only limited industry experience. Associates at some firms can receive promotions to the vice president or principal level, but often are told to gain industry experience before they can return to the firms and become partners.

COMPENSATION

Venture capital is not a business in which one makes a quick kill and walks away with a fortune. Financial success comes from a long period as an investor, which creates credibility with entrepreneurs and the know-how to help good business ideas become profitable ventures. "A lot of people perceive venture capital to be a business in which they're going to [rapidly] make a lot of money. That is 180 degrees from the truth. If people want to make a quick hit, trading on Wall Street is the number-one place to go, hedge funds are number two, large private equity houses are number three, and venture capital is number four. Venture takes the longest. It probably has the fewest people that make massive fortunes," cautions Jeff Hurst.

Bruce Evans adds, "The way you make money in the venture-capital and private equity businesses is staying in them for a long time. You are making long-term bets on companies that pay off over the long-term. Partnerships are ten years in length, so you have to stick with it in order to see the fruits of your labor."

Associates at later-stage VC firms, such as Summit Partners and TA Associates, tend to be compensated at levels comparable with LBO firms—around $250,000 per year. Given the nature of their investment process, they are recruiting the same people as leveraged-buyout firms. At early-stage VC firms, the compensation of associates (who usually have completed business school) is more in line with management consulting—around $150,000 to $200,000 per year. However, associates at smaller firms have opportunities to co-invest in the businesses they help to find and close.

HIRING PRACTICES

Because venture-capital firms are generally quite small, they often look for people with very specific backgrounds. Firms' ideas about the ideal candidates vary, depending on the organization's approach to investing. Later-stage venture firms, such as TA Associates, want to hire former investment bankers (or at least people who have experience in analyzing financial statements and conducting valuations of companies). Although Summit Partners, one of the largest venture firms, also makes later-stage investments, it often hires people directly out of college or with only a year of finance experience. "We like to train people ourselves through our own apprenticeship model. The people that work best inside our firm have presence, charisma, and the raw material that we believe we can turn into sales skills," explains Bruce Evans, a managing director at Summit. Therefore, Summit likes to hire recent undergraduates who will devote the majority of their time to sourcing deals. Intersouth's Kip Frey says, "Sales skills are number one for us . . . In the interview process, we evaluate how the candidate gets along with us on a personal level as a proxy for how entrepreneurs will respond to him or her."

In firms that focus on investing in earlier stage businesses, entrepreneurial experience is highly valued. If a firm is trying to convince an entrepreneur that he or she should take its capital, nothing is more convincing than an invester who can talk about his or her own experience as a successful entrepreneur.

PART 3

INSIGHTS FROM INDUSTRY LEADERS

BRUCE EVANS, MANAGING DIRECTOR, SUMMIT PARTNERS

Bruce Evans studied engineering at Vanderbilt University and then sold mainframe computers for IBM. After graduating from the Harvard Business School, he joined Summit Partners, which he has helped to develop into a firm with a capital base of more than $11 billion. He has applied his technical and business acumen to become one of the industry's top investors. On multiple occasions, he has been listed in the top twenty-five on *Forbes'* Midas List, which ranks the top tech dealmakers in the world.[22]

What did you learn from your early career and from business school that helped you to succeed at Summit?

The principal thing that I took away from IBM was the sales experience, which was quite useful to me later in my career in the venture-capital business. I also received some technical training and developed a high-level understanding of computers, computing, and local area networks. At Harvard, I received technical training in business and took classes in business decision making. The case-study method gave me a first-hand chance to think about, discuss, and argue the soft points of business. It illustrated how decisions often are made based on imperfect information and how, despite having imperfect information, it often can pay to take a risk.

I worked as an investment-banking summer associate at Salomon Brothers, and investment banking felt very confining and grinding. At the same time, I liked the deal part of the business and the variation from day to day. One of the partners at Summit called me because they had seen my résumé. The partner told me that a guy with my background—an engineering degree, sales experience, and geographic history—would probably fit pretty well. In February of 1986, I joined Summit while I was still in business school.

I have generally thought of Summit as a VC firm, but the majority of your investment dollars are designated for later-stage private equity purposes. How do you classify the investments that you make?
We try to straddle the line between the late-stage venture business and the private equity, leveraged-buyout business, so we do both. The term that best describes what we do is "growth equity." We try to be flexible with regard to the type of company and industry that we invest in, whether we buy control or not and whether we use leverage or not.

NOAH GLASS, ENTREPRENEUR, FOUNDER AND CEO OF GOMOBO

While in his twenties, Noah turned a frustration with waiting at New York coffee shops into a successful technology startup. Noah, who had previously developed software for Shutterfly.com and worked at an international development nonprofit, was recognized a few years ago by *Business Week* as one of the best entrepreneurs under twenty-five years of age.

How did the idea for GoMobo develop?

I saw the congestion at coffee shops and lunch spots in New York during certain parts of the day and recognized the advantage for consumers of being able to order and pay in advance so as to avoid waiting. Although the idea of using cell phones to pre-order had potential, I was having a great time working at Endeavor [a not-for-profit], coordinating the creation of an operation in South Africa and working with inspirational people. Through Endeavor, I became connected with entrepreneurs in South Africa. I met some people with experience in mobile/web development and sold them on the idea of mobile food ordering in the United States as a startup. I was still working fulltime at Endeavor but, in my free time, I began working with the South African developers on creating the technology for GoMobo.

How has your role at the company evolved?
When the developers from South Africa first signed on, I had no money, so I gave them founder's equity in the company. Initially, I played the role of product manager for the service. I worked closely with the systems architect to design the service and website. We went through lots of iterations as we figured out how to make things work well for the restaurants and for the customers.

I also managed the process of structuring the funding from David Frankel and working with the lawyer to make sure that we established the finance structure appropriately, giving David participating preferred stock as opposed to common stock. At the same time, I took classes in finance, which was very helpful. In 2005, I focused on going to market with GoMobo. I had to convince restaurants to sign up for a program with nothing except a sales idea and charm. I had to convince them that the idea of products being ready and paid for when customers arrived would boost their sales. It took a while to get the pilot restaurant. I was also handling business-planning issues. For a while, I was working from home, and it was not until 2006 that we hired our first employee. At this point, we are all taking salaries, but they are about 50 percent below the market wage for the senior people whose financial interest is based more on our ownership of the company.

What has been the greatest challenge?

The real challenge for us in the second half of 2006 was to get people to use the service. Initially, we planned to adopt a model like Fandango. Fandango charges users $1.50 for the convenience of buying movie tickets online. We had planned to charge users 25 cents per transaction, but found that most users were unwilling to pay anything. The restaurants, however, were willing to pay a fee per transaction because they saw the service as boosting their overall business.

We wanted to get people to use the service before they had to sign up and create an account. People are naturally averse to creating accounts and giving personal information, especially credit card numbers, for services they have never used. To overcome this, I created a promotion by which individuals could text promotional codes to restaurants and receive free products when they arrived, like a free cup of coffee, small fries, or a scoop of ice cream. The participating restaurants covered the costs of the food, and we covered the costs of the text messages.

How have you liked being an entrepreneur?

I am hooked on entrepreneurship. It is certainly not all roses and glory; half the time, working in a startup is a worst-nightmare scenario. You need a good stomach for it; it is difficult to persist against all the negative feedback. There was an eight-month period during which all I heard was negative feedback. Today, thanks to all the great publicity, half the feedback is good, while the other half is still bad. There is a quote from Zig Ziglar that has stuck with me, "Outstanding people have one thing in common, an outstanding dedication to their mission." You have to believe that you will get through it. Today, I am able to get through the bad stuff a lot easier than when we started. The feeling of closing a big account for a company you helped to build is a sensation far more satisfying than anything I could do at a nine-to-five job or even at an organization like Endeavor.

SAM CLEMENS, ENTREPRENEUR, CEO OF MODELS FROM MARS, FORMERLY OF GREYLOCK PARTNERS

Sam Clemens never wanted to be a venture capitalist. Despite being recruited by and working for one of the oldest and most successful venture firms in the world, he left after a few years to join a startup and has worked at two others since then.

What was your experience at Elance?
Elance was the quintessential ground-floor startup experience. I was the second employee after the two founders; the first was a java engineer who later became our CTO. The company's premise was to become eBay for services. My responsibilities, in chronological order, were:

- First year: product management and getting funding
- Second year: business development and partnership negotiations
- Third year: marketing and user-acquisition programs

How did you make the transition from Elance to Greylock Partners?
Through business school. A lot of people use business school as a stepping stone, either from one function to another (for example, engineering into product management) or from one industry to another. Business school is a way to broaden your résumé and get yourself in front of recruiters. I took an unorthodox approach; I was intending to stay in the same function in the same industry, and, even worse, in an industry [tech startups] that doesn't necessarily value an MBA above a similar amount of time spent working in the industry.

I knew that the thing that I enjoyed doing as a profession was being on the operating side of business and building companies. One of the partners at Greylock called and said that they were looking to hire into their Boston office. One of my professors had recommended me. My response was, "Thank you, but I am not interested." He said, "No pressure; let's just have breakfast next week. We will talk it over, just a chat, get to know each other." His pitch at the breakfast was, "Why don't you come work for us for a year or two? You will source deals, help us evaluate them, and, meanwhile, you get to look for something that you can join. Help us find a company; you join it, we fund it, and everyone is happy." So I agreed.

When did you make the transition to BzzAgent?

About a year and a half after I joined Greylock, a company came in to pitch its business. It was a consumer software company with a really interesting idea and a great team. Greylock looked at funding it, but we passed because it got too expensive. Halfway through the discussions, though, when the team was pitching us, they started asking me what my deal was. Suddenly, they were inviting me to join them. My comment was, "Let's finish the pitch discussion before you try to recruit the person who is evaluating you." But I did end up joining the company.

CHAPTER THREE

THE BILLIONAIRE
BORROWERS

PRIVATE EQUITY AND

LEVERAGED BUYOUTS

What are the most compelling reasons for someone to work in private equity aside from compensation?

Aside from compensation, working at a private equity firm teaches you skills that you can utilize outside of the firm. Buying and investing in companies is something that you can do on your own and internationally. However, asking the question that way is like asking Mrs. Lincoln, how she enjoyed the play. The remarkable compensation can't be ignored.

—David Rubenstein, billionaire and cofounder of The Carlyle Group

PART 1

A HISTORY AND DESCRIPTION OF PRIVATE EQUITY

At 3:00 A.M. on a Thursday morning, John is at his desk, thirty stories above the street in the immaculate offices of the private equity firm for which he works. The seeming disorder of the piles of paper covering his desk and the floor is in contrast to the unadorned, wood-paneled walls of his office. A whiteboard, covered in nearly illegible debt-repayment calculations and sketched organizational charts, is the only object John has had the time to hang. He is busy typing formulas into an Excel model to calculate alternative sales-growth scenarios for a manufacturing company that his firm is interested in buying. John[1] is not the only person in the office; other associates are at their desks, analyzing the target company's cash flow and the valuations of similar companies that have recently been purchased. He, along with a vice president and a managing director from the firm, had earlier that week flown to Georgia, where the target company is based, in order to tour production facilities and meet with the management team. Though John was not impressed by the current CEO, he recognizes that the business's large, loyal customer base allows it to charge premium prices. This leads to a very consistent and high level of profitability. Given its customers, cash generation, and strong competitive position, the question is not whether John's private equity firm wants to buy the business, but how much they are willing to pay. The firm wants to win the competitive auction and acquire the manufacturer, but only if they can do so at a price that likely enables them to produce a return of two to three times their invested capital.

At this late hour the secretaries and senior partners of the firm are long gone, but the junior members of the team are still grinding away at the analysis that will determine whether the firm's partners decide to increase their bid in the morning. Though days like this are common, it is a downside to the job that John is willing to take, in exchange for high compensation and the ability to play a key role in some of the financial world's largest deals.

THE HISTORY OF PRIVATE EQUITY

Jerome Kohlberg, Henry Kravis, and George Roberts, founders of the firm Kohlberg Kravis Roberts & Co. (KKR), became financial pioneers in the 1960s when they started making what today are called "private equity investments." Henry Kravis recently joked at a conference of private equity executives that, when he began in the 1960s, a small conference room would have been more than adequate for an industry gathering. "Little did I know in the 1960s, when George Roberts and I bought our first companies—then known as 'bootstrap' investments— that I would ever use the term 'industry' when talking about what I do."[2] Kravis has a lot to be jovial about. He has amassed a personal fortune of over $3 billion and is seen as one of the luminaries of the financial world.[3] KKR was not the first firm to complete leveraged buyouts, but the longevity of the organization and the size of the deals it has completed since its inception have distinguished it.

LEVERAGED BUYOUTS

A leveraged buyout (LBO) or "bootstrap" transaction occurs when an investor or firm acquires a controlling interest in another company's equity by contributing some capital and borrowing a large portion of the purchase price. In this way, the acquiring firm can make large acquisitions without having to commit a lot of capital.

In the early years, many seasoned executives in the financial world dismissed leveraged buyouts as an insignificant financial instrument and rejected any foray into the business. "In 1974, I sat next to Henry Kravis at a lunch," recounted one long-time industry executive. "He told me that he and his cousin were leaving Bear Stearns to go into the 'bootstrap' business. I thought that was quite intriguing and mentioned it to my boss at the bulge investment bank for which I was working. He thought it was interesting and asked me to write a memo to the management committee, which I did. When I presented it, the chairman of the firm slid the memo across the table to me and said that it was one of the dumbest ideas he had ever heard: 'to compete with our clients?'"

In the 1970s, the largest source of profits for investment banks was advising clients—mostly corporations—on the buying and selling of businesses and underwriting their financing.* As a result, the idea that an investment bank would buy companies using private capital seemed, to many, like a bad idea. As the chairman noted, investment banks might end up competing with their own clients; one division could be advising a client regarding an acquisition while another division was seeking to buy the same company. However, in finance, money talks. Years later, when the profit potential of this type of investment became clear, banks joined the field.

In 1979, KKR set a precedent when it purchased machine-tool maker Houdaille for $355 million. It was the first time that a private equity firm took over a public company.[4] At the beginning of the 1980s, KKR was the largest buyout fund, with $135 million, but it faced competition from other deal makers. Available investment opportunities and debt financing changed a small and relatively unknown area of finance into a major economic force.

When Henry Kravis and his partners started their business in the 1960s, it was "an offshoot of venture capital, with individual investors supporting the earliest deals," explains Kravis. Those individual investors were followed by innovative banks and, later, insurance companies. "The real breakthrough came when non-financial institutions [such as endowments, foundations, and corporate pension funds] began to invest in private equity because the returns were attractive. . . . In the early 1980s a few state pension funds launched their private equity programs and became the major suppliers of capital to the buyout industry,"[5] Kravis adds.

During the 1980s, many of the leveraged-buyout investors sought to profit from the existence of large conglomerate corporations, which contained an array of disparate businesses. The dealmakers recognized that the sum of these parts was more valuable than the whole. They purchased these companies with the intent of selling off its divisions

---

*Underwriting occurs when a financial institution agrees to sell equity or debt in a business. By underwriting the issuance, the financial institution generally guarantees that, if it cannot sell all of the financial instrument, it will hold it itself.

over time, taking advantage of laws that allowed them to defer taxes on the proceeds from the sales of the divisions.

Divestiture, the process by which private equity dealmakers sell off assets of a newly acquired business, was just one of many approaches that investors took. Another was the roll-up: when a firm buys multiple companies in one industry sector and combines them to generate a large return. Turnaround deals involve purchasing distressed companies in the belief that they can be revitalized with better management and operations. All these types of transactions are still done today.

At first, private equity firms borrowed money from banks in order to purchase businesses, using the assets of the businesses they were purchasing as collateral. As the size of the businesses the investors sought to purchase increased, private equity firms needed to find additional sources from which to borrow money. They turned to other financial institutions and, eventually, to the public debt markets. The large deals completed by private equity firms such as KKR and financial dealmakers Carl Icahn and T. Boone Pickens (among others), were made possible by selling debt in the purchased companies to the public in the form of high-yield bonds. Because high-yield debt was the last to be repaid if the issuer went bankrupt, the debt carried higher interest rates as an incentive to buyers. As a result of the elevated default risk, they became known as "junk bonds." As discussed in the investment banking chapter, the great facilitator of the high-yield debt market was Michael Milken, who arranged the financing for many of the largest leveraged buyouts of the 1980s.

Throughout the LBO boom period, leverage of ten to one (borrowing ten times as much as the investing firm actually commits of its own capital) on acquisitions was not uncommon. It was access to massive amounts of debt that allowed KKR to undertake a leveraged buyout of food and tobacco giant RJR Nabisco for $31 billion in 1988. (The deal inspired the bestselling book and film titled *Barbarians at the Gate.*) Despite the public hype resulting from this deal, the fervor dissipated quickly when an economic recession and the collapse of the junk-bond market dropped the annual value of leveraged-buyouts to a fraction of its previous size. Several prominent companies that were bought out with large amounts of debt went bankrupt. This was primarily caused by the fact that the interest payments on the loans were so large that the acquired companies' operating cash flows were unable to meet the obligations.

GROWTH IN THE INDUSTRY

Despite the buyout bust, the 1980s saw the creation of many of the firms that would later come to dominate the industry. In 1984, partners from the consulting firm Bain & Company started Bain Capital as a fund to invest equity in startups and to do leveraged buyouts. A year later, Steve Schwarzman left Lehman Brothers, where he ran global mergers and acquisitions, to cofound The Blackstone Group with Pete Peterson, who was also at Lehman Brothers and who served as secretary of commerce during the Nixon Administration. In 1987, The Carlyle Group was started by David Rubenstein, a lawyer and former Carter Administration official, along with three partners who had more business-related backgrounds. Today, these funds are three of the largest and most successful in the industry.

In the early 1990s, as the U.S. economy grew, so did the amount of money invested in private equity. Investment banks began raising private equity funds of their own. In some cases, banks circumvented concerns about conflicts of interest by using their funds to co-invest with private equity firms rather than being the primary investors. Goldman Sachs Capital Partners became a huge fund, but it did so without being a lead investor on many buyout deals. Investment banks with co-investment funds can simultaneously invest in, advise on, and underwrite private equity deals. Other investment banks, such as J.P. Morgan, simply started somewhat autonomous funds. The banks benefited from having private equity funds by taking significant portions of the funds' profits. Consequently, a flow of highly successful private equity specialists left investment banks to start their own funds or to join independent firms in which they could reap higher rewards for strong performance.

The recession and stock market decline around 2001 brought another decline in private equity investment, but the downturn did not last long. The years 2003 through 2007 were the most successful ever for LBO fundraising and deal making. In 2007, $228 billion was raised by U.S.-based leveraged-buyout firms.[6] The boom in deal making was fueled by lower interest rates on debt, the huge amounts of capital that private equity firms raised from investors, and, with that rise in capital, the wherewithal for firms to purchase larger and larger companies. Strong performance during those years and favorable economic conditions enabled top firms to raise funds in excess of $10 billion.

Club Deals

As firms' funds grew bigger, the size of top deals increased even faster. The large size of the average private equity deal and the lack of many strategic buyers* led the bigger deals to become less competitive, because the acquisitions were so large that they required multiple firms to partic-ipate as joint investors. When multiple firms join together to form a consortium, it is called a "club deal." The size of top funds, and the willingness of multiple firms to co-invest, created the wherewithal for the purchase of prominent companies such as Hilton Hotels, Hertz Rent-a-Car, and Burger King. However by mid-2008, with less debt (fi-nancing) available to private equity firms, they returned to smaller deals.

GOING PUBLIC

The notoriety and scrutiny of private equity reached its crescendo well before the economic collapse, when The Blackstone Group went public in June 2007. Unfortunately for the private equity industry, the notori-ety was not excitement about the investment vehicle but, rather, scrutiny of the taxation on partners' profits. Private equity investors pay taxes at the capital gains rate on the percent of a fund's profits they retain, rather than at the higher personal income tax rate. The impact of that favorable tax treatment was illustrated in the Blackstone IPO. Despite compensation of hundreds of millions of dollars, Blackstone

---

*When a corporation buys another company, it is referred to as a "strategic buyer" be-cause, presumably, the purchase is made as part of the corporation's long-term strategy within its industries of focus. In contrast, investment firms generally make acquisitions to drive high investment returns.

CEO Steve Schwarzman had most of his earnings taxed at a lower rate than that of people who earned less than a million. Additionally, when Blackstone went public, Schwarzman and cofounder Pete Peterson cashed out over $2.5 billion from the transaction.

Taking Blackstone public served three major purposes. The first was to allow the firm's founders to liquidate some of their ownership interest. Schwarzman and Peterson owned a significant portion of the firm, and given how valuable the business had become, the other partners would have had to put up a lot of money to purchase the founders' share of ownership when the cofounders chose to retire. The second was that being public helps to institutionalize a firm. Blackstone's founders have diversified the business from leveraged buyouts to real estate, mergers and acquisitions advisory services, and hedge funds; they presumably want the business to continue long after they are gone. The third was that taking the firm public created a permanent source of capital for its investments. Each fund in a private equity firm frequently requires new capital. For a business that has multiple funds, capital must be raised almost constantly. In boom times, a firm with a strong track record has a relatively easy time raising capital; during tough economic times, the limited partners (the funds' investors) can exercise more leverage on the firms and, in some cases, can negotiate lower management fees or carry rates (the percent of the profit they retain). Issuing shares on the public market provides a firm with a permanent source of capital that can be reinvested. These rationales were also relevant factors in KKR's decision to become a public company.

There is irony in private equity firms going public because the industry has long asserted that businesses taken "private" through leveraged buyouts benefit from not having the pressures and obligations of being public. A private company does not have to report its financial results every quarter (as publicly traded ones do), so, in theory, its management can be more focused on the best strategy for growing the company over the long term. Publicly traded private equity firms have to report the values of all the companies in their portfolios on a quarterly basis. That's not a big issue when values are going up. However, when investments go bad, it can be both embarrassing and distracting for the firm's managing directors.

TROUBLES IN 2008

The recession of 2008 and 2009 has hurt private equity firms, but the full extent of the impact will not be known until the funds operating during this period exit their investments. Nevertheless, the carnage resulting from bad investments was evident by 2008. Texas Pacific Group (TPG) lost its $1.3 billion investment in Washington Mutual; Linens 'n Things, which Apollo Management bought in 2006, declared bankruptcy; and Cerberus' equity in Chrysler was largely wiped out in the company's government-orchestrated bankruptcy.[7] A private equity portfolio company can be more susceptible to bankruptcy because the debt used in buying it requires the company to pay large amounts of cash to cover the interest and principal payments on the loan. If sales dip sharply, cash on hand decreases, and a business can find itself in trouble.

A saving grace for many portfolio companies is the flexibility that the private equity owners build into the structure of the loans (such as allowing a company to delay paying back the principal of the loan), which makes it harder for creditors to push an underperforming business into bankruptcy.[8] In its 2008 Annual Report, the founders of Carlyle wrote that, for the foreseeable future, "Operating conditions for our portfolio companies will remain challenging. Transactions will be fewer and smaller. More equity will be required and debt terms will be less favorable. And hold periods will increase while returns will decrease."[9]

THE SEARCH FOR CREDIT

A large amount of inexpensive (low-interest) debt—a key ingredient for the business—is not always available. The credit-market freeze in October 2008, when Lehman Brothers went into bankruptcy, essentially put all new debt issuances on hold. Although the credit markets began to thaw during 2009, banks and investors were hesitant to issue and buy leveraged loans, a reality which impeded private equity buyouts. As a result, private equity firms began to explore other opportunities. Some raised funds explicitly focused on buying distressed businesses at bargain prices, while others explored deals with acronyms other than LBO, such as PIPE, TALF, and PPIP.

PIPE stands for "private investment in a public equity." For example, in the fall of 2008, Green Equity Investors believed that Whole Foods' stock was trading at a depressed level, and worked with management to buy 17 percent of the company for $425 million.[10] In contrast to the leveraged buyout of a publicly traded company, in which a private equity firm pays a premium above where the stock is trading, in a PIPE, the firm usually arranges to buy a minority interest in a company (from the management), at a discount from where the stock is currently trading. TALF and PPIP are two of the U.S. government's initiatives to restart the credit markets. TALF is the Term Asset-Backed-Securities Loan Facility, which provides investors with leverage to buy securities backed by automobile, credit card, education, small business, equipment, and commercial real estate loans. PPIP is the Public-Private Investment Program; it is focused on residential and commercial real estate assets on the balance sheets of investment banks.[11] The PPIP program allows the government to utilize money from TARP (the original bank-stabilization fund) in order to partner with private investors in buying real estate securities. Participating funds have the opportunity to profit by making leveraged investments (through debt financed by the government) without having to borrow money from banks or other investors.

PRIVATE EQUITY TODAY

Whether the recent downturn in private equity is reflective of problems with the financial model is up for debate. Investor Warren Buffett, who often sees private equity firms as competition when looking for acquisitions, lashed out at the industry in his 2008 letter to Berkshire Hathaway shareholders: "A purchase of a business by these firms almost invariably results in dramatic reductions in the equity portion of the acquiree's capital structure compared to that previously existing. A number of these acquirees, purchased only two to three years ago, are now in mortal danger because of the debt piled on them by their private-equity buyers."[12]

Despite this criticism, long-term data suggest that the industry has produced tremendous investment returns with far less collateral damage than Buffett's comments suggest. A 2008 paper by the World Economic Forum, which examined nearly 22,000 leveraged-buyout transactions between 1970 and 2007, found that the majority of leveraged-buyout investments are held for more than five years and that companies that are bought out have lower default rates than the average for U.S. corporate-bond issuers.[13] Historically, private equity has also produced strong returns in comparison with public capital markets.

MOVING FORWARD

The success of private equity between 2002 and 2007 drove a dramatic increase in the number of new, mid-size, private equity firms ($200 million to less than $1 billion). The growth in the number of these funds meant an increase in competition for mid-size deals ($50 million to $250 million), which drove up acquisition prices and decreased returns to investors. Steve Pagliuca, managing director of Bain Capital, believes that many of these new funds will not last and that the increase in the total number of firms does not jeopardize the long-term prospects of the large established funds. "I think there has been a persistence of top quartile funds [the top 25 percent, with the highest returns for their investors], and money gravitates, regardless of the size of the fund, to the people who have had success over a long period of time. The firms that stay disciplined and add value to businesses they own will continue to stay around."

Pagliuca's comments are supported by a Boston Consulting Group study that estimates that over 20 percent of private equity firms will go out of business in the few years following the recession. The firms that do not survive, the study argues, will be those with poor historical performances and a lack of capital with which to make new investments.[14]

The historical success of top private equity firms will allow them to continue to raise large funds. The question is how long it will take for debt markets to again provide the wherewithal for such firms to purchase huge public companies. Regardless of its trajectory over the next few years, private equity remains a large and important part of global finance. With an estimated $1 trillion dollars in capital to invest (as of

2009), private equity firms will continue to play a prominent role in the world economy.[15]

HOW PRIVATE EQUITY WORKS

The bootstrap investments first made by Henry Kravis employed the same general approach as the leveraged buyouts executed today. Kravis and his partners raised money from investors, identified companies they believed were operating below their full potential, and financed the acquisition of these companies using money that was mostly borrowed from banks or issued as debt to the public market. If the investments proved successful, the cash flow generated by the acquired businesses could cover the interest payments on the loans or bond debt. The term "leverage" connotes the use of borrowed funds to increase one's rate of return on an investment. For example, if a firm purchased a company for $10 million, paid all $10 million itself, and then sold the business for $15 million, it would have generated a 50 percent return on its investment. If, on the other hand, the firm paid $1 million from its own fund and borrowed the other $9 million, when it sold the business for $15 million it would have generated a 500 percent return (less the cost of the interest on the borrowed money). Leverage can significantly increase the returns of profitable investments.

EXAMPLES OF FINANCING STRUCTURES

	Cost	$ Invested	$ Borrowed	Sale Price	Return
No Leverage	$10M	$10M	$0M	$15M	(15-10/10)*100%= 50%
90% Leverage	$10M	$1M	$9M	$15M	((15-9)-1/1)*100%= 500%

FINDING INVESTMENT OPPORTUNITIES

At a private equity firm, the most important group is the investment committee, comprised of the firm's partners, which makes the final decision on acquisitions. At Bain Capital, one of the largest private equity businesses, the committee meets every week to consider investment opportunities. It looks primarily at the customers, costs, competitors, and business plans of the companies the firm is considering buying. The committee examines each potential purchase (or "deal") several times, which helps to focus the work of the team responsible for the transaction.

Most firms consider a large number of deals for every one that they end up completing, and it can be very frustrating to work on many deals that never happen. "One of the worst parts of the job is following leads you think are not going to matter and knowing that the firm is only going to win a fraction of the deals that you do bid on," says JB Cherry, a managing director at One Equity Partners. Steve Pagliuca, of Bain Capital, echoes that sentiment, "To work so hard and then lose the business you are trying to buy by ten cents a share or because the buyer decides not to sell, is one of the least enjoyable aspects of the job. That is a pretty disappointing experience after you have spent three months of your life on the deal."

At THL Partners, approximately 150 deals are considered for every five that are completed in a given year. "Everyone at THL learns from the deals they examine and follows industry trends and values of companies for long periods of time," says Richard Bressler, a managing director at the firm. In addition to following the pertinent industries, maintaining relationships with industry executives is crucial. Bressler gives an example: "I had known the people at Univision for years, so when it came up for sale, my knowledge of the company and its management allowed us to move very quickly and with confidence. I had a good sense of what we should be willing to pay for the company. After we won the bid, we began to search for the next CEO of the company. The person we selected was someone who I had worked with for a number of years at Turner Communications."

The sources of investment opportunities have changed dramatically over the past few decades. A lot of opportunities still come from the large personal and business networks (the two are often intertwined) that the firm's partners have built during their careers. Nevertheless, the success of the private equity business has led to more competition in the purchasing of attractive businesses. Increasingly, investment bankers serve as intermediaries (brokers) between private equity buyers and sellers. "I used to see guys drive in from Ohio in a Buick, spend a few days with me, and be delighted to get five times cash flow for their companies," one long-time investor remarked. "Now they take a private jet, visit Goldman Sachs, and interview us. There is an auction process, where the auctioneer has 'stapled' a financing of eight times cash flow to the deal, and you get a few hours with management in a highly orchestrated minuet. The deal flow now has moved to the investment banks."

Analysis

Private equity firms engage in a tremendous amount of quantitative analysis of the companies that they consider buying. Complex Excel models are painstakingly constructed by associates at the firms (who often work day and night) in order to allow senior partners to assess the range of financial outcomes possible from owning a target company. These models enable a firm to see how variations in future sales, interest payments on debt, and other factors could affect the possible financial return. The inputs into these models (for example, estimates of future revenues, costs, and market growth) are informed by research conducted by the associates, the partners' knowledge of different industries, and the advice of outside consultants. Before making a large investment, a firm might spend $10 million on due diligence, including hiring accountants to analyze the target company's financials, consultants to analyze the industry, and lawyers.

On a given day, junior-level employees research the customers of a target company, create the financial models, work with hired accountants to analyze the target's financial statements, and lead the technical learning about the products of the business. Principals manage much of the due-diligence process, develop the structure and variables of the financial model, and assess the growth prospects of the target company's industry.

THE ROLES OF PARTNERS

Partners pick the best financing sources, deal with the other LBO firms if there are multiple buyers working together in a consortium, and negotiate the purchase. When they complete a deal, they select the management of the acquired business (either keeping the existing leaders or finding new ones), and sit on its board. As members of the board, they are updated regularly and advise the company's management in order to maximize the return on their investment.

Senior partners—often referred to as managing directors—have to anticipate future business trends and macroeconomic changes in order to maintain a portfolio of investments that will produce strong returns for investors over the long term. For example, a fund could have invested in a high-performing newspaper in 2003 and today find itself losing money because the entire newspaper industry has lost share to the Internet.

ADDING VALUE

Large private equity firms continually change the ways in which they add value to the companies they buy. Many of the strategies they have introduced have become widely known and have been adopted by corporate America. For example, LBO firms first thought of giving a company's management part ownership of the business so that they would be financially encouraged to produce better returns. Management ownership is now commonplace in publicly traded companies. Similarly, some of the financial tools used for assessing deals have become more widely understood and utilized.

To deliver the returns investors demand, firms have to bring more to the table than capital when talking about a buyout with a business's management. As a result, many large private equity firms have developed internal expertise in specific industries and operational functions. THL Partners has a "strategic resources group" that provides operational expertise to the companies in its portfolio. CCMP Capital has senior partners with designated operational responsibilities, such as human resources. KKR creates post-acquisition plans to map out exactly what the firm seeks to do during the first one hundred days of owning a company and Bain Capital employs an extensive number of people dedicated to working exclusively with the firm's portfolio companies. Senior leadership in the industry has also changed to include more former CEOs and experienced business operators. For example, John Snow, the former CEO of CSX, is the chairman of Cerberus Capital. Jack Welch, the former CEO of General Electric, is a special partner at the firm Clayton, Dubilier & Rice. Former IBM CEO Lou Gerstner served as chairman of The Carlyle Group.

FEES

The standard fees that firms annually charge their investors are 2 percent of the total amount of money invested with them plus 20 percent of the profits that the fund generates. In comparison, mutual funds generally charge less than 1 percent of assets and 0 percent of profits. Therefore, to justify their fees, private equity firms must consistently outperform the stock market. The private equity (and VC) fee structure is called the "2 and 20" formula. The ~20 percent share of profits that firms retain is referred to as "carried interest" or "the carry." To illustrate, if a firm manages $2 billion and has profits of $400 million, it will take a $40-million management fee (based on 2 percent of assets) and $80 million in carried interest (based on 20 percent of profits). Firms that have produced exceptionally high returns are often able to charge even larger fees because there is such high demand among potential investors. This fee structure has propelled top private equity investors into the ranks of Wall Street's wealthiest.

EXAMPLES OF INVESTMENT-FUND FEES

	Assets	Return	Management Fee	Performance Fee	Total Compensation
Mutual Fund	$2B	20%	$20M	$0M	$20M
Private equity Firm	$2B	20%	$40M	$80M	$120M

As a general rule, most firms have only a few partners per billion dollars managed, so their pay can be enormous in good years. To illustrate, assume that a top firm has $10 billion under management, produces a return of 20 percent, and has twenty partners. The firm would bring in $600 million of carry and management fees. If salaries, professional services, and other expenses take a third of that, the partners would be left with $400 million to be divided among the twenty of them. That makes for a pretty good payday. However, during bad years, when portfolio firms do not issue dividends (distributions of profits to owners) or are not sold, partners receive few or no performance fees.[16]

SIMILARITIES AND DIFFERENCES BETWEEN PRIVATE EQUITY AND VENTURE CAPITAL

Private equity (leveraged buyouts) and venture capital are both businesses in which investors buy partial or full ownership of a company in a manner that is not possible on the public markets. Technically, each is a form of private equity (ownership in a business that is not traded on a public market), but today, "private equity" is assumed to refer only to late-stage growth investments and leveraged buyouts. The term "venture capital" generally encompasses earlier-stage investments.

Similarities

Private equity and venture capital are alike in many ways. Both fields raise money from investors that have large pools of capital and are willing to commit to a fund for a set number of years. They are principal, rather than service, businesses, which means that the partners can choose all the professional service firms with which they work, rather than serving clients on a daily basis. As long as the limited partners are kept happy, private equity and venture-capital partners do not have to "serve" anyone. Perhaps most important, both businesses are high-risk, high-reward fields. Partners are responsible for managing millions (or billions) of dollars. If they invest successfully, they can earn seven- or eight-digit compensation. If their firms do not produce good returns, they will struggle. Partners invest their own money in their firms' fund, so when a fund does poorly, they not only may lose their ability to raise another fund, they will likely lose large amounts of their own money.

Differences

In private equity, firms invest in large, established companies with professional CEOs. The CEOs may lack the technical skills of entrepreneurs, but they are seasoned in finance and management. In venture capital, the firms work directly with entrepreneurs, often people with deep technical knowledge but limited business experience or savvy. Venture is also more volatile in that there is a greater chance for huge successes (for example, early investments in Google or Apple), but there are also more failed companies.

PART 2

INSIDE A PRIVATE EQUITY FIRM

ORGANIZATIONAL CULTURE AND LIFESTYLE

One of the major distinctions in the business world is between advisors and principals. Advisors are the investment bankers, consulting firms, lawyers, and accountants who provide services to companies and investment firms. They have the advantage of usually being paid for their services regardless of whether a deal is ultimately successful; therefore, they have less risk than those who earn significant compensation only if their investments do well. Principals in the investment business—hedge-fund and private equity managers as well as venture capitalists—hire the advisors. They ultimately are beholden to their investors but are able to exercise more control over their schedules than people who advise them.

An associate at a middle-market private equity fund recalls,

> Right before July fourth, we were working to close a major deal. We had worked hard all week to make this deal happen, but on Friday afternoon we sent a slew of requests to the investment bankers, energy consultants, and lawyers who were working on the deal and said that we expected them to be completed by early the following week. I had a great holiday weekend and never did an hour of work, but throughout Saturday, Sunday, and Monday, I received countless e-mails from all our advisors with answers to the questions we had

sent. Since we were the client, we were able to relax, while none of those guys had much of a holiday weekend.

Although the rewards are large for those who succeed in private equity—in terms of both autonomy and compensation, private equity is no cakewalk. Firms have to engage in a number of activities simultaneously in order to be successful. They must raise money from investors, find companies in which to invest, close deals, increase the values of the acquired companies, and exit their investments by selling the companies or taking them public. That variety and challenge is one of the aspects of the job that many insiders enjoy most.

CHARACTERISTICS FOR SUCCESS

One seasoned executive boiled down success in the private equity business to five characteristics:

1. *Being a self-starter.* "There isn't a very good training program at most PE firms. You are thrown into the fray."
2. *Good judgment.* "Knowing which battles to fight, knowing how to judge other people, and knowing when you are convincing them rather than just annoying them."
3. *Linear thinking.* "Being able to analyze a set of facts and come to a sensible conclusion."
4. *Seeing the world the way it is* "without being too greatly influenced by your fears, prejudices, expectations, hopes, and desires. The very best people see the world about 55 percent the way it really is. Most of us are below 50 percent. The margin is that slim."
5. *The ability to manage risk.* "Many people strive to eliminate risk. In this business, you have to take risk to get returns. Internalizing and managing that risk is a real skill."

He adds, "You would be surprised how few people have all these characteristics." Said another way, a high IQ can get you to first base, but, in this business, you'll need to develop high EQ (emotional quotient) to put points on the board.

COMPENSATION

The fee structure of private equity firms enables them to pay individual employees hundreds of thousands of dollars per year. The base salary for associates is around $100,000 but, with annual bonuses added, their total compensation can be triple or quadruple that. At top firms, compensation for post-business-school associates is over $500,000 per year, and, after a few years (assuming that the funds do well), annual compensation can exceed a million dollars. Their salaries and bonuses put associates in the top few percent of U.S. income earners. However, because associates invest significant portions of the money they earn in the funds for which they work, they often do not have piles of cash lying around to spend. Although downturns can take a toll on the value of an associate's co-investment in a firm's fund, compensation at the junior levels is relatively resilient because of the industry's fee structure, which generates income year after year.

During good years and bad, the perks tend to be quite appealing. Most firms occupy large offices with impressive views in the centers of the cities in which they are located. Associates have their own offices, often sharing an assistant. To optimize their time (and comfort), private-equity professionals often fly in private planes when traveling to difficult-to-reach locations in the United States and in first class for international travel. Partners' travel schedules frequently can look like those of presidential candidates, with stops in three states (or even multiple countries) in one day. "There is an enormous amount of travel, because this has become a global business. That travel can wear on you," says Steve Pagliuca.

Despite the undeniable upside of bypassing the hassles of security and commercial travel, flying private can have its downsides. Missing a conference call or meeting is not acceptable when your airplane has telephones, and flying in a private aircraft (often a small plane with four or six seats) can mean sitting face-to-face with your boss for hours, requiring at least the appearance that you are working during the flight.

Business travel can bring private equity employees to appealing U.S. and international destinations, where they stay in top hotels, but they don't have a lot of time to enjoy it. "The little time you are in your hotel room, you are often just ordering room service and working, so after the first trip you don't really have the chance to appreciate where you are," laments one associate.

HIRING PRACTICES

The large compensation packages and the allure of working for a firm that is buying and selling prominent companies have made getting a job in private equity very competitive. JB Cherry, a managing director at J.P. Morgan's private equity fund, One Equity Partners, says, "We have very high standards. We look for people with investment banking or consulting experience. Often, we will call a firm and ask who its best analyst is. All the candidates we interview are smart, went to good schools, and have distinguished themselves at their previous jobs." It is not uncommon for One Equity Partners to receive more than two hundred résumés in a week.

Although candidates are up against fierce competition for coveted positions in private equity, the firms feel equivalent pressure to hire the very best available talent. Headhunting firms, most notably SG Partners, the Oxbridge Group, and the McKibben Group, specialize in placing people in private equity and hedge-fund jobs. The career offices of colleges and MBA programs regulate hiring practices so that students are not put under undue pressure; however, there is no one to regulate the way firms hire associates out of investment-banking and management-consulting analyst programs. Only a few years ago, Blackstone, KKR, and TPG interviewed candidates for the associate position eighteen months into their banking and consulting analyst programs, about six months before they would start to work at a private equity firm. However, a dilemma became evident. Evaluating candidates closer to when they would actually start working allowed the firms to assess how many associates they wanted (based on current market conditions), and the candidates would have longer work histories on which to base evaluations. However, firms that begin evaluating earlier get a head start on identifying the best talent. As a result, most of the big firms now are making offers to people who have been in their jobs only nine months and will not start working at private equity firms for another year or more.

Most private equity firms have relationships with the top consulting firms and investment banks from which they hire. Part of the associate-vetting process includes managing directors calling consulting and banking partners to discuss top analysts. Although the consulting companies and banks don't like to lose talent, their partners know that the more former employees they have working at a private equity firm, the more likely they are to get business from that firm in the future.

The interview process can take many forms, but it is always rigorous. "In their spare time, the Goldman investment bankers I worked with would build leveraged-buyout models in Excel from scratch," said one former banker. "These guys, who worked over a hundred hours a week, most of that time using Excel, would take some of their few free hours to drill themselves on LBO modeling. They knew that, as part of the interview process at firms like KKR and Apollo, candidates are handed a company's 10-K financial statement when they arrive for their interview and are told to build a leveraged–buyout model."

Bain Capital and Golden Gate Capital, firms born out of the consulting business, eschew Excel modeling drills in their interview process, and instead they focus on case interviews—similar to the evaluation described in Chapter 5, on management consulting. The interviewer generally selects a business in which the firm has considered investing and asks the interviewee to think through whether it is a business the firm would want to own. Interviewers expect strong candidates to be able to logically break-down a business and discuss the different aspects of the investment thesis (the rationale for buying the company). For example, "We are thinking of buying a company that makes roofing materials; what are the drivers of that industry, what would you want to know about the company, and what concerns would you have about buying a roof business today?"[17] [Example answer explained in Notes section.]

Because private equity firms are small, and associates play an integral role in the analysis that gets completed, partners play an active role in the interview process. A candidate may be evaluated by a deal maker who he or she recently read about in the *Wall Street Journal.*

The interviewing process can create some challenging situations for candidates as they simultaneously seek to demonstrate that they are comfortable around senior finance people while not appearing cocky or arrogant. "When I was interviewing for a position, two of the managing directors at the firm took me to lunch at a fancy restaurant in New York in the middle of a day of interviews," recalls one PE associate.

> I had been to fancy restaurants before, but I was trying particularly hard to both demonstrate good manners and engage in interesting conversation, so I was scarcely listening while the waiter rattled off the specials in a thick Italian accent and then asked if we wanted menus. Of course, per Murphy's law, the MDs declined the menus and then deferred to me to order first. I remembered hearing the waiter mention a linguine dish, so I ordered that, assuming that it would be reasonably priced compared to the steak, lobster, and other elaborate dishes. I realized that I had made a mistake when one of the MDs turned to me and said "So you're going with the truffles?" Sure enough, for my entrée, the waiter brought out a glass jar containing imported white truffles and then ceremoniously shaved them over a plate of pasta. At the end of the meal, I learned that the "linguine" had cost $250; it was the most expensive item the restaurant offered! Thankfully, half the partners thought that the order showed bravado rather than arrogance, so I ended up getting the job, but I probably could have made a better first impression.

As this story shows, determining the right way to act in a PE evaluation is tough, because the personalities within firms range so dramatically. Once an offer is made, a candidate may find herself or himself in the office of one of the firm's founders, being pressured to accept the offer on the spot. Many firms give candidates only twenty-four hours to decide whether to accept.

MULTIBILLION-DOLLAR BUYOUT DEALS, as well as bankruptcies at private equity–backed companies, have brought increased public awareness of the industry. "Awareness always creates scrutiny, and awareness of wealth creation tends to bring particularly negative scrutiny," notes Joyce Johnson-Miller, a cofounder of the Relativity Fund and a former managing director at Cerberus Capital Management. However, as one of a small number of females and African Americans in private equity, she hopes that the increased public awareness of private equity "will attract more people to pursue this field, especially women."

PART 3

INSIGHTS FROM INDUSTRY LEADERS

ANONYMOUS PRIVATE EQUITY VETERAN

Given a request by one of the private equity executives with whom we spoke to remain anonymous, we had not planned to include his interview. However, his insights, drawing from more than thirty-five years in finance, were so provocative that their inclusion seems merited.

What is your firm's investment strategy?
We are basically opportunistic investors. My belief is that changing times require changing strategies. A lot of other people specialize in healthcare, consumer goods, real estate, media, and so on. My feeling is that everything is cyclical, and you need to roll with the cycles. I like to think of us as omnivorous. We will be minority investors, majority-control investors, even debt investors; I don't really care where we are on the spectrum of investment as long as I can have enough control through my security to influence or change management when I need to. We are a hedge fund when we have to be. In foreign assets, I will protect myself with currency bets; in some assets, with commodities bets. We are a vulture investor from time to time and will buy companies out of bankruptcy. So we are omnivorous through business cycles, investment types, and industries.

What do you see as your position and what experiences helped to prepare you for this role?
I think of myself as chief of strategy, investments, and marketing. It is my job to see what trends are brewing, coming, or going. You can get

the micro right all day long but, if you miss the macro, you get clobbered. I am also in charge of marketing our funds, performance, and
wares to institutional investors. I try to stay out of administration and
a lot of the things that I find to be the opposite of money.

Being a lawyer helps me navigate a lot of issues, all of which are
more legally intensive today than they were twenty-five years ago. The
regulatory environment post-Enron has run amok. But, I think that
thirty years without a paycheck was the most determinant factor. My
last paycheck was in 1977. I got to New York with no cash, $30,000 in
debt to Harvard and a 1963 Pontiac that I had to pay someone to take
away. I had no family wealth as a backstop. I have always had to eat
what I kill. Unlike in big corporations, every acquisition, every dinner,
every new office chair, was paid for by my money, not the shareholders'. I also think a healthy curiosity helps. I travel all over the world. I
have invested all over the world. That helps.

DAVID RUBENSTEIN, COFOUNDER OF THE
CARLYLE GROUP

David Rubenstein is a testament to the fact that neither an MBA nor
extensive financial training is a prerequisite for success in the investment world. The self-made billionaire is a model of the virtues of hard
work and self-discipline. He was a practicing lawyer and served as a
domestic policy advisor in the Carter Administration before cofounding Carlyle in 1987.

**When you started Carlyle, what role did you play and how
has that evolved?**
When we started the firm, my background was in government and
law. The other partners had more standard, corporate-finance backgrounds and had attended business school. At the beginning, we did
everything together. We took on roles where we believed that we could
add the most value. Given my background, I focused on working with
the press, managing government relations, and raising capital. The
others focused more on investments. Bill Conway ended up taking on
a chief investment officer role, Daniel D'Aniello a chief operating officer role, and I took on the position of chief strategist and the public

persona for the organization. The three of us sit on all the investment committees and keep up with what the others are doing.

What characteristics are common among those who have been most successful in private equity?

The complicating aspect with the management of private equity firms is that the people attracted to the business initially were financially focused. They loved doing deals. As the firms grew, they have needed to take on different roles, including lobbying government to ensure that legislation is not enacted that would inhibit business practices, dealing with the press, and managing global organizations.

What do you look for when hiring junior associates? Would you hire someone today with the background that you had in 1987?

In a small organization, you hire people that you know and trust because you do not have the time to train them. As a firm grows, it becomes more process oriented in nature, and hiring gets more pigeon-holed. If I were running recruiting, I would focus more on hiring Supreme Court clerks, Rhodes Scholars, and White House fellows. Carlyle and other major private equity firms tend not to do that. We also are not taking people out of college, because we believe that they do not have the requisite experience. We are hiring at two points, when people have completed two or three years at a top Wall Street training program and after business school.

Can the growth and compensation in private equity be sustained?

Only in the last few years has private equity become institutionalized and global. In the 1980s, private equity firms were small. Today Carlyle has 900 people in the firm and 300,000 people employed by the companies we control. We have been receiving 20 percent of the profits from our deals, and that generates significant financial compensation. As long as our investors stay happy, that level of compensation can be maintained.

STEVE PAGLIUCA, MANAGING DIRECTOR AT BAIN CAPITAL

Early in his career Steve Pagliuca aspired to be an economics professor. However, he greatly enjoyed his summer internship at Bain & Co. and decided to pursue business rather than academia. His desire to be more entrepreneurial led him from consulting to raise an investment fund with Bain Capital. From that first $60 million fund, he has become one of the premier private equity deal makers, overseeing Bain Capital's involvement in LBOs ranging from Burger King to Hospital Corporation of America.

What made private equity appealing to you when you transitioned into the industry in the late 1980s?
I had tried to leave Bain & Company several times, because clients offered me jobs to run companies, and I had an entrepreneurial spirit. I ended up getting involved with Harry Strachan, who started the leveraged-buyout consulting group at Bain & Company. I was on the consulting side, working with leveraged buyouts in the early days. I really enjoyed that acquisition work, so I decided that it would be a good move for me to switch to the acquisition side of things, where I could still apply my consulting skills. Bain Capital was a natural fit.

Bain Capital is generally thought of as a private equity firm, although it has a fixed-income group, hedge fund, and venture-capital practice. Do Bain's VC practice and hedge fund differ substantially from firms set up exclusively around one investment area?
People at our firm work together across Bain Capital funds. We take the business practice and apply all those things, since, regardless of the fund, we do the same fundamental analysis. Our core is business analysis. When we hire for Brookside Fund, we are not looking for hedge-fund people. As a result, the people at Bain Capital have a lot of opportunities.

What is the value added by a private equity fund going public? Do you think more funds will follow Blackstone's lead in doing that?
I think only some will do it. The biggest value is to help an early transition from older partners to newer partners. Bain Capital has already undergone that transition, so we don't have the liquidity issues for the partners. We don't have a person who owns 40 percent of the firm and

has to get liquid and cash out. Under that circumstance, I think going public would be helpful. I believe it has pros and cons and, frankly, I don't know what the result will be. It happened to the investment banks, and it gave them a strategic advantage by being public and having more permanent capital. I think it is still a question at this time.

CHAPTER FOUR

THE MARKET
MAVERICKS

HEDGE FUNDS

There has been a piercing of the illusion that anyone can start a [hedge] fund and, in some ways, the younger and more inexperienced the [manager, the] better. It was as if investors believed there was a magic alchemy in managing a hedge fund, that it was a secret recipe for making money.

—Seth Klarman, value investor and president of The Baupost Group

A HISTORY AND DESCRIPTION OF HEDGE FUNDS

The Standard & Poor's 500 Index had been down 3 percent the previous day; the price of oil was erratic; and unseasonable weather had unexpectedly decreased orange crops, which increased their commodity price. However, at 7:30 A.M., when Jack entered the office of the hedge fund for which he worked, the mood was calm. Another analyst greeted him as he settled into his desk chair and logged on to his Bloomberg terminal, which provided him with up-to-date market information. Jack had become accustomed to the fact that, regardless of market fluctuations, the investment professionals at his firm never showed in their demeanors whether their investments were up or down.

Earlier, during his first few months on the job, Jack[1] had encouraged a vice president to consider investing in the stock of a European telecom company, because he believed that a new European Union regulation would create growth opportunities for the business. He had read all the company's quarterly and annual reports from the previous three years, examined its competition, and built a financial model to predict how revenue growth would affect the company's valuation. The investment was vetted by senior people at the firm, and the decision to commit capital came from a partner who focused on the media and telecom industries. When the European telecom announced quarterly earnings below analysts' estimates, Jack started sweating. The partner who authorized the investment walked by, and Jack was afraid that he was about to receive a verbal thrashing. The partner looked at Jack's facial expression and said, "Jack, you are not going to last very long in this business if you freak out at every unexpected market movement. We made this investment with an expected time horizon of six to twelve months, and I am still confident that this will prove to be profitable." Jack was momentarily relieved by the partner's words. However, he knew that, if he wanted to succeed in the hedge-fund business and take home bonuses of $250,000 or more, he would need to produce impeccable analyses and profitable investment ideas.

Although Jack was focused on technology, media, and telecom companies, the fund for which he worked invested across a number of asset classes: stocks, bonds, commodities—wherever the partners felt that there was money to be made. The previous day's drop in the stock market was not cause for concern, because the fund's positions were hedged. This meant that, for nearly every stock investment they owned, there was an associated short investment that went up in value if the underlying security went down. Therefore, the fund had little exposure to market fluctuations and needed only to predict the winners and losers in each industry accurately to make money. Yet the recent volatility in the market was making it harder for the firm to produce consistently positive investment returns.

Jack enjoyed the intellectual challenge of discerning how micro and macro events would influence public markets. On the other hand, he did not enjoy the knowledge that, if the fund performed poorly for a few straight months, investors might pull their money out. Were this to happen, Jack could be out of a job if the fund needed to cut costs. Hedge funds have the wherewithal to quickly generate large profits, but conversely can incur fast and significant losses.

THE HISTORY OF HEDGE FUNDS

Hedge funds originated primarily from the business models of early private investment partnerships. For most of the nineteenth century, the only option for Americans who wanted to invest in public corporations was to buy certificates of stock. In the late 1800s, investors began to establish private investment funds. These funds had appeal because they diversified an investor's holdings. People could invest in a fund with others, and the pool of money would be used to buy an array of stocks. This business model expanded into public investment funds, the precursors of today's mutual funds. The funds grew rapidly in size and number during the 1920s, until the stock market crash of 1929. The sharp decline in the stock market, coupled with the use of borrowed money (used to boost returns during the boom years), pushed many of the funds into extinction.

In the wake of the financial devastation, the U.S. government sought ways to protect investors better and to regulate public markets more heavily. In the 1930s, as the U.S. economy recovered, the government created the Securities and Exchange Commission (SEC), and Congress passed laws requiring mutual funds to register with and make public disclosures to the new government agency.

Government regulators were not the only ones who learned from the stock-market crash. Benjamin Graham, who had been a star student at Columbia, went to work on Wall Street in 1914. He amassed a sizeable fortune, most of which he lost in 1929. Graham carefully analyzed the failings in his previous strategy, and in 1934 he published *Security Analysis,* which described his new, well-researched method for evaluating securities. He sought to be a "value investor," buying stock in companies that were valued at less than the sums of their parts. Graham's writings laid the groundwork for investing savants such as Warren Buffett and Seth Klarman, and provided support for the idea that talented investors could produce returns far better than the overall market.

As the stock market started to move upward in the 1930s, the number of collective stock funds—both mutual funds open to the public and private partnerships—began to grow. Because the private partnerships had small and restricted groups of investors, they were not subject to the same regulations as mutual funds.

THE FIRST HEDGE: BUYING LONG AND SHORTING

The first true hedge fund was started by Alfred Winslow Jones in 1949. Rather than just buying stocks as peer-investment partnerships did, he determined that he could neutralize overall market trends by buying some stocks long and shorting others.[2] Buying a stock long means that one purchases the security. An investor buys long when he or she believes that the value of the company for which the stock is issued will rise. Shorting a stock means that one borrows the stock at the market price and sells it. If the price goes down, the investor buys the stock at the lower price and returns it to the party from whom it was borrowed, netting the difference. If the stock's price goes up, the investor has to pay the difference out of pocket to buy the stock back at the higher price. An investor who shorts a stock pays interest to "borrow" the security. As a result, it can be expensive to hold a short position for a long period of time. Traditional investment funds seek to buy the stocks of companies that will outperform the overall market, but do not short securities. The downside to this approach is that, even if a manager is able to pick companies that outperform the market, if the market goes down, the investments may still lose value. By buying some stocks long and shorting others, Jones hedged the performance of his fund (that is, it was less affected by the direction of the stock market).

Although the hedge-fund concept intuitively has merit, for decades it remained a rare investment vehicle. When Julian Robertson started his hedge fund, Tiger Management, in 1980, he faced few competitors. Robertson recalls, "There were Soros and one other fund. I would estimate that there was less than half a billion dollars invested in hedge funds, total." Tiger Management and George Soros' Quantum Fund started as traditional, long-short equity funds, but they developed far more sophisticated strategies. By the late 1980s, the three hedge-fund operators with any widespread recognition were Soros, Robertson, and Michael Steinhardt. However, it was not until 1992 that a hedge fund gained public notoriety for a particular investment.

SOROS AND THE BANK OF ENGLAND

The industry tends to keep a very low profile, but when Soros' Quantum Fund forced the Bank of England to devalue the British pound, netting a $1 billion profit, it was hard for people not to notice. The British government, as part of an effort toward European economic coordination, had joined the European Exchange Rate mechanism and sought to keep its currency at a specific rate of exchange with the German currency, the deutsche mark. However, Britain's inflation rate was far higher than Germany's. In order to justify the pound's exchange rate, Britain increased interest rates to boost demand for the pound. Investors, like Soros, recognized that Britain's currency position was not sustainable and began buying pounds short—an investment that would pay off if the exchange rate went down. This stymied the government's efforts to increase demand for the currency, and the Bank of

England (the entity that controls monetary policy for the country) was eventually forced to withdraw from the European Exchange Rate. The value of the pound dropped, and Soros' Fund netted over a billion dollars in profit.

Soros' investment was particularly noteworthy in that it demonstrated that hedge funds could not only make huge sums of money but also affect a country's macroeconomic policy. By the mid-1990s, there were roughly 3,000 hedge funds managing an estimated $300 billion. That was a considerable sum but was still less than one-tenth the $3 trillion or more in assets managed by mutual funds that were focused on buying stocks.

ARBITRAGE

Over time, the strategies that hedge funds employed became more complex, and some funds began to rely increasingly on elaborate financial models to identify profitable trades. In the mid-1990s, a group of Wall Street veterans and Nobel Laureates believed that they had an unbeatable model to make money; they started the firm Long-Term Capital Management. The group developed a proprietary system that allowed it to take advantage of tiny differences in the pricing of similar types of debt (such as bonds, stocks, commodities, and currencies)—a strategy known as arbitrage. Arbitrage takes advantage of differences in prices between two or more markets. One buys an asset at a low price in one market and sells it immediately for a higher price in a different market. The amount of money Long Term Capital made on each arbitrage trade was tiny, so, in order to generate large returns, the fund used huge amounts of borrowed money to leverage its capital. The financial models that the firm employed used historical data, and the firm's managers felt confident that they would make money in all possible market scenarios.

Given the impressive backgrounds of the fund's managers and its outstanding performance during the first few years, the organization was able to raise billions of dollars in equity from investors. Additionally, it was able to secure loans from investment banks to permit unprecedented levels of leverage. However, in 1998, a confluence of global and economic events without historical precedent threatened to destroy the institution. The East Asian and Russian financial crises caused significant diversion from the expected behaviors of stock and bond markets. In the case of most hedge funds, a potential collapse would be a cause for concern only for its investors. In this case, the lenders, many of whom were also investors, had so much at stake that they were petrified by the possible consequences of the fund's failure. Long-Term Capital Management had roughly $5 billion in equity and an additional $125 billion in loans. The financial community believed that the collapse of the fund could cause massive disruption to the entire financial system. The Federal Reserve Bank of New York coordinated an effort by the major investment banks to step in and collectively bail out the fund by essentially buying it out and assuming its debts.[3]

EXPANSION OF THE INDUSTRY

Undeterred by this very public failure, the hedge-fund industry continued to grow through the late 1990s and into the new millennium. The public focus turned, however, toward venture capital and the new fast-growing technology companies. For a short time, the chance to start a company and become a millionaire in a couple of years captured the attention of many aspiring entrepreneurs. Despite the bursting of the tech bubble and the drop in the stock market, during the resulting recession hedge funds continued to perform well. "The hedge fund industry's returns were generally quite good during the tech blow up. That gave the industry a lot of credibility among institutional investors and is one of the reasons why there were such large inflows into hedge funds during the following years," explains Tim Jenkins, who worked at Tiger Management from 2003 to 2007 and is now a managing partner at Marble Arch Investments.

Compared with private equity and the venture-capital business, starting a hedge fund appeared to have few obstacles. In order to gain access to attractive deals, the first two types of firms have to develop relationships with investment bankers and business owners. The barrier to starting a hedge fund was principally a group's ability to raise capital. Although success as a hedge-fund operator requires as much skill as other investment businesses, the nature of the fast transaction cycle allowed people far younger than traditional investing professionals to build track records, raise large funds, and become fabulously wealthy. In the previous ten years, the number of hedge funds had more than tripled and the money the industry managed expanded five-fold.[4] Until the economic downturn in 2008, there had been meteoric growth in the number of hedge funds and the amount of money invested in them. Along with that growth, the hedge-fund industry turned hundreds of people into millionaires, and a few fund managers into billionaires.

THE ECONOMIC DOWNTURN AND LOSS OF CONFIDENCE

The massive increase in the amount of money invested in hedge funds between 2003 and 2008 was a combination of organic growth in firms' portfolios and new capital allocations to the sector by investors. When institutions and wealthy individuals looked at the impressive returns of hedge funds, however, many missed some important nuances in the data on performance. First, everyone had done well for a number of years because the market had been up. Second, there is a survivor bias. If you look at the existing hedge funds over the last ten or twenty years, their returns look good because the firms that produced poor or even mediocre returns no longer exist.

When the market dropped precipitously in 2008 and 2009, many hedge funds with heavily bullish investment strategies, and those concentrated in certain debt markets, experienced significant losses. Although the hedge-fund industry was down far less than the U.S. equity markets, two-thirds of hedge funds lost money in 2008. Three factors led to a period of decline that claimed hundreds of funds and decreased the size of the industry.

1. Some hedge funds borrow money because, as long as their investments increase in value by more than the costs of the loans, the debt enables them to boost their returns. When the markets

became choppy in late 2007, investment banks and other financial institutions pulled back from this type of lending. As a result, the funds were impaired by this loss of access to leverage.

2. With the irregular movements of the market in 2008, particularly the massive collapse in October, asset classes (such as equities, bonds, and money-market funds) that historically had moved independently of one another all decreased in value simultaneously, and the stock market fluctuated up and down along a sharp downward path. This made it difficult to hedge investments effectively. Many of the hedge funds, which had told their investors they could make money in any environment, lost significant amounts of capital. In 2008, the industry ended down 18 percent for the year.[5] Although the stock market's decline was double this amount, the hedge-fund losses severely diminished the industry's reputation for consistent success. Many hedge-fund investors withdrew money, which struck another blow to many firms.

3. Madoff Securities, a fund that had a respected founder and a long record of strong performance, was revealed to be a fraud. In order to protect their competitive advantages, some hedge funds provide limited details to investors about their strategies. Many investors had not questioned investment strategies they did not understand as long as they were making money. The realization that a hedge fund could be a Ponzi scheme scared some investors away from legitimate firms.

HEDGE FUNDS TODAY

One consequence of the market volatility in 2008 and 2009 was investor flight away from startup funds. "There is a big chunk of the community which believes that the larger, well-established firms will be stable survivors and that the smaller, newer funds will have trouble existing at all," said Seth Klarman, president of The Baupost Group. "I am not sure I believe that statement, because it basically means that people who were born between 1955 and 1965 are better than people born between 1965 and 1975." Nevertheless, many relatively new operators who did not have long track records to point to during volatile times were forced to close as skittish investors pulled out.

Unless the fee structure or regulation changes radically, the industry will expand again and continue to attract bright and driven people. "It is so lucrative to be in this busines; the desire from people who want to go into this is enormously high," says Julian Robertson. "Where there is that much will, there is going to be that much way."

The proliferation of hedge funds prior to the recent downturn had made the market more efficient in terms of eliminating arbitrage opportunities and other quickly profitable trading strategies. Arbitrage is enabled by market inefficiencies. With the advances in computerized trading programs, it has become extremely difficult to profit from uneven pricing in the market. Many traders monitor fluctuations in similar financial instruments, and uneven pricing is usually remedied very quickly. This moved the market toward an arbitrage equilibrium or arbitrage-free market.

Yet, the closing of many funds, as a result of the economic turbulence in 2008 and 2009, has created greater opportunity for the firms that continue to exist. Decreased asset prices also create opportunities for profitable investing. "The market will never be efficient because the market's efficiency is determined by the behavior of human beings, and human beings are not always rational," notes Klarman. He explains that major events create investment opportunities. "For instance, you had the Asian contagion in 1998, and a lot of emerging market stocks got very cheap. You had the technology bubble bursting, and a lot of tech stocks were oversold because people were pulling money out of mutual funds. Before that, when the bubble was at full-bore, you had opportunities in value stocks because people sold value stocks in order to buy tech stocks."

POSITIVE EXTERNALITIES

The hedge fund industry has been criticized for producing very wealthy fund managers but not social good. Most in the industry disagree. They argue, first, that successful funds produce returns not only for high-net-worth individuals but also for public institutions, such as museums, foundations, and university endowments, and for thousands of Americans whose retirement savings are managed by large pension funds. Second, many hedge funds are designed not necessarily to produce the highest possible returns, but to have low risk. Funds that are able to achieve consistent returns with relatively low risk are very reassuring to many investors. "I think that enabling clients to sleep well at night is the single most important thing a money manager can do," says Seth Klarman.

Hedge funds can also play a role in efficiently allocating capital in financial markets and serving as checks against poor management decisions by public companies. One fund manager describes that relationship through what he calls "the equity contract": "Company A is going to have customers, to whom it provides services; senior managers, to whom it provides salaries and incentive plans; bondholders, who will be paid interest on their principal; and vendors, who will be paid for services rendered. At the end of the day, after those parties have been given their due, everything that is left belongs to the equity owners." He says that companies should not put themselves in positions in which constituents who already have gotten what they are entitled to (whether it be salary, interest, or accounts receivable) receive the benefits of the companies' being successful while equity holders get very little. Companies that operate inefficiently, sometimes with the justification of not wanting to fire any employees, are likely to end up bankrupt, which causes more harm than if they had initially improved operations. Hedge funds add value both by providing capital in the form of equity to companies they expect to perform well and by pressuring management when their actions do not serve shareholders.

In addition, many hedge-fund managers have become major philanthropists. The combination of their dollars and brain power has been beneficial to a large number of charitable institutions, even during tough economic times. The Robin Hood Foundation, an organization started by hedge-fund managers, focuses on fighting poverty in New York City and raised record amounts in the middle of the recent recession. The Children's Investment Fund, a British hedge fund, commits a portion of its profits to a foundation dedicated to helping children in developing countries. In the fiscal year 2008, the fund contributed $812 million to the foundation.[6]

MOVING FORWARD

Of the investment vehicles described so far—venture capital, private equity, and hedge funds—hedge funds are in many ways the most agile. Unlike the first two, which raise money and invest it once in specific businesses, hedge funds control a pool of capital that they can continually reinvest. The nature of public markets also allows hedge funds to move in and out of positions in very short periods of time. This flexibility can be a great asset and it also allows funds to be more secretive about their strategies and investing techniques. Although venture capital and private equity may not always be successful, their investors know what they are doing. That is not always the case with hedge funds. The recent poor performance of many funds and the Madoff scandal will pose obstacles for firms seeking to raise money in the short term. However, if the industry produces a series of years with market-beating returns, the industry will quickly grow and regain its clout. Although downturns inevitably cause many investors to lose money, in all market conditions, savvy hedge funds can find ways to prosper.

HOW HEDGE FUNDS WORK

STARTING AND RUNNING A FUND

The most challenging step in starting a hedge fund is raising capital. The founders must provide a compelling case to potential investors for why they will be able to produce better returns than the overall market. Finding investors who are willing to make a long-term commitment to the fund and not bail out at the first sign of trouble is key. "The problem with most startups is that they start with guns to their heads. If you lose 10 percent in your first year, you are very likely not going to have much of a second year, because your investors will pull out," says Seth Klarman. "You should try to find a way to lock up your clients and prepare them psychologically for what you are doing and the risks that you are taking. Otherwise, everything is a gamble on whether you get off to a good start. You can't buy stocks for the long run and have a view on how they are going to do in the short run. If you change your view from long-run to short-term, you are going to be just like the herd and you will not be able to outperform."

In addition to raising new captial, senior managers are responsible for selecting investments, monitoring risk, overseeing relations with investors, securing financing (if borrowing is necessary), and managing operations. Amid the recent economic turmoil, many fund managers who use borrowed money to invest have had to spend more time finding and negotiating with providers of debt financing.

When either a fund or the market is in turmoil, partners may also spend a larger portion of their time managing investor relations. In down times, there is generally more capital coming out of the hedge-fund industry than entering it. Whether the investors in a fund remain patient depends on their trust in the managers and their reliability as investors. "People often will go out and raise low-quality money—meaning that it comes from sources that are not reliable," explains Tim Jenkins, who raised a fund in early 2007. "There are certain kinds of investors who consistently pull out at the first sign of trouble. You need to understand the stability of your capital."

The economic volatility in 2008 caused even traditionally reliable investors to try to withdraw investments from hedge funds. "Some hedge-fund investors did not like their liquidity profiles [the intervals at which they were allowed to make withdrawals from their investments]," explains Jenkins. "They were very unhappy when they were not able to obtain liquidity when they wanted it, regardless of whether they were entitled to it. Many institutional investors also mismatched the liquidity of their own funds with that of the investment managers with whom they had invested their clients' money. There are many examples of institutional funds that had quarterly liquidity for their own investors but committed capital to hedge funds that had lockups of two years or more."

Strategies differ, but many firms that make large investments in public equities meet with the management teams to discuss the businesses and assess the managers' ability to run them effectively. Partners at large hedge funds often set up meetings with managers directly, and investment banks periodically bring managers around to the funds. The executives want to "sell" the funds on their stocks, and banks endeavor to keep strong relationships with the corporations.

Managing a hedge fund entails not only thinking about single investments but also overseeing the entire investment portfolio. "Running a portfolio is very different from being a stock picker," explains Seth Klarman. "You have to think very hard about position sizing and diversification. It might be tempting when you have a great idea to put 25 percent of the fund in one position, but you are effectively betting the ranch. You are not treating your clients right, nor is it smart for business because, if that 25-percent position goes down by half, you now have caused yourself a massive business problem."

Managing the non-investment side of a firm is also critical. Klarman advises someone starting a fund to "invest as heavily as possible in the operations side of the firm. For example, hire a good CFO. While you can only succeed on the investment side, you can fail on the investment side or the operations side. If you send financial reports to the wrong clients or report the wrong net worth on their statements, your clients will be extremely disillusioned."

INVESTMENT STRATEGIES

"Hedge fund" has become a catch-all term for any private investment fund focused on public markets (and able to charge large fees). As a result of this broad use of the term, not all hedge funds actually hedge their investments or focus on buying stocks. Some focus exclusively on trading debt, commodities, art, or wine (one even focuses on adult entertainment companies).[7] All these funds seek investments for which they believe they can accurately predict the direction of an asset's value.

Successful fund managers are cognizant of what their edge is. They continually ask, "What is this security worth? Where is it trading?" They use their insight or structural advantages to drive investment decisions. Some firms have large enough staffs that an analyst can focus more deeply on a few companies. Some have proprietary computer models that identify trends in certain markets. Some have

the advantage of being able to wait two or more years for an investment to pay off. Some have senior managers who are from an emerging market and understand the business environment there better
than other investors.

Comprehending how markets and global economies are interre-
lated can also provide opportunities for valuable trades. "I think it is
important to have an interest in macro analysis," said Julian Robertson,
who has invested successfully in everything from U.S. stocks to Asian
currencies. "I hate people who make light of an investor that makes a
lot of money in currencies. There is a tendency to think that currency
trading is limited to the people who currently do it. No one has ever
been precluded from currency trading. I think it is very smart to be
well-rounded. There is not that much difference between currencies
and stock. A country can be thought of as a company when you are
looking at currencies and credit differences between various nations."

Other large and successful funds focus on only one asset class,
often stocks. This is the case with Maverick Capital, a multibillion-
dollar hedge fund. Maverick invests exclusively in public equities, buying companies both long and short to enhance returns and hedge risk.[8]

Value Investing vs. Speculation

One investment approach employed by many investors across asset
classes is "value" investing. Seth Klarman, one of the preeminent value
investors, notes that although most investors claim to be "value investors," few truly deserve the title:

> Value investors look at what things are worth today and are not
> dreamy-eyed about the future, although a value investor necessarily
> needs to consider the future—whether the numbers today are sus-
> tainable or are likely to be on a strong growth trajectory. Growth in-
> vestors make the mistake, often, of being so excited about growth
> that they forget that it matters what you pay for a security. Momen-
> tum investors have no anchor. They buy things that are doing well
> and sell them when they stop doing well. They are rudderless. What
> do you do if you own a momentum stock that acts well and then, all
> of a sudden, there is a very short-term jolt? Momentum is a confus-
> ing term; people can be referring to momentum of earnings, of rev-
> enue, of share price. When the momentum stops, what do you do?
> Sell, buy more, or wait? Value investors have a very valuable road

map. They figure out what an investment is worth, look at where the security is trading and, if it is at a substantial discount, they buy it. If it goes down, they reassess, try to figure out why it went down, and if they are convinced that the value is still there, they buy more.

Everyone wants to be a value investor; even growth investors will say that they are buying things for less than they are worth, but they have flimsy definitions of value. These days, there are articles about people collecting wine or rare porcelain or stamps as investments. Those are not investments; they are speculations. An investment is something that has an intrinsic value that primarily consists of its ability to generate cash. If you own a building and it's filled with tenants, if you own a bond and it pays coupons, those things are throwing off cash; they are investments. If you buy a bottle of wine, its only value is what someone will pay you in the future to drink it or to resell it. When you are totally dependent on the whim of a future buyer, you are much closer to speculation. An investment throws off cash and has downside protection, a margin of safety. If you bought a restaurant company that owned its stores, but was bad at selling hamburgers, its buildings still have value to somebody else. An investment may have many types of downside protection and many ways that it can be profitable. A speculation has one: you hope you find a buyer at a higher price.[9]

Although value investing has proved to be an effective strategy when well executed, it is not the only approach that has been successful. Historically, there have been five types of funds: long-short, arbitrage, global macro funds, managed futures, and event-driven. Some firms manage a fund using one or more strategies; other firms have multiple funds, each employing different strategies. Certain hedge funds also invest in private markets, such as venture capital, growth equity, leveraged buyouts, and real estate. The investment focus of firms can evolve over time. For example, Cerberus Capital Management, which long had a focus on distressed debt, now allocates a huge portion of its capital to leveraged buyouts of distressed businesses.[10]

Long-short Funds

Long-short funds follow the method of industry pioneer Alfred Winslow Jones, buying some securities long and shorting others. All long-short funds hedge their investments to some extent, but managers can vary their long and short exposure based on their expectations of where the market is going. If they are bullish, they will likely allocate more than half their invested capital to long positions; if they are bearish, they will do the opposite.* A manager may allocate more than 100 percent of a fund's value between long and short investments, often without having to borrow money. When a firm shorts a stock, it sells the borrowed shares. It then has the cash value of the shares until it decides to close the position and buy back the shares (in order to return them to the party from which they were borrowed). As the firm does not have to commit equity to hold short positions, it can invest more than 100 percent of the fund's value without any loans. For example, a $100 million hedge fund might have $50 million invested short in companies X, Y, and Z. Simultaneously, it might have $100 million invested long in Wal-Mart, Coca-Cola, and Google. If the fund managers accurately predict the direction of its investments, and the short stocks go down 10 percent while the long stocks go up 10 percent, the firm will return 15 percent without having to borrow money. This investing approach is a form of leverage, but not necessarily one that increases risk. "I could make a very good case that a fund that has 100 percent of its value invested long, and that borrows to have 50 percent of its value invested short, is more conservative than a fund with no leverage that is invested 100 percent long," says Julian Robertson. In this example, the firm has invested 150 percent of the fund's value, but its net exposure to market movements is only 50 percent.†

One of the largest and most successful hedge funds that principally employs a long-short strategy is SAC Capital, founded by Steven A. Cohen.[11] Unlike long-short funds that have average hold times of three months or longer, SAC often moves in and out of equity positions very quickly. Because of the size and frequency of its trades, it is one of the most active participants in U.S. equity markets, comprising as much as 3 percent of the New York Stock Exchange's daily trading volume.[12] The use of rapid trading, as opposed to buying securities for a longer

---

*Being bullish is having a belief that the market will rise. Being bearish is having a negative view of a security's or market's prospects.
†Net exposure is the exposure of a fund to changes in the equity markets. It is calculated by subtracting the percent of the fund's capital invested short from the percent invested long.

period, has significant tax consequences for investors. If a fund owns a security for over a year, the profits from the sale are taxed as capital gains. If a trade is made when the security is held for less than a year, the profits are taxed as income. Capital-gains tax rates can be as much as 20 percent lower than income-tax rates, so the tax efficiency of a firm's strategies can be an important consideration for investors.

Arbitrage

Arbitrage funds try to exploit the differences in the price of an asset across multiple markets or the mispricing of two or more assets that are correlated. Because many investors look for arbitrage trades, successful firms generally need advanced computer systems and financial models to quickly take advantage of opportunities and to identify correlations. Arbitrage opportunities can arise from:

- pricing variation between securities and their underlying components (such as a convertible bond that allows the holder to convert the security into equity);
- asset prices deviating from the historic levels for yield curves and credit spreads (the two underlying measures of the value of a bond)[*]; and
- historical mathematical relationships between different assets.

There are also capital-structure arbitrage trades, in which a fund owns some debt/equity in a company long and owns another component of the same business short. For example, if a hedge fund thinks a company will go bankrupt, it might buy secured debt (which would likely be paid off in the bankruptcy) as well as short, unsecured debt (which would decrease in value).

One of the most successful statistical arbitrage funds is D. E. Shaw, which hires talented computer scientists and mathematicians to con-

---

[*]*Yield curves relate to the time before a bond matures. Normal yield curves indicate that longer-term bonds pay higher interest than those with shorter periods of maturity. "Credit spread" refers to the amount of interest that debt pays above the interest on U.S. Treasury bonds. The riskier the entity issuing the debt, the higher the credit spread.*

struct and operate complex models by which to identify arbitrage opportunities. Not surprisingly, the multibillion-dollar firm is incredibly secretive about its strategies. Finding opportunities at D. E. Shaw requires extensive research, which David Shaw believes gives his firm a competitive advantage.

> It's been our experience that the most obvious and mathematically straightforward ideas you might think of have largely disappeared as potential trading opportunities. What you are left with is a number of relatively small inefficiencies that are often fairly complex and which you're not likely to find by using a standard mathematical software package. . . . Even if you were somehow able to find one of the remaining inefficiencies without going through an extremely expensive, long-term research effort of the sort we've conducted over the past eleven years, you'd probably find that one such inefficiency wouldn't be enough to cover your transaction costs.[13]

Given that many arbitrage opportunities are very small—often fractions of a cent—and that trading incurs transaction costs, high volume can be key in the profitability of arbitrage.

Event-driven Strategies

Event-driven strategies try to take advantage of occurences, such as mergers and debt downgrades (when ratings agencies deem that a company is less financially sound), that impact individual securities. The announcement of a merger of two publicly traded businesses can cause significant volatility in the stock prices of the two companies. Public markets often overreact, driving the shares of one player in a merger higher or lower than fundamental analysis would suggest is warranted. This creates an opportunity for hedge funds. Similarly, many investors do not want to be invested in companies that are perceived as distressed. Funds that have expertise in valuing ailing companies can profit from buying their debt at a discount. A large player that utilizes this strategy is London-based Centaurus Capital. It buys stock and debt in companies, primarily European ones, that it believes are being affected by major changes or corporate events, such as earnings releases or acquisitions. Some long-short funds, such as SAC Capital, also employ event-driven strategies.

Global Macro Fund

Global macro funds (also called "directional funds") try to identify and profit from macroeconomic trends (for example, inflation, unemployment, and GDP growth) that will cause changes in the values of assets. A prominent asset class that these funds invest in is currencies. Successfully predicting currency changes can yield large profits, as is illustrated by Soros' bet against the British pound and Julian Robertson's trades in Asian currencies. The adoption of the euro has eliminated many currencies and decreased the variety in possible trades of this type. Nevertheless, these funds continue to be opportunistic, looking for trades across asset types and international markets. As a result, it is challenging to clearly define their investment parameters.

Managed Futures

Managed-futures funds invest in a broad array of markets, including metals, commodities, currencies, and market indexes. They utilize financial instruments, such as options, to buy positions in areas as disparate as Japanese yen, platinum, and soybeans. As a result of such diversification, these funds are intended to have lower risk and not to move in line with stock markets. Given the impact that these funds can have on commodity markets (markets for tangible goods), they are regulated by the Commodity Futures Trading Commission.

Other Strategies

Firms can hedge stock investments by industry (for example, by buying McDonald's long and Wendy's short) or by the overall market (by buying long and short positions in market index funds).

Hedge funds also use options to invest and hedge investments. A "call option" is a contract that allows an investor to buy a security at a specified price during a certain time frame. For instance, someone might purchase a call option for $5 that gives him the ability to purchase a share in Apple for $140 during a four-week period. If the price exceeds $140, the holder of the call option can buy the stock at $140 and sell it immediately for a profit. If Apple stock rises to $146, the option holder will make a 20 percent profit on the $5 investment (versus only a 4 percent profit if he had owned the stock outright). However, losses from price declines are equally magnified.

A "put option" works the opposite way: it gives the holder the right to sell a stock at a specified price—an investment that pays off if the stock goes below the specified level. Options have the advantage of potentially producing far greater returns than if one bought or shorted stocks, but they are also riskier because expired options are worthless.

Of course, just because a fund believes that its positions are hedged does not mean that it will never lose money. For example, in the fall of 2006, Amaranth, a multibillion-dollar hedge fund, was forced to close when a highly leveraged bet on natural gas prices went bad and the firm lost $6 billion. Funds often use leverage to increase returns. However, when significant leverage is used, funds can find themselves exposed to much greater losses, as Amaranth's fall illustrates.

Activist Shareholders

Large hedge funds can sometimes affect their returns in public equities by being activist shareholders. An activist shareholder builds up a large position in a company—perhaps buying 2 to 5 percent of the company's stock—and then pressures the company's management to give the shareholder a seat on the board and/or to take specific actions, such as selling an asset or division of the business. "There are two sides to that coin," notes Klarman, who is not an activist investor. If a company "had a bunch of inefficient businesses lying around with badly utilized resources, you might well be making the economy more efficient and might even be creating jobs by forcing a business to redeploy those resources." However, he cautions that applying pressure to well-run companies in order to extract short-term shareholder benefits can have negative repercussions.

> The problem is that nobody can know which shareholders are right and which management groups are right. I have sympathy on both sides. I would not be universally applauding the shareholder activists who, I think, can sometimes force companies to do things that cause those companies problems later. For example, when the fashion is to leverage up [to use debt rather than equity to finance operations and expansion], the activist investors force companies to leverage up and give back money to shareholders, and, then, when the fashion is to de-leverage, the company goes broke because it has too much debt. Is it on the hedge-fund manager's conscience that 10,000 people are laid off when that happens? I think it cuts both ways.

ANALYSIS

Analysis within a hedge fund often resembles the work of associates in private equity in terms of evaluating industry trends and valuing businesses. Hedge fund analysts who focus on the equity market spend a lot of time reading SEC filings (in which companies report their financials and provide operations details) and trying to understand the value and future prospects of companies. Analysts dedicated to currencies and commodities might focus on changes in government policies and macro-level supply-and-demand drivers, such as wages, inflation, and governmental monetary policy. In all cases, the analysts want to examine information that will enable their firm to identify investment opportunities for which its outlook diverges from the consensus on Wall Street. "You are trying to answer the basic question, 'Why is there a misperception about this stock's value in the market? Why is this stock cheap or expensive?' Financial models are built around the relatively few variables that determine a company's earnings and the valuation it deserves," such as earnings power and free cash flow, explains Tim Jenkins, who has worked in both private equity and hedge funds. "In private equity, price is what you negotiate. That is not a consideration for hedge funds. Private equity is 80 percent process, and most private equity firms pursue similar strategies. In public market investing, people can have very different strategies and perspectives."

Investment decisions at most hedge funds are based on very in-depth research. "When I worked for Tiger, it was always very important to spend time assessing a company's management team, not just its business model. We wanted to understand who the managers were and how they thought about their business, industry, and balance sheet," says Jenkins. "We would visit companies; meet with senior managers as well as business-unit managers; attend conferences; and speak with competitors, customers, and suppliers. Although we generally didn't go this far, some firms would hire private investigators to perform background checks and create detailed studies of management teams."

Not only do good and bad investment decisions impact the performance of a fund, they also affect the partners' wallets, as a significant portion of the capital base at most funds is committed by the senior leadership. "Every day, you are looking at the guy whose money you're investing," says Jenkins.

FEES

The standard hedge-fund fee structure is the "2 and 20" model (2 percent of assets under management and 20 percent of profits). However, funds with particularly strong performances can charge much higher fees. The Renaissance Technologies Medallion Fund is known for charging the highest fees: 5 percent of assets under management and 44 percent carry on profits.[14] The firm's tremendous returns in excess of these fees have kept investors happy and made the firms' management billions of dollars. In 2007, the top ten hedge-fund earners each made over $500 million, with Renaissance Technologies' founder James Simons earning $2.8 billion, and John Paulson of Paulson & Co. netting a staggering $3.7 billion. Each earned over $2 billion in 2008.[15]

High-water Marks

In order to attract investors and make them comfortable with paying hefty fees, many firms have a high-water-mark clause. This means that investors do not pay carry fees in a given period unless a fund's value grows to exceed its previous highest level. For example, if the value of the fund goes down 20 percent in one year and up 15 percent in the next year, the fund will not collect a carry fee (percentage of the year's profits) because the fund's value is below its highest level (the high-water mark). As a result, a hedge fund that does not make money for investors will be out of business quickly. Without profits on which to charge carry fees, its managers cannot pay big salaries to top investment professionals (or themselves), and top talent leaves the firm.

Fund of Funds

An important component of the overall hedge-fund market is the fund of funds. These investment vehicles raise capital from investors and then select a diverse group of fund managers with whom to invest. They offer three advantages over investing directly in a hedge fund:

1. They generally have far lower investment minimums than hedge funds (often $250,000 rather than $1 million or more), which allows more people access to hedge funds.
2. They offer diversity of investments, which potentially minimizes the risk of one bad fund destroying an investor's return.
3. Hedge-fund strategies and the performance of fund managers can be difficult to assess; it is the job of a fund of funds to carefully research all the managers with which it invests.

A fund of funds charges a fee on the assets under management, often 1 or 1.5 percent, and a 5 to 20 percent carry on its annual profits. Because those fees are on top of the fees charged by the managers of the funds in which the fund of funds invests, there is no guarantee that the performance will exceed that of the overall stock market (given annual fees for investors of 3 to 3.5 percent of assets managed and 25 to 40 percent of profits).

Although the economics of fund of funds seem highly attractive for those running them, in turbulent economic times even their founders may not come out on top. For example, in 2006 Ron Insana left his job as an anchor for CNBC to start a fund of funds. He believed that his relationships with some of the world's most successful hedge-fund managers could be turned into a successful investment business, even though his personal investment experience came only from covering markets as a reporter. Top hedge funds often do not accept new investors. This is because they believe either that their investor base is adequate to support increases in the capital under management or that expanding too much will hinder their high returns. Insana convinced managers of top funds to allow him to invest with them. Although he was able to raise over $100 million, it was far less than the billion dollars he sought. His fund charged 1.5 percent of assets under management and 20 percent of profits. Insana had the terrible luck of starting his fund just as markets began to become more volatile. In just over a year, his fund was down by 5 percent.[16] Even though the market was down much more significantly, the fund did not have any profits on which to charge the 20 percent carry fee.

The management fee brought in over a million dollars, but after he paid all the firm's employees and the expenses of running the business, Insana was left with little and decided to close the business. His fund's failure was attributed largely to bad timing, though others have failed because of negligence in conducting diligent investigation of the funds in which they have invested (their most important responsibility). Many poured millions into Madoff Securities, while apparently asking few tough questions. Fairfield Greenwich Advisors invested more than half of its $14 billion fund with Madoff's firm.[17]

REGULATION OF HEDGE FUNDS

Although relatively unregulated, hedge funds have to abide by certain constraints in order to maintain their autonomy from government agencies. Funds that actively trade in commodities submit limited filings to the Commodity Futures Trading Commission, and funds with more than $100 million under management report their holdings to the Securities and Exchange Commission on a quarterly basis. Funds can have no more than ninety-nine investors, each worth $1 million plus, or up to 500 investors if each has a portfolio valued at $5 million or more.[18] The rationale for the lighter regulation of hedge funds, as opposed to mutual funds, is that wealthier, presumably more sophisticated, investors can discern the risks of investing with a particular manager, while the average mutual-fund investor may not have the resources to conduct due diligence. The logic of this argument was severely challenged by the Madoff scandal. Given the number of investors in Madoff Securities, it should have been registered with the Securities and Exchange Commission. However, in order to avoid SEC scrutiny, Madoff did not allow the feeder firms that invested with him to mention Madoff Securities in the materials they sent to their clients, which kept his investor count hidden from authorities. Sophisticated investors in his fund, which included the large European banks Crédit Agricole, Banco Santander, and HSBC, apparently had no greater visibility into his illicit behavior than did non-financial clients.

PART 2

INSIDE A HEDGE-FUND FIRM

ORGANIZATIONAL CULTURE AND LIFESTYLE

Hedge-fund offices are often set up in one large room, with the investment professionals who direct trading decisions sitting at desks in this open space. Each desk has three to nine computer monitors that display stock prices, corporate news, and financial data. The lack of separate offices for traders makes it easier for people to discuss transactions on an ongoing basis.

The tone of the environment varies by firm. Funds that make longer-term investments tend to be more tranquil than funds that move in and out of positions within minutes. "People do try to stay unemotional with the investments," said an analyst at a fund with multimonth investment periods. "If you came into the office, you would never be able to discern a good day from a bad day. We take an analytical rather than an emotional approach. If a company in which we own stock has a bad earnings report, we analyze the holding. We decide if the report changes the reason we bought the stock. If the report proves us wrong, we sell. If it provides us no information, we'll probably keep the position at the same size. Sometimes a bad earnings report can contain information that gives us more confidence that we'll be right in the future and, in that case, we might buy more." Other firms take on the feel of investment-banking trading floors and are more charged with adrenaline when the market is open.

Regardless of the level of outward expression of emotion, a sense of competitiveness pervades even the most collegial investment funds. Unlike in most businesses, people's performance can be measured constantly in terms of profits and losses. At firms with sector heads who oversee specific types of investments, there is competition in terms of who can produce the best returns. Competition exists even at the analyst level. It is generally less pronounced, because it is harder to measure people who do not have a final say on all of their investments, but a competitive environment is contagious. Some funds encourage and reward team-based collegial competition, and other institutions embody an "eat what you kill" mentality. There are even firms where employees function like independent contractors, earning large portions of the profits they generate and giving the rest to the firms' senior leaders. In such organizations, loyalty often extends only until a trader has a more lucrative offer. That allegiance cuts both ways, as two to three months of bad performance can cause someone to be phased out of the firm. Speaking about his experience at a fund with this type of setup, a former analyst commented that "people didn't work for the quality of life, they went to the office every day in order to do their best to make as much money as possible. They left the office camaraderie and cultural stuff at the door."

There is also diversity in dress and demeanor. "I run my own fund, and I am wearing a suit today," said Tim Jenkins, cofounder of Marble Arch Investments. "It is part of the mindset that I took from the firms in which I learned the business." He believes that a more formal approach is an important part of the culture at his fund, where executives meet with many management teams. However, he adds that there are tremendously successful funds that have more casual environments.

Like traders at investment banks, people who work for hedge funds have hours that correspond with the times when stock markets are open. However, that does not translate into a short day. "My hours are pretty much around the clock," says Tim Jenkins. "Although the U.S. markets are only open for a set period each day, there is usually a market open somewhere in the world at any given time. In the public markets, you are constantly assessing new pieces of information and you have nearly unlimited control over your portfolio, which makes the pace of the job much more active. However, I do have control over my schedule in the sense that I'm the one deciding which investment ideas to pursue." In general, there are fewer all-nighters and weekends worked than in private equity, but there are also fewer moments of downtime during the day. Senior leaders (fund managers) even have to coordinate their vacations in order to ensure that the business can continue to invest if someone is out of the office and difficult to reach. Public markets wait for nobody, so being away on vacation for a week can be difficult to arrange, because stock prices change and new information that shapes how investors perceive the values of assets is constantly being released.

CHARACTERISTICS FOR SUCCESS

Success at most hedge funds takes more than just analytical talent; it requires a high level of business judgment in order to understand securities and markets well enough to drive large financial returns. Some firms look for deep expertise in a specific industry or asset class (such as currency, commodities, and bonds); others look for raw talent. Many funds look for specific personality traits. "We want people to fit into our team-based, collaborative culture," explains Klarman. "We like people to have outside lives that are interesting. We like people who are well read. People need to be problem solvers. Can they learn and are they interested in learning? If people think they know it all before they start, they are probably not the right fit. If someone wants to leave immediately and start his or her own firm, he or she is probably not the right person. We tend to hire people who want to be long-term employees and potentially partners at the firm some day."

PROMOTION AND MOBILITY

When people first start at a hedge fund, their work tends to focus on the analysis that underlies the decision making of seasoned investors. Hedge-fund analysts work with more senior people who help guide the industry, companies, and other asset areas on which the analysts focus. "In general, when people first join the firm they are assigned to senior professionals whom they work with for the next two, three, or four years," explains Julian Robertson. "They get the grunt work of ratios and statistical stuff, but that can change fairly quickly. If they are successful, the promotion rate is very quick. We had a thirty-year-old president at one time, so people get very important positions quite soon. I think that is why so many people like the hedge-fund industry."

In order to advance within most firms, analysts are expected to develop their own investment ideas. That can be a stressful opportunity, because the performance of an investment is associated with the person who advocated it. Individual performance is transparent, and mediocrity is not tolerated for long. "The results of your work in the hedge-fund business emerge in a relatively short period of time, compared with private equity, where the success or failure of an investment may take years to determine," says Tim Jenkins.

COMPENSATION

Compensation is largely determined by the performance of the fund in a given year. As in private equity, base salaries start at around $100,000 and increase with tenure. However, the majority of compensation comes in the form of annual bonuses, which can range from nothing to millions of dollars. Employees also have the opportunity to co-invest in the funds for which they work. Some firms allow people to invest as soon as they are hired, while others permit employees to co-invest only by allocating portions of their annual bonuses to the funds.

HIRING PRACTICES

Most hedge funds have small staffs, so they hire few people. In looking for candidates, they sometimes rely on personal networks and recommendations. Although some funds, such as Bridgewater Associates, hire analysts right out of college, most look for people with some financial experience, such as participating in an investment-banking analyst program or experience at another investment firm. "Very few hedge funds have any interest in training or teaching," notes the founder of a large firm. "They have an interest in hiring fully developed people."

From an applicant's perspective, the first question one should ask in evaluating whether to work at a fund is, "Would I want to invest my money here?" The ability to produce strong returns is the primary driver of whether a hedge fund will stay in business. The interview may be one of the few opportunities for a potential hire to gather key information about a firm, such as its track record and strategy for producing high returns in the future. Seth Klarman advises, "If someone says, 'I have a computer model, and we are up 72 percent a year,' then you would say, 'Can you tell me a little about how the model works?' Why would there not be competition in the development of computer models like there is with everything else? Because there clearly is. I would be skeptical of too good a record, but I would particularly focus on if they made most of the record when they had only $20 million under management and now they have $2 billion or $20 billion. I think you would want to ask, 'Do you do what you say you are doing? Are the people here now the same ones that were here when you produced those strong returns? Is it credible that this will be replicable into the future?'" Picking a firm carefully is critical because poorly run funds can go out of business quickly. This would result not only in being out of a job, but also in having a negative association to overcome. "There is a certain type of notoriety that surrounds certain funds," said one industry veteran. "If you were to join one of those funds, and it blew up, I think that it would be a tough burden to overcome."

PART 3

INSIGHTS FROM INDUSTRY LEADERS

JULIAN ROBERTSON, FOUNDER OF TIGER MANAGEMENT

Julian Robertson was one of the pioneers of the hedge-fund industry when he started Tiger Management in 1980. His fund began with $8 million in capital and, by the turn of the century, he was managing roughly $22 billion. Although he closed his fund to outside investors after two down years, he continues to invest successfully and to manage a large personal fortune through managers who he oversees and mentors. Robertson is credited not only with creating massive financial returns but also with developing some of the most talented hedge-fund operators. His "tiger cubs," as those who work for his fund are called, have gone on to build tremendously successful firms of their own.

Given the proliferation of the fundamental long/short equity strategy, do you think the market has become more efficient? Has it

therefore become more difficult for hedge funds to outperform other investments?

Yes, it is more efficient, and that is because of the proliferation of hedge funds. In general, hedge funds are much tougher competition than investment banks or mutual funds. There are exceptions, but most hedge funds have very smart people in them.

Do you expect major shifts in the hedge-fund industry over the next decade as a result of that increased efficiency?

I think that twenty-five years from now, as hedge funds continue to proliferate, the excellence of the investment process will bring about an efficient market theory. This will cause the statistical results of funds to be much more similar.

What will be the long-term effects, if any, of the recent economic turmoil on the hedge-fund business?

I do not think the effects will be terribly profound. If you look at the industry performance average, hedge funds performed twice as well (or, more appropriately, half as badly) as other investment mediums in 2008. Nothing has happened in terms of performance that invalidates hedge funds.

SETH KLARMAN, PRESIDENT, THE BAUPOST GROUP

Seth Klarman is regarded as one of the most successful money managers in the world. He is a practitioner of the value-investing principles laid out by Benjamin Graham, and his own investment book, *Margin of Safety,* commands prices above $1,000 on eBay. Klarman's first opportunity to demonstrate his investment skills came immediately after business school, when he was asked by a professor to help manage a pool of money for a group of families. Failing to find managers whom he trusted to invest the money effectively, Klarman took on the task himself and has consistently produced exceptional returns ever since.

Tell us about starting Baupost.

I was there at the beginning, but I really didn't start it. Baupost was a collaboration of several families that were monetizing some of their illiquid assets. They came together, and I entered the picture, and I think I changed their plan a little. They were going to parcel out most or all of the money to other investment firms. When I came along, the decision was made that we would become an investment firm ourselves. I did not take the entrepreneurial risk of starting Baupost.

What came together was serendipitous, and the good things happened after that. My advice to a young person entering the job world would be, don't worry so much about what you get paid the first year. Don't worry about how you get rich right away; worry about how you can learn a lot, how you can get responsibility as quickly as you deserve it, and how you can get connected with good people who will care about you—about your advancement and about your learning. When I joined Baupost, I started with a relatively modest salary [only $35,000[19]] and a promise that I would participate in profits when there were some. There were no guarantees and no ownership on day one. I ultimately became owner of the controlling interest of the company. It was because the founders were high-quality people; they saw that I had talent and let it grow and flourish. They knew when to back off.

You have extended the investment scope of Baupost over time. How do you think about investments in different asset classes?
We invest everything in parallel, although there are several entities. We have expanded the scope of our opportunity set to include private investments, including real estate, and to be fully international, but the philosophy hasn't changed at all.

Are there advantages to having that diversity, or is it more about having the ability to see additional opportunities across different arenas?
It is not automatically good to be in all sorts of different things. It is good to look at lots of different things, because we want to have our money in the cheapest things that are out there. If you look as broadly as possible, you are more likely to have cheap things fall within your search.

TIM JENKINS, COFOUNDER OF MARBLE ARCH INVESTMENTS
Tim Jenkins started his career as an analyst at Morgan Stanley's private equity fund. Believing that an independent private equity firm would

offer more opportunities, he joined Madison Dearborn, a large Chicago-based private equity firm. During business school, he interned at Viking Global Investors, a large hedge fund started by a former employee of Tiger Management. After graduating in 2003 he went to work for Julian Robertson at Tiger Management. After four years he cofounded his own firm, Marble Arch Investments.

What will be the long-term effects, if any, of the recent economic turmoil on the hedge-fund business?
Clearly, performance across the industry was quite poor in 2008, although it was better than the broader market. A lot of firms need to re-earn investor trust. Some funds imposed gates to reduce investor liquidity. I suspect that, over time, those funds will sustain some reputation damage, because investors have long memories. However, if the industry starts to produce good returns again, those memories may be shorter-lived. I do not think there will be large structural changes in the industry, although it will likely be harder for new funds to raise money for a while. I suspect there will be consolidation and a progression toward larger funds over time, which is not unlike what happened in the mutual-fund industry over the last thirty years.

Will funds lower their fee structures?
I do not think the fee structure will change materially, if at all. What will change are liquidity terms. It used to be the case that people could raise multiyear locked-up money with a small number of liquidity windows [times when investors can withdraw money]. That has been the biggest area of pushback from investors, since liquidity has become very important.

Will the prevalence of leverage in the hedge-fund industry ever return?
Long-short funds like ours use a very modest amount of borrowed money, if any. The funds that use a lot of leverage typically pursue arbitrage strategies that seek to exploit very small profit opportunities. For these strategies to produce attractive returns, leverage is required. What I hear from other people is that, to no one's surprise, leverage has

been sharply reduced, because the people providing lending—namely the prime brokers [investment banks]—are themselves under pressure. However, asset prices have dropped, so the "real" un-levered returns of these strategies have been fine.

Has the stock market acted rationally over the last couple of years, or has volatility been driven more by fear than fundamentals?
It's difficult to say; I'm sure that question will be debated for some time. The financial crisis and global economic collapse that followed created a very challenging investment environment. The unprecedented government interference in the capital markets that followed further complicated the investment landscape. But I'm not sure that the market's huge swings were irrational. People were scared, and investors in just about every asset class sold investments en masse. That will result in a lot of price movements that appear irrational. Looking back on the recent volatility, you can certainly see how fear and greed were at work, sometimes on the same day.

The most surprising thing to me, and to many other investors, was the power of de-leveraging in the market. As a result, a lot of odd things occurred in the second half of 2008. You would come in to the office in the morning and find that all your long positions were down and that your shorts were up. You wondered how this was possible day after day. It was because people were simply ripping their exposures off [investors were reducing investment exposure by selling longs and covering shorts]. Most investors had never seen that degree of de-leveraging, which is why you saw poor returns from nearly every fund, no matter the strategy, with only a handful of exceptions.

What is the fallout of the Bernie Madoff scandal? Is it contained to the fund of funds?
Certainly it is very bad press for the industry. It affects the fund-of-fund business most, but, of course, the fund-of-fund business impacts the direct hedge-fund business. The degree of the scam was egregious. What is interesting is that anyone who had done more than five minutes of research would never have invested in Madoff's fund. It shows how little due diligence people had done. Nearly all our investors have internal

due-diligence teams. They review our fund documents, investor correspondence, and systems, and conduct on-site visits with our investment and operations teams. They perform orders-of-magnitude more diligence than it would appear anyone did with Madoff.

Ultimately, the incident may prove to be a good thing for the hedge-fund industry if it results in healthy scrutiny from investors and regulators. We don't believe that greater oversight would hurt us because we do everything by the book already. But people running loose operations may find themselves in trouble.

What type of regulatory change do you expect?

I think there will be a lot of discussion and probably some modest reforms, but it's unclear how much substantive, long-term change there will be. Although politicians everywhere want to demonize the industry, hedge funds did not cause this problem. It was widespread, systemic greed throughout the system, lax risk controls, and ineffective government regulation. The businesses that facilitated much of the trouble—the banks and government-sponsored mortgage enterprises [Fannie Mae and Freddie Mac]—are all regulated businesses. It is easy for people to blame Wall Street and anyone who is affiliated with it, but the only way Wall Street was able to do what it did is the greed that compelled people to buy houses and other products that they could not afford. The blame goes up and down the system. I think there will probably be more regulation and scrutiny of the hedge-fund industry, but I do not think it will be damaging in the long run. Encouragingly, regulators seem to be conscientious about proposed rules that could prove disruptive. For example, regulators considered forcing public disclosures of short selling but backed off after complaints from the industry. We now submit data to the SEC about what securities we short, but the SEC has decided not to publish that data, which might have caused a lot of problems.

CHAPTER FIVE

THE MILLION-DOLLAR ANALYSIS OF MANAGEMENT CONSULTING

We were the original arbitrage talent business. Meaning we hired some-one, paid them $100,000, and charged them out for $300,000 because we could hire better talent than others could.

—A management-consulting partner

A HISTORY AND EXPLANATION
OF MANAGEMENT CONSULTING

Within weeks of starting at the consulting firm, Laura[1] found herself sitting at a large conference table in the executive wing of the bank for which her team was working. She was tasked with analyzing the performance of peer financial institutions to determine how the client's performance in the third quarter of 2007 compared to that of the competition adjusted for the business mix of each firm. It was exciting to know that the materials she was compiling would be shown to the CFO of this corporation. Nevertheless, she was afraid that she would make some novice error as she pored over the financial statements of other banks.

She was staying at a beautiful, modern hotel in midtown Manhattan, ordering room service, and taking taxis to and from the client's office. Her team spent three or four days a week in New York, with the partner, manager, and consultants sharing one large conference room at the client's headquarters in order to make it easier to gather data and meet frequently with people at the bank. The remaining days, the team members spent at their own desks, where they were often more efficient than when sharing a conference room in New York. The days were long, but splitting her time between the lavish corporate headquarters of the client and the elegant hotel made Laura feel pretty important.

As the junior associate on the team, she took the initiative on food runs and printing documents, but the real work that she completed was valuable for the project. The assignments were outlined and later checked and tweaked by her supervisor, a Harvard Business School grad who had been in consulting for just over a year. She was as sharp as anyone Laura had ever worked with and, more important, she was supportive. Nevertheless, even her positive attitude could not overcome the contagious nature of pre-client-meeting stress. Because of the time-sensitive nature of the work, the tension in the conference room would rise before meetings with the client's representatives. Everyone would scramble to complete analyses and PowerPoint slides. The senior people would rush off to a meeting, and Laura would be left with a few others to briefly decompress and check the *New York Times* online before the manager returned with new analysis requests, which Laura would be expected to quickly complete. Though operating on clients' schedules often made work stressful, she enjoyed the variety of analytical challenges that consulting posed, as well as the opportunity to gain an inside perspective on multiple industries in a very short period of time.

IT CAN BE difficult to understand the rationale for management consulting. Why do large, profitable corporations hire outsiders who have never worked in those corporations (or perhaps even in that industry) to solve their business challenges? Why do private-equity firms, whose core function is finding companies that will be good investments, hire consulting firms to analyze the growth prospects of the businesses they are considering buying? The answer is that corporations often find themselves lacking either the experience or the staff resources to address key business issues. The scale of large private-equity buyouts makes the cost of consulting services worthwhile when such services can provide deeper understanding of the dynamics of a market and the position of the target company.

The multibillion-dollar management-consulting industry is rarely talked about in the media. The focus has always been on the client; consequently, consulting firms rarely receive public recognition. They do not list their clients on their websites or discuss them with the media. The reason is that many firms believe that being discreet builds trust with their clients. At some boutique firms, senior partners keep company information close to the chest in order to minimize the temptation for a manager or junior partner to try to steal clients and start his or her own company.

Venture-capital firms and investment banks also tend to keep low profiles, but when their investments perform well or deals close, they take credit. Consultants tend to be behind every major corporate merger, significant cost-reduction initiative, and large private-equity deal; however, unless the client mentions the consultants, they do not receive public recognition. "I am a professional third party. My satisfactions are all derivative," said one consulting partner.

THE HISTORY OF MANAGEMENT CONSULTING

In 1926, James McKinsey, while working as an accounting professor at the University of Chicago, started a firm to provide financial and budgeting services to other businesses. From that venture came McKinsey & Company, the world's best-known management-consulting firm. Prior to that, there were business consultants, but they were focused almost exclusively on improving operations in manufacturing businesses and were referred to as "management engineers." Though James McKinsey's name is on the door, it was Marvin Bower who was largely responsible for building the firm into what it is today. He came to the company in 1933 and during his career developed many of the operating principles that still govern the firm: placing the interests of clients first, emphasizing employee training, and maintaining professionalism. Bower put management consulting on the same plane as law and accounting. It was not until thirty years after Bower began at McKinsey that its first lasting competitor was established.

NEW INSIGHTS

In 1963, Bruce Henderson left his job as a vice president at the Westinghouse Corporation to head a new "consulting" division of the Boston Safe Deposit and Trust Company, an investment-management firm. His division, which eventually became the Boston Consulting Group (BCG), distinguished itself by developing new ideas about the ways in which businesses grow, decline, and compete. Over the years, BCG's business insights have been adopted by many of its peer firms and used in their consulting analyses. For instance, the "experience curve" introduced the principle that the costs of producing a good decrease as the length of time a firm has produced the good increases. Another key insight was the "growth-share matrix," a framework for evaluating multiproduct businesses based on their cash usage and generation.

As is shown in the illustration that follows, the most valuable type of business lines are "stars"—ones that grow rapidly and generate a large amount of cash. As markets mature, stars often become "cash cows"—businesses that produce a lot of cash but are no longer growing rapidly. Businesses with low growth that are not producing much cash are "dogs" and should be exited or improved. "Question marks" are business segments that are growing quickly but not generating cash.

GROWTH-SHARE MATRIX

| | | Relative Market Share (cash generation) | |
		High	Low
	High	Stars	Question Marks
Market Growth Rate (cash usage)	Low	Cash Cows	Dogs

SPINOFFS

A few years after starting his consultancy, Bruce Henderson met Bill Bain on a trip back to his alma mater, Vanderbilt University. Bill Bain was working in the alumni office after graduating from college and Henderson was so impressed with him that he recruited Bain to join BCG. Although lacking the pedigree of an MBA from a top business school, Bain distinguished himself as one of the most insightful consultants at BCG and developed strong client relationships. In the early 1970s, he became frustrated with BCG's focus on producing reports for clients; he wanted to create a more results-driven management-consulting firm. In 1973, he left BCG with six others and started Bain & Company out of his apartment in Boston. The firm sought to differentiate itself by partnering with executives who were willing to undertake dramatic changes at their companies in order to make them more profitable. Unlike McKinsey and BCG, Bain worked with only one company per industry so that the firm's clients would gain real competitive advantage. Bain's business model proved effective, and the firm began to expand its base of clients. Bill Bain took a highly secretive approach to the business, both internally and externally, which led a *Fortune* writer to refer to the company as the "KGB of consulting" in 1987.[2] The firm did not advertise; it relied solely on client referrals and word-of-mouth.

Bill Bain was not the last consultant to believe he could go it alone. In the 1980s and 1990s, partners from established firms and people new to the industry started numerous other consulting practices, including LEK Consulting, Parthenon Group, and Katzenbach Partners (which was acquired by Booz & Company in 2009). "When spinoffs occur, it often is because people are unhappy with what they are being paid, who their boss is, or the fact that they didn't become the boss," explains Joe Fuller, a cofounder and CEO of Monitor Group, a global consulting firm. Although most spinoffs have not overtaken their predecessor firms, they have been successful in carving out their own places in the consulting market. Ram Charan never worked for a major consulting firm, yet, by winning the trust of CEOs, he has established himself in the industry. Charan, who essentially runs a one-man consulting operation, has authored nearly a dozen business books and has advised senior executives at GE, DuPont, and Verizon.

A CYCLICAL INDUSTRY

The consulting industry generally moves in boom-and-bust cycles, in line with the economy. During downturns, large institutions—both companies and governments—often redefine what constitutes a discretionary expenditure, sometimes cutting out consulting services. Consultants can add a great deal of value when companies encounter tough times, but these are often the periods when businesses most need to preserve cash. Ironically, a 2008 article in the *McKinsey Quarterly* suggested that one of the areas in which investment banks could cut costs without damaging employee morale was in slashing fees paid to consulting firms.[3] During recessions, consulting firms cut back on hiring and may increase the difficulty of promotion hurdles.

The nature of specific downturns also affects certain firms disproportionately. For example, Accenture—with its focus on information
technology—was especially hard hit in the 2001 downturn, as companies delayed installing new technology infrastructures. McKinsey has a
huge financial-services practice that felt the effects of the financial
meltdown in 2008. On the flip side, firms with strong cost-reduction
and turnaround practices may find new customers during times of
market tumult. FTI Consulting and Huron Consulting—firms that advise companies on litigation, forensic accounting, and crisis/risk management—saw their business increase in 2008 while most other firms
experienced revenue declines.[4]

A DIVERSE INDUSTRY

There are consulting firms of all types, such as legal, financial, and information technology, but only some are true management-consulting
firms. However, the distinction is a little blurry. Because working with
CEOs on company strategy is thought of as the most alluring type of
consulting, many firms seek to position themselves as management
consultancies. Bain, McKinsey, and BCG have clearly distinguished
themselves as the three big management-consulting firms; however,
large consulting firms, such as Booz Allen and Accenture, have strategy
practices, as do industry-focused boutique consulting firms.

Booz Allen traditionally has specialized in manufacturing
processes and operations, as well as serving the defense industry and
the U.S. government. Booz Allen's government consulting practice was
purchased by The Carlyle Group in May of 2008. The firm was split,
and Booz & Company was spun off as a stand-alone commercial
consulting practice.

Accenture is the largest consulting firm in the world. It focuses primarily on consulting in information technology. The firm is traded on
the New York Stock Exchange and has over $25 billion in revenues.[5]
Accenture consults on process management, technology installation, and
cost reduction and, in some of those functions, it competes with traditional
management-consulting firms; however, firms like Accenture typically
have much longer cases than most management-consulting firms.

Accenture is one of the consulting practices that came out of the accounting industry. All of the major accounting firms used to have consulting practices. This was a practical offshoot for these firms, as they already served major U.S. corporations. However, they began to be criticized for the apparent conflict of interest in having both services under the same roof. Accountants were supposed to audit a company's financial statements fairly and independently. That impartiality and independence can be compromised when a service firm is simultaneously trying to win favor with the corporation in order to garner consulting business. When there were eight or ten major accounting firms, the consulting divisions of those firms were able to serve different corporations than the accounting practices. However, as the accounting industry consolidated significantly, the restrictions on consulting clients began to pose greater challenges. Accenture used to be called Anderson Consulting and was created out of the accounting firm Arthur Anderson. Another consulting firm, Bearingpoint, formerly was the consulting division of KPMG. The most significant consulting practice still within an accounting firm is Deloitte Consulting.

COMPETITION FROM BANKS

Prior to the downturn in 2008, consulting firms were experiencing business interference from the investment-banking field. As part of their sales processes, investment banks were approaching clients with strategies derived from capital markets, such as the idea of stock repurchases.[*]

Banks played to the fact that the compensation programs of many executives were rooted in share prices. Joe Fuller asks, "If you were going to listen to someone about how to improve your share price as a CEO, between Goldman Sachs and Monitor, which would you listen to?" He adds, "Goldman Sachs, even today, can call any CEO in the United States and say, 'We really need to see you,' and they can have a meeting next

---

[*]*Stock repurchases or "buy-backs" occur when a company purchases outstanding public shares of the company. Companies generally do this in the belief that decreasing the supply of shares on the public market will increase the value of those that remain public.*

week. I can call any CEO in the United States and say, 'I really need to see you' and, of the Fortune 500, about 440 would say, 'Who are you and how did you get this number?'" The banks have brand credibility in that arena. However, credibility does not always mean reliability.

In the eyes of some, having banks do advisory work was bad, not only for consulting firms but also for their clients. Fuller cites a telecommunication-services company as a victim of bad strategy advice from an investment bank.

> The investment bankers convinced the CEO, who wanted to sell the company, that if he wanted to get the maximum value he had to get certain operating ratios near the high end of the industry. That advice was derived from the idea that the high-performing companies in this industry have this ratio and get this multiple [of earnings when they are acquired]. Therefore, if this company could achieve a higher operating ratio, it would get a larger multiple. Based on the bankers' advice, the CEO decided that one of the costs he had to cut in order to meet this operating hurdle was customer care. When he cut customer care, customer satisfaction fell through the floor, and he started losing customers, particularly his higher-margin customers. His brilliant campaign to get the ratio up to a level that would drive a higher share price actually caused his revenue to drop. His company became the slowest-growing firm in the industry. The company declined in value by about 30 percent, and then he sold it.

Although Fuller tells this story to illustrate why bankers should not offer strategy advice, it also shows how destructive bad guidance from any type of advisor can be.

THE IMPACT OF THE DOWNTURN

The economic crisis of 2008 and 2009 provided some new opportunities for consultants as businesses looked to cut costs or merge with other companies. Overall though, 2009 was a down year for the consulting industry as companies became more conservative with their cash on hand. Unlike the downturn in 2001, which occurred mainly in the United States, the 2008 and 2009 downturn had a global reach. Given that most consultants do not serve operational roles in their firms, when clients dry up, layoffs can come quickly and unexpectedly. The vast majority of operating costs for a consulting firm are salaries and benefits. As a result, when firms decide that they need to cut costs, it often means letting people go. On the whole, consulting jobs are far more stable than finance jobs, but in really bad economic times, nearly everyone in the business can feel vulnerable.

MANAGEMENT CONSULTING TODAY

To be successful, firms must be able to adapt to changes in the market. The consulting industry has increased its revenues by expanding its offerings into newer businesses, such as serving hedge funds and private equity; by creating new practice areas; and by expanding geographically. One industry veteran predicts, "Private equity is a real economic force and is going to be around for a long time. The trend toward globalization has been occurring for a while; China, India, even some parts of Africa, all are going to be increasingly important." Ron Daniel, former global managing partner at McKinsey notes that "China today is like what the United States used to be, where generalist consultants with excellent analytical skills can be successful (granted that they speak Chinese) without special competence in a specific practice area. In the United States, there are a few McKinsey people who remain generalists, but this requires an exceptional level of talent in problem solving. I often say that being a generalist at McKinsey is now the most demanding specialty of all."

The products demanded by companies in emerging markets change over time as the overall economy matures. "Early on, they [customers in developing countries] want data-intensive reports, where they almost judge the product by the pound," notes Joe Fuller. "Over time, they start learning that there are limits to that, so they start asking more sophisticated questions." The countries in which there is demand for management consulting are those with some very large companies. Outside the United States and Europe, that includes Brazil, Australia, China, Japan, Korea, and India. The Gulf nations and Russia tend to boom and bust more than other markets. However, many stable and growing economies do not have businesses seeking management consulting. "Citigroup has larger potential [from the point of view of a consulting firm] than Egypt, Chile, and Thailand combined and multiplied by three," says Fuller.

Consulting dynamics in developed markets are also changing. Consulting services in Germany historically have had the highest profit margins. German companies are very relationship driven and brand conscious. As a result, McKinsey and BCG, which entered the market well before everyone else, have enjoyed high market share in Germany. All the other major consulting firms work in Germany, but they do not have as much presence. Currently, market share seems to be shifting away from the established players as German managers become aware of how high their consulting fees are relative to the rest of the world.

In the United States, as companies become savvier consumers of consulting services, they are demanding more specialization and expertise from the partners with whom they work. "When I started in consulting in 1978, a client would pay us for a couple of months to learn its businesses and then teach it to them. [Clients did not expect deep industry expertise from the consultants and were willing to pay them while they learned the dynamics of the business before suggesting areas for improvement]. Now, in order to have lunch with a prospective client, you have to show up with two people who know a lot about the business. There is just a lot more knowledge out there," said a consulting partner.

Technology has enabled some components of consulting firms' research and basic data analysis to be conducted in lower-cost countries such as India, China, and the Philippines, but not the core functions. "Bill Bain originally created Bain & Co. to do strategic planning software," recalls Chuck Farkas, a senior director at the firm. "Bain believed that the firm could create software programs that would do 90 percent of what we do and that with just a little wisdom sprinkled at the beginning and the end by consultants, you could have a strategy. It didn't work. You can put data in and generate a lot of graphs and charts, but those aren't strategy." Farkas compares the situation to the impact of new medical-screening technologies on the demand for doctors. "You can now input a lot of data, test results, and other basic information into a computer, and it will tell you what ailments a patient might have, but you still want a doctor to complete the assessment and analyze the computer's results. The doctor and that artificial intelligence, in combination, are better than the computer or the doctor alone. I think we will continue to harness all the things that are out there to be better at our business, but I don't see our business going away."

MOVING FORWARD

As long as the global economy grows, so too will the management-consulting industry. Corporations and finance firms continue to face challenging business questions and to find value in utilizing skilled external advisors. Assuming consulting firms are able to hire, effectively train, and mentor top talent, their services will be in demand. Nevertheless, the industry is highly competitive; for individual firms to continue to grow, they will need to stay nimble and develop new strategic tools. Prior to the recent downturn, a host of new, specialized consulting firms that focused on particular industries or corporate issues were started. The recession put some firms out of business and forced others to merge. Going forward, it is uncertain whether boutique firms will steal market share from the industry's large players or whether the recession initiated a period of consolidation that will benefit the largest global consulting firms for years to come.

HOW MANAGEMENT CONSULTING WORKS

Management-consulting firms provide the capacity to answer important business questions for clients. What new business lines should we start? Does it make sense to expand the business into Asian markets? What costs can be eliminated to improve operating margins? Consultants are brains for hire. Partners bring the experience of having worked with many different companies (usually in that specific industry) without the political baggage of working on the client's management team. The rest of the consulting team brings the analytical capacity to tackle business issues. Rarely are a business's challenges truly unique; on some level, good consultants simply have great pattern recognition.

ATTRACTING CLIENTS

A consulting project is called a "case" or "engagement." Prior to a case beginning, there is a sales process. For existing clients, a new case may be an offshoot of previous consulting work, the result of a direct request from a senior officer at a company, or the result of an issue the consulting partner has identified in a meeting with the client. To win new clients, partners use their networks to schedule preliminary meetings with potential clients in order to explain how they believe they can add value. For the large established consulting firms, existing clients provide the vast majority of new work. "Most of McKinsey's client activity comes from our doing good work for them in the past," notes Ron Daniel. Of McKinsey's roughly $5 billion in annual revenue, Daniel estimates that only "10 to 15 percent comes from clients who are newly introduced that year."

However, many projects, even those for previous clients, tend to be sold on a competitive basis. "The procurement departments* of all major companies have gotten fairly sophisticated," explains Chuck Farkas. "Even if a company intends to hire one firm or another, it wants a little competition to keep pricing fair." A corporation or private-equity firm will submit an RFP (request for proposal) to a number of consulting companies. The consulting firms then create proposals that explain their approaches and what they believe distinguishes them from their competitors. McKinsey, for instance, would likely talk about its breadth of experience, perhaps noting the number of times it has completed a study like the one proposed. Monitor's proposal would discuss its proprietary "tools that help management develop better insight into the choices they have to make. We then work to understand what the decision makers' burden of proof is for making that choice, allowing us to do very lean analysis," explains Monitor's CEO, Joe Fuller. He says that, for firms with high market share in a sector,

---

*The procurement or "sourcing" department oversees all major product and service contracts the company enters into. As consulting engagements can cost several million dollars, this department often is involved in the negotiation process.

"The idea that is developed for one client tends to permeate the industry quickly, because the consulting firm's sales force gets out there and calls on the people they know." The salespeople do not tell potential clients that company XYZ is going to build a new plant in a specific location; however, if in the course of a study the consulting firm comes to the conclusion that alternative power plants are economically viable, it might seek to do a study for another power company on whether it should build this type of plant and how it might go about doing that. Firms draw a line between market insights developed during a client engagement and implications for a specific client. The client owns the analysis of the implications, but the consultants own the market insights.

In some instances a request for proposals is more involved and includes what is called a "bake-off." In this situation, consulting firms complete some work for the potential client (for free) and, based on the preliminary work, the client chooses one firm with which to continue working. Bake-offs tend to occur with savvy consumers of consulting services. These clients have experience with consulting firms and, therefore, can use the competitive process to their advantage. In fact, Fortune 500 firms sometimes hire former consultants into strategic roles and use them, in part, to manage company interactions with consulting firms.

When a case is sold, meaning that the client agrees to the proposal for work, the consulting firm finds a manger to lead the consulting team. That person puts together a group of associates and consultants.

THE CASE PROCESS

Once a consulting team is up and running, it spends the first few days learning about the client's business and the particular issues the case is supposed to address. The team members look at presentations from previous projects (if work has been done for the client in the past); search through their firm's knowledge-management system for relevant intellectual property;[6] and use analysts' reports, news services, and financial statements to quickly develop a baseline understanding of the client.

Businesses hire consultants to help make them more profitable, so most cases focus on increasing revenues, cutting costs, or both. This can mean improving production facilities, evaluating new markets the client might want to expand into, eliminating overhead costs, restructuring the client's sales force, or evaluating a potential merger.

Private-equity diligence cases address different areas. Private-equity firms want to know what the overall dynamics are of the market in which the acquisition target operates, who its customers are, how much room for expansion there is, how the business stacks up against its competitors, and what the target company's revenues will be over the next five years. For instance, in investigating an engine manufacturer for a private-equity client, the consulting team would attempt to answer the following questions:

- What is the projected market growth for the industry?
- What regulatory changes could affect the industry and customers' buying patterns?
- Who are the customers and what criteria do they use to select the engines they purchase?
- What are the relative strengths and weaknesses of the target business?

In contrast, had the engine manufacturer hired the consultants, its questions would likely have been something like the following:

- The operating margins of our business have decreased over the past few years. Where can we eliminate overhead or manufacturing costs?
- Many of our competitors have begun selling engines in Asia. What is the initial investment necessary to gain a presence in the Asian market and, given our current product offerings and competition, how much of that market could we capture?

The pure-strategy consulting cases are often thought of as the most intellectually "sexy." However, the truly challenging assignments (and the most rewarding for the client) often involve some degree of analyzing the execution. "The 'what questions' are almost always susceptible to data, and if your data is poor or has gaps, you triangulate," explains Shona Brown, senior vice president of business operations at Google and a former partner at McKinsey. "There are various tools to use. You can take an analytic process and come up with a relatively clear answer to what you should do. People think that 'Should I buy the company?' or 'Should I enter China?' are the really interesting questions. In fact, the most difficult questions in business are the 'how' questions. It's not whether we should buy the company; it's how we should integrate it. Those issues are much more intellectually challenging. Getting 50,000 people to change course is a much more difficult problem than determining what course you think those people should be on."

Not all consulting projects involve highly complicated questions with work being prepared for the CEO of a company, as Joe Fuller explains:

> There is an illusion that, when you start as an associate at a firm like McKinsey or Monitor, you are going to be working on really high-level problems for a senior executive. That happens, but the majority of people in junior staff roles are going to be working on reasonably straightforward, often mundane problems; for example, "How can we get the costs of wiring harnesses down?" The most senior person on the client side who is going to see the work is a vice president. The work is going to rely heavily on work that has been done in the past and does not have a high level of intellectual content.

Analysis

The analyses that consultants execute incorporate a combination of quantitative and qualitative inputs. For a retail client, the work might involve developing key metrics for all the store locations, segmenting the customers and determining how their buying criteria vary, assessing the characteristics of the stores with the highest sales and identifying their best practices. With a cost-reduction situation or post-merger integration, a combination of interviews with customers and managers and a comparison of the company's cost structure with industry benchmarks would be the basis for setting cost- and/or revenue-synergy targets.

The consultant's toolkit includes analytical methods by which to evaluate customers, cost, industries, organizational structure, process complexity, and business functions (such as finance, IT, supply-chain management, and acquisition diligence). Consultants often add significant value to their clients by conducting and analyzing primary research. That can entail designing Web surveys, leading client-arranged interviews with customers or managers, and conducting cold calls (trying to reach people by phone with no previous introduction or connection). Although the latter can be unpleasant, the data collected from cold calls can provide great insights on customer behavior and industry dynamics, especially when a team is working in an esoteric field that is not well covered by the media, market research firms, and stock analysts. Many businesses have huge expertise in their own products but do not have the resources to fully evaluate all their competitors and the overall market dynamics. Management consulting can provide that resource.

Similar to peer professional services, consulting work can also pose ethical dilemmas as people seek to balance the interests of the client, their firm, and their own ethics. "I worked on a case for a healthcare company that had an incredibly effective antibiotic treatment," recalls one consultant. "Because the drug was so powerful, doctors were only using it in rare circumstances to make sure it was not overused to the point that cells might build up resistance. We were hired by the manufacturer to look at how we could expand the drug's use in the market to make the product more profitable for the company. We interviewed a number of doctors to see how they used it now and how changes in the labels might affect their use. Healthcare companies have to be profitable to survive, but the project raised some ethical issues for me."

FEES

Consulting fees vary from project to project but average a few hundred thousand dollars per team, per month. Clients are not always eager to pay such hefty fees for consulting services. However, when consulting is done right, the profits it generates far outweigh the fees. "I started working with a mid-size data processing company after a failed IPO attempt," recalled an industry veteran. "They told me they had never paid anything like what my firm charged for consulting services before.

There was apprehension at first, but they were receptive to our advice and, in the end, the strategic work that we helped them with led to a successful IPO and ten-million-plus dollars in the pockets of all the senior executives who had stock in the company."

THE ROLES OF PARTNERS

Consulting firms are partnerships, and profits are shared among the partners. At small consultancies, all partners may make management decisions together, but as firms expand, that decision-making authority is often assigned to a governing body. "As Bain has grown, decision making has had to shift from the whole group to a smaller group called the 'management committee,'" notes Chuck Farkas. "The management committee reflects the whole partnership, with various tenures, geographies, industry interests, and so on. Management committees and related subcommittees set compensation standards, evaluate whether to open new offices, create new practice areas, and determine whether partners will be promoted to director."

There is a range of seniority and status within the partner group in large firms. Junior partners are responsible for bringing new business into the firm, working directly with case managers, and other day-to-day roles related to client engagements. At the director (senior partner) level, there are still responsibilities in these areas, but less time is spent with the team. "Over the course of a year, my time is probably split evenly across client development, existing clients, and teams," explains Farkas. Partners at consulting firms work for their clients and, to some extent, report to office heads and more senior partners, but they have far more autonomy than do corporate CEOs. If their firm does not do well in a given year, they do not answer to angry investors. Bill Meehan, a former senior director at McKinsey explains that the partnership structure allowed him "the independence to pursue projects without having to frequently report to a corporate hierarchy."

Writing articles and business books is an activity that may seem peripheral to the consulting business, but one which helps attract new clients. Firms send published articles by their partners to potential and current clients in order to spur interest. Articles can be used to draw attention to a point of view the firm has or to a new tool or idea it is implementing. Publications like the *Harvard Business Review,* the *Wall Street Journal,* and *Financial Times,* which are read by thousands of potential clients, are particularly valued. The content of business books published by partners is business theory and, in some case, consulting firms try to build practice areas around this intellectual property. For example, Fred Reichheld of Bain & Company wrote the book *The Ultimate Question: Driving Good Profits and True Growth.* The underlying concept he introduced was the Net Promoter Score, a simple tool by which customers of a business are asked to rate their likelihood of recommending the service/product to a friend or colleague. Bain developed a suite of peripheral tools around this concept and uses the book to position the organization as the consulting firm for businesses that want to measure or improve customer loyalty.

PART 2

INSIDE A MANAGEMENT-CONSULTING FIRM

ORGANIZATIONAL CULTURE AND LIFESTYLE

Nearly every major consulting firm has a presence in New York, San Francisco, Boston, Dallas, Chicago, and Atlanta. These offices tend to have variety in the types of industries served because of the diversity of businesses headquartered in these cities. Smaller market offices often have more of an industry focus: pharmaceuticals in New Jersey, oil in Houston, entertainment in Los Angeles, and industrials in Pittsburgh. Most firms pay the same salaries and have the same benefits in all their U.S. offices, so one definitely feels wealthier being a consultant in Atlanta than in New York.

TRAVEL

The most common downside associated with the consulting lifestyle is the frequent travel. McKinsey and Accenture are on the extreme end of work travel, requiring that teams work from the client site four days per week. To save money, a handful of "nomadic" consultants who work out of New York offices live in hotels during the week in whatever cities their clients are located and stay with family members or friends on the weekends, rather than renting apartments. By having its consultants work from a client's office, McKinsey is able to easily staff case teams from offices all over the country and the world. A team might have a manager from San Francisco, consultants from Chicago, and an analyst from Mexico City. The advantage to the model for the consulting staff is that it affords a lot of cross-office interaction. Bain tends to operate more on a travel-as-needed basis, which results in an average of two days per week on the road; however, certain practice areas at Bain entail relatively little travel at the associate level. Bain tends to staff most teams out of the same office, so it lacks some of the interoffice work connection, but the lighter travel allows for a much more vibrant office culture. At firms in which all the consultants travel four days per week, the home offices can be very quiet except on Fridays, when the consultants return to complete their expense reports and do some work before the weekend.

TRAINING

In management consulting, the key assets that firms offer their clients are industry- and company-specific insights that will help make the clients' businesses more profitable. The only way to do that consistently is to have very smart employees who are fast learners. Although much of the learning is on the job, formal training programs provide some baseline skills and understanding of the firm's approach. The firms hire employees right out of college and business school, so they cannot assume that people come with specific skills. Initial training provides the basics of financial analysis, PowerPoint, Excel, and key consulting frameworks. Training continues throughout one's tenure at a firm. The initial training programs are very content heavy; as one gains experience, the ongoing training is more social. McKinsey sends second-year business analysts to a castle the firm owns in Europe, and Bain sends its senior associate consultants (third-year out of undergrad) to Cancun or Thailand. The training provides opportunities to learn and interact with peers from the firm's offices around the world. Accenture's training is more methodological: employees go to Lake Charles, Illinois, to become qualified in particular areas and processes. At Monitor, in addition to programs on analytical skills, associates receive extensive training in communication and how to give and receive feedback.

SOCIAL LIFE

Given that consulting firms have offices throughout the world, events that allow cross-office interaction are important in creating a one-firm feel. Bain has become famous in the consulting industry for its Bain World Cup soccer tournament, in which over 800 consultants from around the world meet in the home city of one of the firm's offices for an elaborate soccer tournament. Although many firms sponsor offsite retreats that involve sports, the fact that actual work plays no official part in the Bain World Cup is quite unique. The more casual cultures of some consulting firms—including Bain, Monitor, and Parthenon Group—include a number of social events for employees, from Friday-afternoon beers to weekend parties.

One's work life can mix with one's social life in many industries, but consulting is notorious for blending the two. Because most consulting firms have more casual cultures than comparable areas of business and finance, their associates tend to work and play with their colleagues. Intense travel also can foster more social time with other consultants. That can lead to a more collegial environment in the office as well as more activities with friends from the company outside work. When coworkers spend their social time together, interoffice dating is bound to occur. Firms vary in their acceptance of coworkers dating, but many firms count married colleagues among their current and former ranks.

TIME AND COMMITMENT

The hours that a consultant works vary with each assignment, averaging between fifty and sixty hours per week at the pre-and post-business-school level. The number of hours one works is, in large part, a result of how quickly one completes tasks and how much one is trying to impress others at the firm. "McKinsey, like many consulting firms, is an output-oriented firm," explains Ron Daniel. "People are relatively indifferent to the amount of time and energy that individuals spend in order to produce excellent work. If you can do an assigned task in forty hours, and it takes someone else seventy hours, you may have more free time. However, most of the exceptional performers, who can finish their work in forty hours, actually work sixty hours, adding that much more value and becoming partners in the firm sooner."

Although partners and managers seek to maintain a balance between work and free time for consultants, work comes first and cases for new clients can be more intensive. Partners work for long periods of time to foster a new client relationship. Consequently, they may over-deliver on the first case in order to show the value they can provide. This often requires long hours from the team.

Moreover, partners are extremely loath to walk away from even the most difficult clients, because their compensation hinges on the size and profitability of their billings. Given the difficulty in cultivating new clients, partners have a strong incentive to retain their accounts. However, good firms will not sacrifice their principles to keep bad clients. Monitor dropped a European client because of price fixing and planned to resign from another account because of discrimination. "One of the senior managers at a client firm objected to the fact that there was a gay man on the case," recalls Fuller. "So I said, 'Easy, we don't have to worry about it, we quit.' Within thirty-six hours, his boss's boss was on the phone telling me that this was the damndest thing he had ever heard and that he wanted to meet the young man in question and tell him that his company was friendly and embraced diversity."

In seeking to serve the client, consultants may find themselves in strange positions. "I remember a case team that was doing a project for the client's head of strategy, who clearly was having a nervous breakdown," recalls Chuck Farkas. "The manager and partner went to a meeting with him. The guy, whose hobby was knife throwing, began to throw knives into a bulls eye that was two feet above their heads. After three or four knives had been thrown, they didn't want to be sitting within range any longer, so they got up and left."

Consultants in certain practice areas, such as private equity, corporate mergers, and business turnarounds (where companies face bankruptcy pressures), occasionally work ninety-hour weeks. However, these intense cases tend to be followed by some time off or, at least, lighter assignments (unlike in investment banking, where it would be more of the same). The economics of the consulting business model do not allow consulting firms to compete with investment banks and principal investment firms (such as hedge funds and private equity) in the area of employee compensation, so they focus on work-life balance as a core differentiator in recruiting. Nevertheless, in serving sophisticated businesses and investment firms, it often feels as if the work outweighs the life.

One of the perks unique to consulting is time on the "beach." Consulting is a project-based business, and when consultants are not on a case or on client development, they often are able to enjoy their "unstaffed" status. This means that they do not have to come into the office, although they must be within a few hours' range of it. It is most common for this period to last a couple of days between cases, but at particularly slow business times, consultants can end up with weeks of what amounts to paid vacation.

Contributions to Society

Part of the consulting ethos is that you contribute more to the firm than just what your casework requires. Although there is no obligation to participate in activities outside the office, a commitment to the business or the greater community can be advantageous to advancement within the firm. That commitment—sometimes referred to as "the extra 10 percent"—can be in recruiting (a huge undertaking for professional service firms), organizing office intramurals, volunteering at a local nonprofit, or participating in nonprofit consulting programs. One example of this is Inspire, a nonprofit consulting group composed of associates from Bain, Monitor Group, Parthenon Group, L.E.K., and Katzenbach Partners, that completes consulting projects for small nonprofit organizations. Inspire is supported by the consulting firms, but all the work—from finding "clients" to leading the teams—is done by pre-MBA associates. The associates work for Inspire in their free time, so the scope of a case tends to be much narrower than in a "normal" assignment. At the firm level, all the major companies make in-kind donations of free consulting services to a few not-for-profit organizations. Consultants with particular interests in the social sector can also work on projects in their firms' dedicated nonprofit practice areas or, if they work for Bain, can spend six months at the firm's sister organization Bridgespan, which serves nonprofits exclusively.

Even partners are encouraged to participate in activities outside the firm. Consulting partnerships understand that a large part of their business is client development, and service on boards is a great way to interact socially with potential business prospects. "When I was managing partner, I was able to devote 10 to 15 percent of my time to doing other things, like chairing the board of trustees at Wesleyan University. The firm was supportive of my service outside McKinsey," said Ron Daniel. On occasion, consultants also offer free services to the organizations in which they are involved.

CHARACTERISTICS FOR SUCCESS

Successful consultants combine a strong analytical capacity with good business intuition and an enthusiasm for helping organizations tackle challenging problems. Chuck Farkas notes that the best consultants "have learned to think in a very structured way. While they may be creative, this has been subsumed into a linear and logical approach to problem solving. Of course, they communicate well and play well with others on their teams." He also emphasizes the importance of being a good listener and able to quickly pick things up on the job. That learning process continues at even the most senior levels. "You have to continue to learn throughout your career: how to manage yourself, how to manage others, and how to manage a client. The most successful partners never stop asking, 'What will I do differently next time?'"

Savvy consultants also quickly learn the importance of developing allies within the firm—managers and partners who seek them out when starting new cases. "Having senior guys pushing for me is how I ended up with an early promotion," noted one senior associate. Even in the largest firms, having advocates in the senior ranks can make a big difference when it comes to assignments, bonuses, and promotion. Quality of work is a prerequisite for success, but allies are often a key asset for those who set themselves apart.

PROMOTION AND MOBILITY

As one moves up in the consulting business, the role that he or she plays in addressing clients' issues changes. The initial position is very focused on analytical problem solving. "The early part of the job is a listen, execute, add position," says Fuller. "Listen to what you are asked, do what you are told and, if you have any intellectual energy left over, then you can worry about adding value." Within six months, an analyst begins to own more of his or her work and has responsibility for deciding how to approach a problem and how to communicate his or her insights to more senior members of the team. "After a couple of years, you begin to take on project-management responsibilities, maybe leading a team of two or three others. You have a role in determining when and how you are going to communicate with your client and in training younger people on your team," explains McKinsey's Ron Daniel. This position involves designing one's process, executing, managing people who are working on different tasks, and knowing when to interface with those who are more senior. As one becomes comfortable with these tasks, the next step involves more responsibility for developing relationships with clients. Joe Fuller cautions that this change in responsibility can be a challenge. Sales skills are very different from the analytical and management skills required up to this point. "There is a big winnowing of talent at each [of the stages of career progression]."

Many firms have up-or-out policies; after a certain number of years in a company, one is either promoted or encouraged to find another job. Ron Daniel explains that:

We have an annual turnover rate of 12 to 18 percent, which is, in large part, a function of our up-or-out policy. This rate of turnover means that we have ~1,000 jobs being vacated every year that need to be filled. Because of the growth of the firm, we often hire more than 1,500 people a year. The irony of hiring at McKinsey is that, although we only hire associates whom we believe can become partners, we are structured in such a way that only a fraction of those who join the firm reach senior positions. Roughly one-in-five associate-level hires becomes a principal, and 50 to 60 percent of principals become directors. The significant number of people who leave the firm is part of the reason the company has such a large and active alumni group, with whom we endeavor to maintain excellent relationships.

Daniel adds that, "Management consulting trains you to marshal facts; to communicate your ideas effectively to others; and to be perceptive about when to attack a problem head on, when to press forward, and when to back off. When McKinsey people go off to run companies, they often become successful operators."

In addition to starting one's own consulting firm, there are entrepreneurial opportunities within the profession (particularly at the senior level): opening new offices, building new practice areas, establishing new models for human resource development, and starting new ventures within the firm. "McKinsey does not conduct marketing studies to determine where we should start a new office. Usually a group of young partners, or even senior associates, decide that there is an unmet need somewhere and create a startup, building a new geographic location for the firm," says Daniel.

COMPENSATION

The base salary in consulting is comparable to that in investment banking, venture capital, and private equity. The difference is that the consulting bonus is a fraction of the base salary, while bankers and principal investors expect to make one to three times their base salaries in annual bonuses. The imbalance in compensation between consulting and money-management firms is present in all cities, but is most apparent in New York because of the concentration of investment-banking and finance jobs. However, for successful senior partners in consulting firms, annual compensation is over $1 million.

PART 3

INSIGHTS FROM INDUSTRY LEADERS

CHUCK FARKAS, SENIOR DIRECTOR AT BAIN & COMPANY

Chuck Farkas taught middle school and completed projects for the provost of his university after graduating. Afterward, he started graduate school to earn a PhD in history, but realized early in the program that becoming a professor was not his true aspiration. He attended business school and interned at a small consulting firm called Bain & Company. During his career, Chuck has contributed to the firm's success as a recruiter, author, consultant, and practice-area head.

What makes a client experience great or miserable?

At this point, I value the relationships most. The best cases are those in which I have a client that I care about personally and professionally, and where the client feels the same way about me. We truly become partners; we work together to solve the client's biggest problems, and we treat each other like partners. When my clients have problems, they call me and they know that I will tell them when we can help and when we can't and that I'll find the best resources to address their problems.

The worst is when you are a vendor. A client says, "I am going to hire a consulting firm. I have selected you because your proposal was best or your pricing was best. Now deliver on the terms of the agreement. We will meet once every three weeks for 47½ minutes." The case stays impersonal.

Have there been times when clients with whom you had close relationships have tried to hire you? If so, what kept you at Bain?

Yes, clients have asked. I really like what I do and I like the people I work with. The uniqueness of this environment is the sense of partnership that exists among the people who work here. There have been a number of CEOs with whom I felt as though we worked together as partners and I could go join them, but in every instance, they were going to be there for a while. Maybe I would be their successor, but everyone else in the organization would have been as much my competitor as my partner. I have seen many of my colleagues go off to do that. They gain real authority; they become buyers rather than sellers; they become chief executives. But it's a much lonelier environment. That isn't what I wanted.

JOE FULLER, COFOUNDER AND CEO OF MONITOR GROUP
In 1983, Fuller partnered with his brother, Mark Fuller, and Michael Porter—all with ties to the Harvard Business School—to start a new consulting practice. They sought to differentiate their firm by developing innovative approaches to management consulting. The organization, Monitor Group, now spans the globe and employs over 1,500 consultants.

What was the original aspiration of you, Mark, and Mike? Was it to build a global consulting firm?
The first thing was to build a firm that developed and advanced ideas. One thing we had noticed about the industry, which is now truer than ever, is that it had stopped investing in thinking. We looked at the industry rather extensively and came away with the conclusion that there wasn't a firm at that time that was really about pushing the envelope of ideas and strategy. We looked at the history of the industry and we said, "There has been a traditional place for what Christensen [an HBS professor] now calls a 'disruptive competitor' that comes up with new ideas." We thought there was a space for a firm that was about ideas. Picking up on our pseudo-academic backgrounds, we would be about building the capabilities of the client to do things versus just telling them what to do. If you are a good consultant, you advise people in such a way that they are more confident in doing what they need to do. Too often, bad companies and bad managers, served by either arrogant or not-very-good consultants, fall into a model of "the consultants tell you what to do and you go off and do it." That is not the definition of success for anybody over the long term.

What will be the longer-term effects of the recent recession on the consulting industry?

I think that Booz & Company's acquisition of Katzenbach in 2009 is probably indicative of a trend toward consolidation. A self-funding (private) partnership is a difficult structure to manage in volatile times. Scale helps to nullify some of the effects.

RON DANIEL, FORMER GLOBAL MANAGING PARTNER OF MCKINSEY & COMPANY

Just under two decades after joining McKinsey & Company, Ron Daniel became the head of the firm. He is regarded as one of the best consulting-firm leaders of all time and has been active in the profession for over half a century.

What types of people do well in consulting?

People who thrive in the consulting environment are smart, effective communicators, and enjoy a life of the mind. You are, in a way, searching for the truth. It is halfway between academia and the operating world. People at McKinsey enjoy learning and continue to gain knowledge throughout their careers. After fifty years at the firm, I am still doing so. At this point, a lot of my learning comes from firm members much younger than I am. Being a consultant is also a life of service. It is a "helping" profession. You seek to help organizations with their core issues, to solve their most difficult problems.

Recently there has been an expansion of positions for college graduates in consulting. What is driving this?

The growth of the business analyst program (people hired directly out of college) is not because the team structure at the firm requires more analysts. We don't really need analysts to do the work; the program is all about more effective future recruiting. We seek to create franchises at the top colleges whose graduates we want to hire. Having a business analyst program gives us a running start on attracting the best candidates from graduate schools later on.

What are the most and least enjoyable aspects of consulting?

The most enjoyable part is the terrific colleague group that you are working with. It is certainly different from many client situations. In most companies, by the nature of the businesses they are in, there have to be "chiefs" and "Indians," intellectually speaking. At McKinsey or Bain or BCG, everyone is an intellectual "chief." Your colleague group is terrific, and that is a source of enormous satisfaction and one of the important reasons why I am still here. The relationships you build with your clients and the sense that you are serving those clients are also enjoyable. Receiving terrific feedback from your clients and real demonstrations of appreciation for what you have done for them is very rewarding.

The least enjoyable part is travel. In today's era, travel has become more onerous than it used to be. It is more physically taxing. Also, occasionally we may get involved with a client that we shouldn't be serving. That usually means that it is not change-ready. Or the consultant is brought in by the CEO, but there is no buy-in from others in the company, and we discover that we can't change peoples' attitudes. Those assignments are no fun.

CHAPTER SIX

BIG BUSINESS

THE MANAGEMENT OF

FORTUNE 500 COMPANIES

At General Electric people talk a lot about your 'Say-Do' ratio, defined as the ratio between the things that you say you are going to do versus what you actually get done. GE looks for people who make commitments and then go out and meet those commitments. Business is about getting stuff done.

—Jaime Irick, a general manager at General Electric

A HISTORY AND DESCRIPTION
OF FORTUNE 500 COMPANIES

Early in his time at a major Fortune 500 company, Ethan[1] was considered a rising star and was given the reins of a major initiative. The project was to figure out how the firm could integrate its diverse products across business units to create a combined offering for major spectator events. Ethan was reporting to a senior executive and the president of one of the corporation's major divisions. If things went well, he was told, he could end up running the new business.

One of the people on the project was a much older individual who was a corporate-culture torchbearer. He passed himself off as a simple, casual guy with no MBA or sense of business strategy but, given his experience at the company, he knew better than anyone how things actually worked. Ethan was seen as the young hotshot MBA, and the two of them didn't hit it off. That tension boiled over after Ethan called someone in the company to ask a somewhat delicate question. It was an inappropriate move in the old timer's eyes, and he sent Ethan an angry email that evening. Increasingly irate messages flew back and forth. Those messages resulted in a telephone call, during which they yelled at each other. The relationship was strained from that point on, but, because he was doing a good job on the analysis of the project, Ethan did not think there would be any negative repercussions. He had laid out timelines with his superiors and was delivering on everything that was promised.

Two months into the project, Ethan received a call from the division president to whom he was reporting. This man had helped to recruit Ethan, who considered him a mentor. He asked Ethan how things were going, and Ethan immediately launched into a formal update, explaining how he was making progress on all the established targets. The president interrupted him to say, "You are not doing well." Ethan felt beads of sweat on his brow. He tried to think whether he had made a mistake in his financial calculations or had forgotten to validate one of his assumptions. The president continued:

I hear that you and your partner on this project are butting heads. He has been telling senior people that you might not fit into this culture. You are hitting on all the metrics, but you aren't following the process that we use here. We know that you are smart, but you need to figure out how to play as part of this team. You'll have plenty of opportunities to score points later. I have worked with this individual and others like him, so don't worry. Over time, you will see that they bring something to the table. Learning how things work in this culture is as important as producing lots of output quickly.

At the end of the call, Ethan realized that he was lucky to have someone offer him such candid advice and took note of his new understanding; rising within corporate America is a balance between performance and politics.

LARGE CORPORATIONS play significant roles in nearly all the other fields discussed in this book. They are major clients of consulting firms and investment banks, scrutinized and invested in by hedge funds and private equity firms, and, in many cases, the products of venture investments. The Fortune 500 is a list compiled by *Fortune* magazine that identifies the largest U.S. companies, based on their revenues. Revenue is perhaps the simplest way to measure the size of a business; however, it is not necessarily the best metric with which to measure its success. On the 2009 list, 128 of the corporations, all with revenues of over $4 billion, were unprofitable.[2]

This chapter focuses primarily on nonfinancial organizations, as many of the large banks are covered by Chapter 1. Nevertheless, the analysis here is, for the most part, broadly applicable.

THE HISTORY OF BIG BUSINESS
IN THE UNITED STATES

Innovations between the Civil War and World War I provided the foundation for many U.S. businesses. Factory machines, assembly lines, faster steel production, the combustion engine, electricity, and communications technologies provided U.S. entrepreneurs the wherewithal to create U.S. Steel, the Ford Motor Company, AT&T, and

General Electric, among many other companies. "The winning companies of the early 1900s had emerged from the most savagely Darwinian industrial maelstrom in history," writes author and former banker Charles Morris.[3] These businesses served customers in a domestic economy that was growing rapidly, and they used their increasing scale to maintain and strengthen their competitive advantages. The U.S. involvement in World Wars I and II and increased international trade created additional demand for the products of many large corporations. During the 1950s and 1960s, management roles at large U.S. corporations filled the aspirations of most business-school students. Retail businesses with innovative models, such as McDonald's and Wal-Mart, were founded, and existing companies expanded.

In the 1970s and 1980s, high labor costs, little innovation, and a lack of effective forward thinking by management left many U.S. businesses susceptible to strong competition from abroad. Companies such as General Motors and RCA began feeling pressure from foreign competitors, yet at the same time, the seeds were being planted for a new batch of successful U.S. corporations. The growing venture-capital business enabled many new companies to emerge. Although the late 1970s and early 1980s were not banner years for U.S. business, they were formative ones for companies such as Microsoft, Apple, Home Depot, Starbucks, and Cisco Systems.

Businesses that do not adapt quickly to changing customer demands and competitive pressures can enter into periods of decline. Recessions tend to exacerbate that process, as the most recent downturn so aptly demonstrated. Chrysler, Circuit City, and Washington Mutual, all businesses that might have survived for years given a healthy economy, declared bankruptcy.

The length and depth of the 2008–2009 recession reinforced the importance of business leaders' paying attention not only to their profit-and-loss statements but also to their balance sheets (records of the companies' assets and liabilities). During the boom period between 2005 and 2007, Apple and Exxon Mobil were criticized for holding massive reserves of cash rather than giving money to shareholders through dividends or share repurchases. Those critics fell silent during the recession, as that cash gave the companies large cushions with which to operate more comfortably, while cash-constrained businesses were forced to sell assets or to raise additional funding. Companies with healthy balance sheets made strategic acquisitions, such as Oracle's purchase of Sun Microsystems and Pfizer's merger with Wyeth Pharmaceuticals.

Executives also sought to capitalize on market dislocation when they believed that the public markets had overly discounted the prospect for a company's future success. For example, recognizing that its bonds were trading at only 40 percent of their face value, the Ford Motor Company purchased $10 billion of its own debt in April 2009. The debt was trading at this level because many believed that the company would default on its obligations. Ford's management believed otherwise and seized the opportunity. That move decreased interest payments and gave the company immediate earnings, because it received $10 billion in cash from issuing bonds and had to pay only $4 billion to retire its obligations.[4] Along those same lines, Liberty Media's CEO, Joe Malone, who is a veteran dealmaker, identified a unique opportunity. In February 2009, he extended a $530 million loan to Sirius XM radio, which was on the verge of bankruptcy and, in return, received a $30 million financing fee and preferred stock that was convertible to a 40 percent equity stake in Sirius.

BIG BUSINESS TODAY

MANAGING IN A DOWNTURN

"Anyone who says that his or her success leading a business is completely independent of market conditions and what is going on in the world is not being straight with you," asserts Jaime Irick, a general manager at General Electric. Companies of all types and sizes face headwinds when the economy is in recession. Things that have worked in the past are no longer effective. Even businesses that are less exposed to fluctuations in consumer spending, such as healthcare, are impacted. During a recession, "we look carefully at working capital and the health of our customers—the impact that the economy may have on their ability to pay in a timely manner (or at all)," says Peter

Nicholas, cofounder and chairman of Boston Scientific, a Fortune 500 company that manufactures medical devices. In May 2009 he noted that "there have been bankruptcies at the customer level, and in some of the countries that have single-payer healthcare systems, the governments (which are the payers) have simply decided not to pay their bills for now and have stretched out payments over two years or more. There are a myriad of issues that, under normal circumstances, we would approach in a business-as-usual way but that today we look at more carefully."

LONG-TERM BUSINESS TRENDS

Over the past few decades, a number of forces have conspired to make the U.S. business environment more efficient and competitive. Private equity firms have contributed by buying and improving businesses that were operating below their potentials. They have demonstrated the value of effectively using debt financing to increase returns to shareholders and of making management teams financially vested in the performance of the business by giving them partial ownership. Shareholder expectations of high profit margins and continued growth also encouraged increased operational efficiency. "One of the defining characteristics of companies today versus twenty years ago is how lean they are," notes Joe Fuller, the CEO of Monitor Group. "If you go back to the 1980s, major corporations would have thirty-to-eighty-person strategic-planning staffs. There was a lot of slack capacity." Today, he says, "they don't have any slack resources."

Increased market demands have also propelled many companies to increase the formal business training of their employees. "My first client was a major chemical company, and in the headquarters there was only one MBA," recalls Chuck Farkas, a senior director at Bain & Company. "Today, nearly everyone there would have an MBA and could do things that Bain was hired to complete twenty years ago. Projecting growth rates, evaluating investment decisions . . . most of those can now be done in-house by people who are well trained in discounted cash flows and who can go online to access databases. The problems we [Bain & Company] have to solve today are an awful lot harder in terms of complexity, speed of change, and the global natures of most businesses."

MOVING FORWARD

Recessions and tough economic times increase the number of business bankruptcies and lead, inevitably, to significant job losses at all levels. For many companies, the downturn necessitated deep cost cutting, plant closings, and layoffs. When done effectively, these measures can make businesses leaner and better poised for future success. In a 2009 "Special Report on American Business," the *Economist* predicted, "In the next couple of years the businesses that thrive will be those that are miserly with costs, wary of debt, cautious with cash flows and obsessively attentive to what customers want."[5]

Companies that cut costs in ways that cause their product quality and/or customer satisfaction to suffer may find large hurdles in returning to past levels of profitability. In the recoveries that inevitably follow downturns, the demand for goods and services increases. Businesses that weathered the economic turbulence and continued to meet the needs of their customers have an opportunity to capitalize on their performance and gain market share.

COMMON CHARACTERISTICS
OF FORTUNE 500 COMPANIES

THE ROLES OF SENIOR MANAGEMENT
AND THE BOARD

Senior officers in dynamic businesses have three principal responsibilities:

1. **Running the business** entails overseeing the company's products and customer relationships.
2. **Managing the corporation** includes the governance of the corporation and its legal and regulatory aspects.

3. **Leading the institution** involves establishing and communicating the organization's mission, values, and priorities, as well as leading its creativity and new-business-area development.

Running the Business

Positions from the CEO down through mid-level managers have responsibility for running the business. This entails developing new products, anticipating customer needs, pricing effectively, and delivering on promises. That means providing customers with a service or product that is better than the competition's. The CEO may not be involved in day-to-day operational details, but he or she invests time in key initiatives of the corporation. Staying abreast of all the important issues across a large organization and effectively focusing one's attention requires a high level of intellectual capability and curiosity. Being informed also involves spending sufficient time with employees and customers to keep a finger on the pulse of the business.

Managing the Corporation

Managing the corporation includes dealing with compliance issues— such as adhering to the Sarbanes-Oxley accounting and oversight regulations; filing documents with the Securities and Exchange Commission; meeting with members of governmental branches; providing reports to shareholders; following the laws of all the countries in which the business operates; managing intellectual property; and, in some industries, overseeing labor relations. CEOs have to attend most meetings with shareholders and government officials, and they have to be fully informed on the key issues being discussed.

The board of directors of a corporation selects the CEO and has responsibility for approving the company's strategy. The group is charged with helping to ensure that management decisions serve the best interests of shareholders. Within the board, there are committees in which much of the substantive decision making occurs. The policy areas with which the board is involved include governance, finance, strategy, compensation, and human resources. The responsibility of the chairman of the board "is to be sure that the people who are members of that board are vibrant, alive, smart, contributing, committed, engaged, helpful, and bringing best practices and oversight to bear," says Peter Nicholas, the chairman of Boston Scientific.

In some businesses, particularly those run by their founders, the CEO serves as the board chairperson. In other instances, there is a non-executive chair, someone who is not an employee of the company. A non-executive chair leads board meetings and has the responsibility of providing support for the CEO. In a company in which one person serves as both CEO and chair, it is particularly important that the board's committee structure functions effectively, so that sensitive decisions, such as executive compensation, can be made independent of the company's management team.

Leading the Institution

The third area of responsibility for CEOs is leading the institution. Chris Galvin, his father Robert Galvin, and his grandfather Paul Galvin (all who served as CEO of Motorola) defined true leadership as "'taking people places elsewhere,' to a place they would not have gone without you," says Chris Galvin. To them, "true leadership is about initiating and/or embracing significant change." More specifically, they believe that leadership entails fostering a corporate culture with strong ethics, creativity, innovation, and appreciation for process rigor. Additionally, the CEO sets the principles that get communicated to employees and customers about how the company defines and differentiates itself from competitors. Peter Nicholas explains. "That means you spend a lot of time on the organizational dynamic and making sure the organization knows what it is doing and why." The CEO also is the front man for the company. "You are the cheerleader," Nicholas adds.

GROWING THE BUSINESS

Many of the roles that senior managers play involve more than one of the three principal responsibilities. An issue continually on the mind of senior managers is expanding or "growing" the business. Investors expect that companies' revenues will continue to increase year after year. Consequently, maintaining a position as one of the largest U.S. corporations requires steady growth. The two methods that businesses can use to achieve this are internal growth (creating new products, finding new customers and/or new geographies) and acquisition. Many of the Fortune 500 companies that were started in the last few decades accelerated their growth through an aggressive acquisition strategy: buying smaller companies that offered products complementary to their own.

The process of looking for, analyzing, financing, and integrating new businesses can consume the attention of senior executives. At times, their jobs resemble those of private equity firms. However, there are differences between the investment processes of the two. Professional investors, such as private equity firms, have no requirement for strategic fit or match among the businesses they buy. For them, one of the most important aspects of every transaction is the exit strategy: whether the investment will be bought by another organization or go public. Corporations that are looking for growth, however, are "strategic buyers" and look for "value beyond the financial, value that stands alone through the transaction," explains Peter Nicholas. A large part of Nicholas' strategy as CEO was acquiring companies to expand Boston Scientific. In his acquisitions, he was looking for "synergies between technologies, customers, organizations, and geography that generate the kind of leverage that creates synergy across the entire range of the enterprise, as opposed to just financial synergy. If you are in a company like ours," he explains "and you have a core mission, sense of values, and strategy, every acquisition you look at, should, unless you have lost your discipline, fit within all those defining statements." If it doesn't, it is likely that the financial benefits won't outweigh the costs.

Many management teams also invest time in organic growth. During Chris Galvin's tenure as CEO, Motorola focused on investing in the firm's own research and development to create the technologies that would fuel the company's short- and long-term growth, a concept his father and grandfather had instilled in the business. "We believed that for Motorola Inc., high innovation was a matter of survival and it was doable and repeatable decade after decade," notes Chris Galvin. "The new industries and management change processes only come when you are open to new ideas and willing to tolerate trial and error over many years. For instance, Robert Galvin embraced the invention and promulgation of the cellular phone as I did with the cable modem. In both cases people told us over and over again that these were absurd and unworkable ideas. Both initiatives turned out very well."

The pressure to grow at any cost has led some senior officers to manipulate corporations' accounting practices. They create growth "on paper" but, in doing so, they often violate the law. The most dramatic example was the global telecommunications company WorldCom. Between 1999 and 2002, the firm used accounting tricks in order to boost pre-tax income by more than $7 billion. By decreasing estimations of future costs and categorizing operating expenses as capital expenses (which were not deducted from revenue in calculating pre-tax income), the firm made itself look better to Wall Street. However, the accounting maneuvers caught up with the company, and it declared bankruptcy in 2002. The CEO and members of WorldCom's financial team were convicted of fraud (among other charges) and sent to prison.[6]

PRESSURE AT THE TOP

There is great appeal in being a senior officer at a large public corporation. Senior executives manage thousands of people, command seven-figure salaries, enjoy perks like private jets, and often have more flexibility in their schedules than other employees. However, they must report to both the board of directors and the corporation's stockholders.

When businesses are seen as underperforming, there is often immense public pressure for change at the top. That pressure can incentivize business leaders to focus on quarterly profits rather than long-term strategies for growing a business, or find themselves out of a job. Chris Galvin was ousted as CEO of Motorola in 2003 after a difficult three-year period of restructuring and high investment in R&D. He was replaced just before the realization of performance improvements that stemmed from the restructuring efforts he led and the launch of the hugely successful RAZR cellular phone, a product that he had spearheaded. Rick Wagoner, the former CEO of General Motors, was the object of intense public indignation after he asked the U.S. government for financial assistance in 2008. Many of the factors that led to this request were outside Wagoner's control. Nevertheless, a few months after the request, he was asked to resign.

CORPORATE VALUES

Performance Values

General Electric, a business revered for its talent management system, has a program developed by Jack Welch that is called "the 4Es." These "Es" are the characteristics the company looks for from high-performance employees:

1. Energy: Do you bring lots of personal energy to your work?
2. Energize: Can you energize those around you and customers?
3. Edge: Do you have the ability to make the tough call—to fire your best friend, to cut the cord on an investment that you do not think will succeed, to pile money into something when nobody thinks you should and have it turn out to be a good investment?
4. Execute: Do you make a promise and deliver on it?

Chris Galvin liked the concept and, with permission from Welch, modified the GE leadership systems for Motorola in an effort to improve Motorola's supply-performance-management systems. Galvin believed that the company needed to explicitly call out high innovation as a key business leadership expectation in order to maintain its drive to create new industries. Consequently, he added "Envision," meaning envision the future and give support to creating it. Motorola also added "Ethics." "Jack challenged that the business's ethics should be so well-ingrained in the company that you shouldn't have to say it," recalls Galvin.

No question that is the goal, but "uncompromising integrity and treating the individual person with dignity and respect" was so ingrained that if it was [not explicitly stated], the team would feel something was missing. In addition, I knew Motorola was taking aggressive regional risk as it expanded globally, and I believed that you have to make the discussion of ethics explicit because the meaning of "morals," "principles," and "values" is influenced by country cultures, religions, and government systems, and differ widely. So at Motorola we adopted the "4 E's Plus Always 1": Envision, Energize, Edge, Execute, and Always Ethics. I combined Energy and Energize retaining all of GE's substance and added "Envision." The "plus always one" means that ethics should be a part of everything we do.

At Motorola during Galvin's tenure, leaders had to excel across all five "Es." "Some people are great at imagining an idea but can't create the plan. Other people have huge amounts of energy but no edge. Some people had the four 'Es,' but weren't trusted. There were no trade-offs on ethics. The process of being able to integrate all these things is necessary to be a comprehensive leader."

Because business units often have their own profit-and-loss statements, managers' execution can be measured. Among corporations, the culture of the institution can also influence effectiveness of execution. "I was accustomed to an organization that got things done, where people met their commitments," says Larry Bossidy, a former GE executive, about his arrival as CEO of Allied Signal. In his book, *Execution,* he writes that he wasn't prepared for the malaise he found. "The company had lots of hard-working, bright people, but they weren't effective and they didn't place a premium on getting things done."[7] Bossidy assembled a group of effective managers, created a more cohesive corporate strategy, and developed an incentive system that rewarded execution. The financial results were impressive and led to a successful sale of the business.

Corporate Responsibility
Corporate responsibility is an increasingly important subject for business. The concept encompasses the environmental impact of a business, contributions of time and money made by the organization and its employees, and investments in initiatives that are focused more on human betterment than on profit making. Some companies use corporate-responsibility programs as a way to bolster their public images and attract customers; others see responsibility as part of their guiding principles. After much internal planning, in 2004 Google announced to its shareholders that it would dedicate 1 percent of its equity and profits to philanthropic endeavors. For other companies, initiatives can be more opportunistic. For example, Bristol-Myers Squibb's HIV-AIDS program came out of a conversation. The wife of the CEO of the company, Charles Heimbold, was friendly with the wife of the UN Secretary General Kofi

Annan. One night, the Heimbolds and the Annans were having dinner together. Annan said to Heimbold, "No pharmaceutical company has really taken a leadership position on the problem of AIDS in Africa; why doesn't Bristol-Myers Squibb do it?" Out of that came Bristol-Myers Squibb's "Secure the Future" initiative, a $130-million program in southern Africa and French West Africa to combat HIV-AIDS.

PART 2

INSIDE FORTUNE 500 COMPANIES

ORGANIZATIONAL CULTURE AND LIFESTYLE

The work-life balance at most operating companies is better than it is in professional service industries (such as accounting, consulting, and investment banking), where clients expect people to work long hours to justify high fees. Because of their scale, large corporations tend to market themselves heavily, and people know what they are. It may be superficial, but not having to explain the company you work for every time you meet someone is a small perk. There is also something nice about working for a company that actually produces a product or offers a concrete service.

However, working at a Fortune 500 company does have drawbacks. Because the businesses are so large, they can sometimes feel bureaucratic and political. Change comes more slowly, and upward mobility is not always clearly defined. Although the work itself may be interesting, it carries administrative and organizational tasks that are less than pleasant. In addition, the compensation scale generally is not as high as in investment and professional service firms, especially below the senior level.

CHARACTERISTICS FOR SUCCESS

Moving up professionally requires broadening one's skill set beyond a single core area. Peter Nicholas says that to reach a senior level at

Boston Scientific, "You have to develop strong skill sets that deal with the multi-faceted nature of large enterprise. You have to have the analytical capability to understand what numbers are saying in an intuitive way, appreciate and understand technology, and have a sense of how you balance the financial portfolio within an organization among all the various competing elements—production, marketing, selling, finance, control, and technology."

Given the challenges of managing competing resources and leading people in a large company, U.S. corporations often recruit former military officers. In the military, you start in a very specific role, such as infantry officer. As you progress, you move both up and over in the organization's hierarchy, for instance leading infantry and artillery as a battalion commander. You may not have the same technical training or expertise as everyone you manage but you are tasked with leading them. Similarly, in a Fortune 500 company, a manager may have less depth of expertise in a topic than the individual analysts, engineers, and scientists who report to her. Military academies teach their students to lead twenty or more soldiers immediately upon graduating, an applicable training. Coming out of business school, former military officers may be disadvantaged in terms of business practice; however, they bring unusually high levels of leadership experience. "Most of the people coming out of the military today have been in combat, so they have had to make really critical decisions under the gun. I think that's extremely relevant when working in a fast-paced, high-expectation corporate job," says Jaime Irick, a West Point graduate. In venture capital or consulting, the partners can execute the analysis of junior employees if they have to—building financial models or executing due diligence. The art of corporate leadership is knowing enough to lead people who perform highly technical and varied tasks while not becoming buried in the details and losing sight of the broader organizational objectives.

PROMOTION AND MOBILITY

There are some key strategies for rising within large U.S. companies. In the other fields discussed in this book, promotion requires strong performance. In big corporations, there is added complexity. All companies have a wide array of divisions, such as sales, marketing, recruiting, research and development (R&D), finance, human resources (HR), and information technology (IT). In each corporation, specific function areas are seen as more core to the business. Often, people from the departments that are seen as critical and that generate the highest revenues are the ones who ascend most quickly. Positioning oneself in highly valued departments is key, so it is important to find out what a corporation values. In some organizations this is obvious; for instance, the senior management of consulting firms is made up of consultants rather than of people with backgrounds in IT or HR. At a manufacturer of commodity products, operations experience—which informs cost control and the importance of meeting deadlines—may be prioritized. Many companies have multiple core areas. Proctor & Gamble needs senior people with product-development and marketing expertise. Microsoft needs sales people and computer engineers. When Chris Howard was at GE, he kept a file of all announcements about the promotion of senior managers. He read about their backgrounds and looked for patterns in the characteristics that were common among those who received coveted positions. Chris believes that you have to pay attention to changes in what a company values. He found that promotions were the best way of tracking that.

Key roles in corporations involve changing tasks and responsibilities. At professional service firms, many people enter at the analyst level, and there is a defined timetable for increased responsibility. That certainty does not exist in most large companies. Shona Brown, the senior vice president of business operations at Google, says, "We have no idea what you are going to be doing in two years, because we have no idea what we will be doing in two years. But we are confident that there are going to be lots of opportunities for anyone who is doing well."

Operating roles provide experience in how businesses actually run that is not fully understood in consulting, investment banking, or investing. In consulting, "You see more companies, often more industries, but you tend to only see 40 to 50 percent of what it takes to actually get something done in a company," explains Shona Brown, who was a partner at McKinsey before joining Google. "A consultant's operating understanding is much less deep than he or she believes. The types of problems that you deal with in an operating company . . . touch the strategy questions and the very deep-level implementation stuff that you won't get in consulting." This complexity is part of why many large businesses provide mobility and seek to move top talent between divisions; they want employees to have both broad and deep understanding of the issues facing the businesses.

An MBA is generally seen as an asset within Fortune 500 companies. Because junior positions require people to specialize, the MBA is a way of rounding out one's business skills. Companies in technical fields, such as computer science and medicine, value other graduate degrees equally highly. "The engineering degree is very useful, whether you work as an engineer or not," notes Shona Brown, who holds a doctorate in engineering. "An engineering degree teaches you analytical skills, critical thinking, and structured problem solving." Nevertheless, the MBA is the most common graduate degree among CEOs, even those in the sciences. However, neither an MBA nor an Ivy League degree is a prerequisite for being the CEO of a major company. Two of the most common CEO alma maters are the University of Texas and the University of Wisconsin. Only 10 percent of S&P 500 CEOs come from Ivy League schools, and fewer than 40 percent have an MBA (although 67 percent have an advanced degree of some kind).[8] Prestigious degrees can facilitate entry into a fast-track management program, but individual performance and corporate politics determine who succeeds.

WORKING INTERNATIONALLY

Every Fortune 500 company is a global organization. Even those whose customers are all in the United States have manufacturing facilities abroad and use services from international providers. This globalization creates more opportunities for people to work abroad and heightens the importance of understanding the foreign operations of the company. Of the CEOs at the one hundred largest U.S. companies,[9] forty-four have international work experience.[10]

Sidney Taurel, former chairman and CEO of Eli Lilly, says that international general-management assignments provide greater managerial breadth than local ones. In essence, an international general manager becomes an "ambassador, and mimics the role of a CEO in the United States." While in business school, Chris Howard worked on a study that examined the shared traits of senior leaders in the biotech and pharmaceutical industries. The study determined that general-management experience abroad was hugely advantageous for those seeking to ascend to senior leadership. Of the leaders interviewed for the study, the majority felt that the challenge of managing with less institutional support and fewer bureaucratic impediments provided an opportunity to demonstrate their ability to succeed in adverse conditions.[11]

Global corporations can provide opportunities for those who want to travel. Megan Clark, who headed the technology division at BHP Billiton, received her first job as the result of a conversation with a director of WMC Resources, a mining company. "The job offer sounds great, but I can't start until after I go to South America," she told him. When the director asked why, she explained that she had lived there at the end of high school and wanted to go back. "Forget everything I just told you," he said. "You are going to start work in Rio de Janeiro." Although job location is not always as serendipitous, companies with large geographic footprints have significant flexibility in where they place employees. Ken Weg, the former vice chairman of Bristol-Myers Squibb, made travel and exposure to different cultures primary criteria in selecting where he would work. He subsequently ran operations for major pharmaceutical companies throughout the world.

Mentoring

Mentors can be valuable resources. Receiving advice from those who have been around a business for a while can shed light on opportunities and ways to succeed within the company. Even external advisors can be beneficial. When Boston Scientific's cofounder Peter Nicholas concluded his tour as a general manager in Europe for the pharmaceutical company Eli Lilly and received an assignment he was not interested in, he decided it was time to find a new job. Nicholas read a report called "Managing the Threshold Company," about the various stages that companies go through.[12] "It was written by the head of McKinsey's New York office, Donald Clifford. I was so fascinated by the paper that I called him. He was helpful in weighing specific opportunities for me." Mentorship can come from family members, friends, professional contacts, and people within one's company. Guidance from multiple sources can be helpful in weighing opportunities as they arise.

COMPENSATION

Compensation in most corporations is based on a combination of base salary, an annual cash bonus, and stock incentives.* In more senior positions, bonuses and stock options can comprise the majority of an employee's compensation. At many corporations, an employee's annual bonus and stock options are determined by the performance of the company, the individual, and the division in which he or she works. Selective fast-track programs seek to hire the same types of candidates as do management-consulting firms, so the compensation is relatively comparable.

CEO total compensation averages $13 million, but varies based on the size of the business, its performance, and the industry in which it operates.[13] CEO pay has long been a source of public outrage and shareholder resentment, especially when companies' stock prices lag the overall market. Although CEOs do not determine their own salaries, a CEO often serves as chairperson of the board of directors, so he or she determines the composition of the board's compensation committee—the group that sets the CEO's salary. That committee is often advised by the company's vice president of human resources, who reports to the CEO. The committee has information on what the

---

*Stock options allow an employee of a company to purchase shares in the business at a pre-set price. Generally, an employee stands to gain when the share price of the company increases during his or her time there. For example, the price of the option will likely be set at the company's stock price on the day of issue. If, two years later, the stock price has gone down, the option would not be exercised, and the holder would neither gain nor lose anything. However, if the price goes up, and the employee exercises the option, he or she is paid the difference between the current price and the price on the date of issue.

CEOs of similar companies are paid, and the members tend to ensure that the CEO of their company is above average, which propels an upward compensation cycle. This system also enables CEOs to end up with huge benefits. Perhaps the most extraordinary was Nabors Industries' death benefit. At one point, the company was required to pay the estate of its CEO $264 million if he were to die while holding his position.[14]

The Clinton Administration tried to reign in excessive corporate compensation by changing the tax laws for salaries above $1 million that were not tied to performance. This measure has largely been seen as a failure. CEO salaries have continued to go up, while the additional tax costs have been passed on to shareholders and compensation structures have become more complex in order to circumnavigate the restrictions.

PART 3

INSIGHTS FROM INDUSTRY LEADERS

CHRIS GALVIN, FORMER CEO OF MOTOROLA, CHAIRMAN OF HARRISON STREET CAPITAL

Chris Galvin built a career at Motorola, working in numerous positions across the company from sales to venture investments. As CEO, he focused on innovation and developing best practices in talent identification and development, among other things. He now is chairman of Harrison Street Capital, a real estate private equity firm.

Why did you choose to start your career at Motorola in a sales position?

You can start in twelve different places and work your way up: sales into product management, finance into operations. What was interesting about the sales work that I did was that it was conceptual sales. I was selling radios to people who didn't know that they needed them. I would, for instance, go in to speak with the head of a large trucking business and explain to this guy that he ought to buy radios for his trucks. I had to convince this person, who probably had a big house and a condo in Florida, that he wasn't making enough money and that these radios could improve his business. To do this type of sales required me to know a great deal about the customer's business operations to justify the cost and to do a consulting sell.

Three years into my time at Motorola, the management promotion model changed and the company said that those in sales did not have enough broad operation/technical/product development knowledge to become senior management. So I went into marketing and then product management, which involved actually taking a demotion.

It appears that you transitioned from a career in management at Motorola directly into making private equity investments in real estate? Why did you make this transition?

Though real estate has always been my second passion, running Motorola was my first. I never imagined I would need to found a new global conglomerate from scratch. In September 2003 the board of Motorola announced they would seek a new CEO, believing apparently that things were so bad at Motorola that an outsider was needed. They hired Ed Zander about Thanksgiving 2003 to do a massive turnaround of Motorola, Inc. The Motorola that Zander inherited was a $30 billion revenue run-rate company growing at more than 40 percent top line,[*] generating about 10 percent operating earnings, and creating prodigious free cash flow. From 2000 to 2003 my team and I had turned around four sectors in our company, each the size of a small Fortune 500 corporation, as well as two smaller business units. Motorola was the fastest-growing Fortune 60 corporation in America when the board handed the reins to Ed Zander. Regardless of the obvious questionable judgment in governance, the events required us to face a tough reality. I knew that I was not coming back to Motorola and had moved on. I, along with members of my family, have founded The Galvin Projects (a virtual global think tank), Harrison Street Capital

---

[*]*Sales are referred to as "top line growth," since revenue is the first line of the net income statement.*

LLC, Harrison Street Real Estate Capital LLC, Gore Creek Asset Management LLC (a capital investment company), a software company, and began a rollup in defense services. We are seeking to create a multi-business private conglomerate. In the first quarter of 2005 I was the only employee, and today we have approximately 700 employees distributed globally with offices in Washington, D.C., Chicago, and Shanghai.

PETER NICHOLAS, COFOUNDER AND CHAIRMAN OF BOSTON SCIENTIFIC CORPORATION

Peter Nicholas spent a number of years in established healthcare companies before realizing that he would be fulfilled only by starting his own business. Serendipitously, he met John Abele, with whom he cofounded Boston Scientific Corporation, a medical device company. The two men grew the business into a Fortune 500 company.

How did you come to the conclusion that there was a real opportunity for a new medical device company? What gave you the confidence to pursue this venture?

I had been in healthcare for ten years and I was casting about for different opportunities. I thought that I ought to be doing something that traded on my knowledge of medicine, hospitals, physicians, specialty technology, and all the dynamics of the healthcare system. In my last years at Lilly, I had been part of a team that acquired a pacemaker company, so I became aware of the device industry and its promise. When John [Abele, the other cofounder of Boston Scientific] and I were talking about the potential for less-invasive medicine to deliver alternatives to surgery in a kinder, gentler way—less money, less trauma, less aftercare—it fit the paradigm. The market opportunity and my business experience suggested, to me, that if we started a company in this field, we were going to be very successful.

What was your initial plan for building the business?

My ambition for BSC was for it to become a global leader, the major share player in its business, and a sustainable long-term enterprise. When you start with that idea, it suggests a whole different mindset around financial structure, organization, competence, skill sets, the kinds of people you hire, and the way in which you propose to stage the development of the company.

Boston Scientific operates in the medical-device industry, whose products are largely non-discretionary. How has the company felt the recession?

In many ways, we are more recession-proof than other companies—and certainly other industries. In our world, people keep getting sick, regardless of the weather or the economy, and they need healthcare to get better. Specifically, we are in the business of diagnosing and treating very serious diseases and, therefore, the procedures we are involved with are non-elective and non-discretionary. Nonetheless, credit markets pose certain threats; working capital is always a challenge; and cash really does become king. That means carefully reviewing discretionary spending. High-risk, long-term program spending may be modulated downward or stretched out a little. Acquisition opportunities, ironically, may become more available, because weaker companies are less able to weather the economic storm. While we have to be prepared to be opportunistic, we also must be more disciplined than is the case when we are in a more predictable (and more forgiving) economic environment.

SHONA BROWN, SENIOR VICE PRESIDENT OF BUSINESS OPERATIONS AT GOOGLE

Shona Brown collected a plethora of academic degrees before entering the business world. She joined McKinsey in Canada after having completed extensive research at Stanford. Leaving McKinsey in 2003 after nearly a decade, she was approached about a position at a mid-size technology company called Google. She accepted and has played a role in the meteoric growth of the business.

Having spent your professional career in management consulting prior to joining Google, were there surprises when you moved into an industry role at a very senior level?

Conceptually, I understood that I had not seen fully what it takes to implement things administratively. Even in an extraordinarily fast-paced industry and in a company with exceptional talent, it takes longer to get things done than it does from the perspective of a consultant doing a project that costs millions of dollars for the CEO. People are going to drop other things and pay attention when it is a project for the CEO. I don't think you can fully understand that until you are on the operating side. Whenever we bring people in that have primarily consulting backgrounds, we see the transition they have to go through. Those coming from academia or large bureaucratic organizations adjust to a more action-oriented environment. The consultants have to go through this wave of understanding that, just because everyone in the room has agreed that something makes sense, it doesn't mean that it's been done.

Describe risk and decision making in a business operations role as opposed to an advisory role.
It feels very different when it is your company. One of the things in a technology company is that the employees are meant to live and breathe as if it is their company. To foster that, at places like Google, all our employees own some portion of the business. They care passionately whether we do X, not just because it's their project, but because they think it's the right thing for the company. For the people in the more strategic roles, it is very different standing and presenting to the executive team at Google and talking about something they want to do, than if they were in the same position presenting to a client.

In terms of making a mistake, one of the things you drum into people in the consulting profession is that the clients are paying millions of dollars for our services; if you add your numbers up wrong, it is a big deal. That can be very high risk for an individual in an up-or-out environment, but it's not as if you are ever actually building something. Here, you could make a mistake and cause some of our services to fail and have a bunch of companies not be able to make money for seventy-two hours. Those types of operating risks do not exist in professional services.

For folks who are adrenaline junkies, I find it amusing when they try to argue that they get more adrenaline from being in professional services than in an operating role. I think that no matter how you cut it, ultimately advising is advising. I loved advising, but one of the reasons I moved is that I wanted to have to live with my own advice.

CONCLUSION

The worlds of business and finance changed dramatically during the writing of this book. In a matter of three years, we watched a huge period of economic expansion turn into the worst recession in decades. Although world-renowned organizations that thrived in 2007 no longer exist (at least as stand-alone entities), the major industries of finance and business have persevered and are adapting to the new economic environment. We still believe in the tremendous power of free enterprise and the value that is created through the private sector. Nevertheless, the failings of some have wrought consequences for many, from new governmental regulations to public skepticism about the ethics of the private sector. Those in finance and big business need to earn back the trust of both the people they serve and the greater community.

Each of the industries described in this book will be affected by factors outside its control. The future growth of the investment professions is dependent on institutional money managers (pension funds, endowments, et cetera) increasing their capital allocations to alternative asset classes, such as venture capital, private equity, and hedge funds. The Fortune 500 will need consumers and other businesses to increase their spending, and investment banks and management-consulting firms will require corporate and investor clients with cash to spend on their services. The prospects for expansion among these industries are intertwined. A full and robust economic recovery will, in many ways, require the regained health of all of them. We are confident that, for decades to come, the leading firms in investment banking, venture capital, private equity, hedge funds, management consulting, and the Fortune 500 will be money makers for the constituencies they serve: clients, investors, and shareholders.

The interviews we conducted for this book reinforced our belief that there are no prerequisites for success in these fields, except perhaps hard work and a passion for one's profession. The industry leaders we interviewed come from a broad array of educational and professional backgrounds. What they share is a genuine enthusiasm for the work they do, whether it is manufacturing life-saving medical devices, making investments in exciting companies with high growth potential, or finding ways to increase the profitability of their clients. In every case, that passion was pursued with extraordinary devotion, diligence, and hard work.

Historically, the periods following recessions are times of immense opportunity. New ventures have a greater chance to gain market share amid dislocated industries; junior employees are given increased responsibility as hiring lags business growth; and decreased asset prices lead to tremendous wealth creation for skilled investors. It is a valuable time to understand these industries and the growing positions they hold in the global economy. This book is a blueprint for understanding the new world of finance and business; for those interested, there are excellent resources for deepening one's knowledge of the topics explored. Below are some that we believe are particularly valuable.

INVESTMENT BANKING

- *Den of Thieves* by James B. Stewart
- *Liar's Poker: Rising through the Wreckage on Wall Street* by Michael Lewis
- *The Myth of the Rational Market: A History of Risk, Reward, and Delusion on Wall Street* by Justin Fox
- *The Two Trillion Dollar Meltdown: Easy Money, High Rollers, and the Great Credit Crash* by Charles R. Morris

VENTURE CAPITAL AND ENTREPRENEURSHIP

- *The Acton MBA for Entrepreneurship* (www.actonmba.com)
- *Crossing the Chasm: Marketing and Selling High-Tech Products to Mainstream Customers* by Geoffrey A. Moore
- *Life Entrepreneurs* by Christopher Gergen and Gregg Vanourek
- *Startup: A Silicon Valley Adventure* by Jerry Kaplan

PRIVATE EQUITY

- *Barbarians at the Gate: The Fall of RJR Nabisco* by Bryan Burrough and John Helyar
- PEHUB.com (A forum for private equity and venture capital news)

HEDGE FUNDS

- *Institutional Investor* Magazine (www.iimagazine.com)
- *The Intelligent Investor: A Book of Practical Counsel* by Benjamin Graham
- *Margin of Safety: Risk-Averse Value Investing Strategies for the Thoughtful Investor* by Seth A. Klarman
- Seekingalpha.com
- *When Genius Failed: The Rise and Fall of Long-Term Capital Management* by Roger Lowenstein

MANAGEMENT CONSULTING

- *Competitive Advantage: Creating and Sustaining Superior Performance* by Michael E. Porter

MANAGEMENT OF THE FORTUNE 500

- *Execution: The Discipline of Getting Things Done* by Larry Bossidy, Ram Charan, and Charles Burck

- *Good to Great: Why Some Companies Make the Leap . . . and Others Don't* by Jim Collins
- *The Innovator's Dilemma: The Revolutionary Book That Will Change the Way You Do Business* by Clayton M. Christensen
- *Winning* by Jack Welch and Suzy Welch

LEADERSHIP

- *On Becoming a Leader* by Warren Bennis
- *True North: Discover Your Authentic Leadership* by Bill George

APPENDIX A

FIRM PROFILES

To provide further insight into the industries covered in this book, we have provided below a series of short profiles detailing many of the largest and most influential firms. The profiles include a brief history of the firm, its investment or operational focus, and its senior leaders. The metrics used to measure the relative size of firms varies by industry and (in some cases) within them. For investment banks, we list total bank assets and mergers & acquisition (M&A) league tables (a measurement of the volume of banking deals on which the organization advises). For venture capital, private equity, and hedge funds, we show assets under management to indicate how much capital the organization invests. Because most consulting firms are private companies, they do not publicize total revenue, so the number of consultants is used as a proxy. We do not profile Fortune 500 companies since the biggest ones are all well-known businesses (Exxon Mobil, Wal-Mart, General Electric, etc.).

INVESTMENT BANKING

Though there are a large number of firms offering investment banking services, the nine profiled are the largest players in the United States. The array of services offered by each varies. Some have large consumer banking business units while others are principally focused on capital market activities. All of these institutions contain the functions described in the banking chapter. Total bank assets is one metric for the size of a financial institution. However, given the diversity of business segments across the firms, this should not be seen as a proxy for relative performance. For instance, banks that have significant consumer retail business tend to have larger amounts of assets than banks that do not offer these services (e.g., Citi versus Goldman Sachs). M&A league tables rank the total value of the deals announced on which the bank provided investment banking advisory services. This is a measurement for the performance of the investment banking division of these firms.[1]

BANK OF AMERICA

Total assets: $2.3 trillion

M&A league table[2]: $180 billion

Establishment: Bank of America is the product of a long series of banking acquisitions. Though it has offered investment banking services for a number of years, it became a major player in the industry with its 2008 acquisition of Merrill Lynch. The principal architects of the modern Bank of America were Hugh McColl and Ken Lewis. McColl was the commercial banking leader who took over a regional bank in North Carolina and, through a series of acquisitions, built the largest bank beyond Wall Street. Lewis, who worked for McColl, took over as Bank of America's CEO in 2001 and initiated the acquisitions of MBNA (a credit card company), U.S. Trust, Countrywide Financial, and Merrill Lynch.

Leadership: Ken Lewis was the president and CEO of the bank until early 2010. (At the time of writing his successor had not been named.) He also served as chairman of the company until 2009, when shareholders voted to remove him from this position, as a result of losses related to the Merrill Lynch acquisition. Lewis started his career as an analyst in 1969 and played an active role in many of Nation Bank's acquisitions under Hugh McColl. He is a graduate of Georgia State University.

BARCLAYS

Total assets: $1.9 trillion

M&A league table: $111 billion

Establishment: Barclays is a British bank dating back to the late 1800s. The firm went public on the London Stock Exchange in 1902 and became one of the United Kingdom's five largest banks in 1918. Though Barclays had been growing its presence in U.S. investment banking throughout the last decade, its efforts were catapulted forward by its acquisition of Lehman Brothers' North American investment banking and capital markets businesses in the fall of 2008. Prior to the acquisition, Barclays had its own U.S. investment banking operations; however, after the merger,

Lehman's head of investment banking, Skip McGee, took over U.S. banking operations for Barclays.

Leadership: CEO John Varley has worked at Barclays since 1982. During that time he has headed the Asset Management Division and Retail Financial Services. President and chief executive of investment banking Bob Diamond joined Barclays in 1996 after working in fixed income trading at Morgan Stanley and heading the fixed income business at Credit Suisse First Boston. He graduated from Colby College and has an MBA from the University of Connecticut.

CITIGROUP

Total assets: $1.8 trillion

M&A league table: $245 billion

Establishment: Citigroup was the creation of Sandy Weill, who orchestrated the merger of his company, Travelers Group, with CitiCorp. Under Weill, Citigroup became the first full-service bank offering everything from securities brokerage to insurance to retail banking and M&A advisory work. Weill was succeeded by Chuck Prince, a lawyer by training, who had worked with Weill on many of his acquisitions. In 2007, the company began experiencing multibillion dollar losses. Many of its troubles stemmed from its significant business operations in financial products tied to the U.S. housing market. Amidst the turmoil Chuck Prince was ousted and replaced by Vikram Pandit. During the recent recession, Citigroup accepted more than $45 billion in support from the U.S. government to maintain its financial stability.

Leadership: CEO Vikram Pandit originally came to work at Citigroup when the firm purchased Old Lane Partners, a hedge fund that Pandit cofounded. Previous to his tenure at Old Lane, Pandit worked in institutional securities at Morgan Stanley and Credit Suisse. He holds a BA and MA from Columbia State University and a PhD and an MBA from Columbia University. Chairman Richard Parsons was the former CEO of Time Warner.

CREDIT SUISSE

Total Assets: $1 trillion

M&A league table: $160 billion

Establishment: The firm traces its history back to 1856 when the Swiss business leader Alfred Escher set up a bank to finance the expansion of his country's railroad system. The bank opened its first U.S. branch in 1940 and expanded its American customer base to individuals (rather than just corporations) when it gained the ability to accept deposits in 1964. The bank significantly increased its U.S. investment banking presence in the last few decades with the acquisitions of First Boston and Donaldson, Lufkin & Jenrette, Inc., both large New York–based firms.

Leadership: CEO Brady Dougan worked in the derivatives group at Bankers Trust before starting at the newly renamed Credit Suisse First Boston in 1990. He held leadership positions in equities, global securities, and institutional services before becoming CEO in 2007. He holds a BA and an MBA from the University of Chicago.

Deutsche Bank

Total Assets: $2.4 trillion
M&A league table: $213 billion
Establishment: Deutsche Bank is a German firm founded in 1870. During the years of Germany's Weimar Republic the banking industry went through a period of significant consolidation, leading the institution to become a central player in the German economy. Consequently, it played a large role in the economic policies of the Third Reich and was heavily dismantled in the aftermath of World War II. However, in the mid-1950s the firm reconsolidated with some of the businesses that had been broken apart. The bank grew in the 1960s and 1970s and expanded globally. In 1999, it gained a large position in the U.S. financial services market through its acquisition of Bankers Trust.

Leadership: The firm is headed by Josef Ackermann. Formerly, he was President of SKA (the original name of Credit Suisse). He joined Deutsche Bank in 1996 as the head of the investment banking division and became chairman of the management board in 2006. He holds a doctorate from the University of St. Gallen.

Goldman Sachs

Total Assets: $890 billion
M&A league table: $343 billion
Establishment: Goldman Sachs was started in 1869 by Marcus Goldman, who was later joined by his son-in-law Samuel Sachs. The business remained a family-run operation for more than fifty years. In the post–World War II era, the firm played an important role in many of the largest IPOs in the United States. Nevertheless, it was not until 1999 that Goldman Sachs followed many of its banking peers and became a publicly traded company itself. Throughout the past two decades the firm has not only

produced billions in investment profits, but also a long list of senior government officials, particularly at the Treasury Department. Amidst the financial crisis of 2008 the firm accepted a $5 billion investment from Berkshire Hathaway and became a bank holding company. However, by mid-2009 the bank was back to generating large profits for employees and shareholders.

Leadership: CEO Lloyd Blankfein was a practicing lawyer before joining Goldman Sachs's currency and commodities business. He rose to head the firm's Fixed Income, Currencies and Commodities Division before taking increasingly senior roles in the company. He holds degrees from Harvard and Harvard Law School. President and COO Gary Cohn also rose within the firm's FICC division. He is a graduate of American University.

JPMORGAN CHASE

Total Assets: $2.0 trillion

M&A league table: $303 billion

Establishment: Like Citigroup, JPMorgan Chase is the amalgamation of a great number of financial institutions. The firm traces its history back to 1799 when Aaron Burr founded the Bank of the Manhattan Co. to supply water to the lower part of New York and compete with the Bank of New York (which had been founded by his political rival Alexander Hamilton). However, the most well-known player in the bank's history was J. Pierpont Morgan, who founded J.P. Morgan & Co. in 1871. He played a large role in the consolidation of the American railroad industry and the financing of some of the country's largest corporations. The modern JPMorgan Chase evolved out of a series of large mergers and acquisitions. Chemical Banking Corp. merged with the Chase Manhattan Group in 1996, Chase Manhattan merged with J.P. Morgan in 2000, and Bank One merged with JPMorgan Chase in 2004. More recently, the firm acted opportunistically and acquired Bear Stearns and Washington Mutual in 2008.

Leadership: CEO Jamie Dimon began his career working for Sandy Weill at American Express. A few years later Dimon followed Weill to Commercial Credit, from which they built Citigroup through a series of mergers and acquisitions. In 1998 Dimon left Citigroup and later became CEO of Bank One, a large Chicago-based bank. In 2004 when Bank One merged with JPMorgan Chase, Dimon became president of the business and shortly thereafter CEO. He holds degrees from Tufts University and Harvard Business School.

MORGAN STANLEY

Total Assets: $677 billion

M&A league table: $331 billion

Establishment: Morgan Stanley was formed in 1935 by Henry Morgan and
Harold Stanley, bankers who had previously worked at J.P. Morgan. In its
early years, Morgan Stanley focused primarily on advising corporate
clients on their equity and debt issuances. In the early 1970s the firm
started sales and trading operations and in 1986 it went public. In 1997
the firm acquired Dean Witter, Discover & Co., expanding its offerings to
include the Discover credit card and Dean Witter's asset management
and brokerage services. In September 2008, under the strain of the financial crisis, Morgan Stanley converted to a bank holding company and
sold a minority stake in the firm to Japan's Mitsubishi UFJ Group.

Leadership: James Gorman became CEO of Morgan Stanley in January 2010.
Previously he served as co-president and head of the firm's wealth management division. He was hired by firm chairman John Mack in 2005
from Merrill Lynch, where he held a leadership position in wealth management. Prior to Merrill, he was a partner at McKinsey. He holds a BA
and a law degree from the University of Melbourne, and an MBA from
Columbia Business School. Mack has spent most of his career at Morgan
Stanley. He left in 1997 after the Dean Witter merger, in part because
Phil Purcell, Dean Witter's top person, became CEO of the newly merged
firm. Mack became head of CSFB, but returned to Morgan Stanley in
2005 to become CEO. He is a graduate of Duke University.

UBS

Total Assets: $1.5 trillion

M&A league table: $170 billion

Establishment: UBS dates back to 1897 when the Swiss Bank Corporation was
formed. However, the organization in its current form stems from the
1998 merger of Swiss Bank and Union Bank of Switzerland. Prior to the
merger, Swiss Bank made some significant acquisitions, including S. G.
Warburg and Dillon Read, which gave the firm a large U.S. presence. The
Swiss Bank–Union Bank of Switzerland merger made the company one of
the largest commercial banks and wealth managers in the world. In 2000,
the then renamed UBS AG, purchased Paine Webber, a large U.S. wealth
management company. Though wealth management in the U.S. continues
to be a large and important business unit for UBS, the firm has recently
had to deal with significant scrutiny from the U.S. Department of Justice.
The government demanded UBS release the names and accounts of U.S.
citizens who are using the bank to avoid paying taxes on their assets.

Leadership: Oswald Grubel became CEO of the firm in 2009. Previously he had served as CEO of Credit Suisse, where he worked for nearly four decades. He served in leadership roles within Credit Suisse's private banking and trading operations before joining the firm's senior management.

VENTURE CAPITAL AND ENTREPRENEURSHIP

Determining the top venture capital firms is difficult since they range widely in size and scope. Certain companies, most notably Intel, have internal venture funds to foster the growth of new technologies in their sector. Some large investment firms like Bain Capital and Goldman Sachs, who manage a vast array of investments, have venture funds. Summit Partners, TA Associates, and General Atlantic are investment firms that make equity investments at multiple stages of a company's development, (though only a portion of their investments can be characterized as venture or early stage). Lastly, there are the traditional venture capital firms like Kleiner Perkins and Greylock, who focus on helping entrepreneurs build businesses. The firms profiled below fall into the latter two categories. The firms that focus on earlier-stage investments tend to have fewer assets under management because the investments they make are smaller than those made by later-stage firms. Given the diversity of the backgrounds these firms look for in their entry-level investment professionals, we have included a short section on the junior members of the firm. We have also profiled three famous entrepreneurs since this group features prominently in the chapter.

BENCHMARK

Assets under management: $2.5 billion
Establishment: Founded in 1995 by Robert Kagle, Andy Rachleff, Bruce Dunlevie, and Kevin Harvey.[3] Robert Kagle worked at the Boston Consulting Group before joining Technology Venture Investors. Andy Rachleff and Bruce Dunlevie were at Merill Pickard, another venture firm, and Kevin Harvey was a successful entrepreneur. The initial focus was to limit the size of the fund raised to be able to focus on small, early-stage investment opportunities. All partners had an equal stake in the firm's financial success to ensure a high level of cooperation.
Investment focus: Early-stage venture firm, making initial investments ranging from $100,000 to $15 million in technology companies.
Notable investments: eBay, Red Hat Software, ZipCar, 1800flowers, AOL
Leadership: The firm's founders still work at the company, but the organization has expanded to include additional partners in Silicon Valley, Lon-

don, and Israel. Most partners have run startup ventures, though a few have only had experience on the investing side of the business.

Profile of junior-level people: One associate worked at an investment bank that focused on venture deals. Another associate worked at Bain & Co. before joining Commonwealth Capital Ventures and attending business school.

DRAPER FISHER JURVETSON

Assets under management: $6 billion

Establishment: In 1985 Tim Draper left the investment bank Alex Brown & Sons to found a venture fund, becoming the third-generation in his family to start a venture capital firm. He was joined in 1991 by John Fisher, a former colleague at Alex Brown. Steve Jurvetson became their third partner after writing to Draper and Fisher during his second year of business school and proving himself on some investments. Previously he had worked at HP and Bain & Co.

Investment focus: Information technology, life sciences, and clean energy.

Notable investments: Skype, Hotmail, Baidu

Leadership: The firm is run by its three founders and seven other managing directors.

Profile of junior-level people: The firm's analysts generally work in finance prior to joining the firm, but often have varied backgrounds. Out of college, one spent a year working with nonprofits in Central America, and another worked for the Center for Strategic and International Studies, a Washington think tank.

GREYLOCK PARTNERS

Assets under management: $2 billion

Establishment: Founded in 1965 by Bill Elfers and Dan Gregory who were shortly thereafter joined by Charlie Waite. Elfers started the firm after working at American Research and Development, which he joined after serving in the U.S. Navy.

Investment focus: Early-stage investments in consumer, Internet, biomedical, semiconductor, services, software, and systems companies. The firm has also made some investments in bricks and mortar (meaning not medical or technology) companies, such as Filene's Basement. Greylock is open to funding anything the partners believe is a great business opportunity.[4]

Notable investments: DoubleClick, Facebook, Millennium Pharmaceuticals, Evite, Filene's Basement, Stryker

Leadership: Chairman Henry McCance joined Greylock in 1969 after two years in the office of the secretary of defense. He is a graduate of Yale and Harvard Business School. Partner Bill Kaiser worked for seven years in sales and marketing at HP and Apollo Computer (a Greylock investment). He has a degree in electrical engineering from MIT. Partner David Sze consulted at the Boston Consulting Group and Marakon Associates before working in marketing, products, and sales for Excite and Electronic Arts.

Profile of junior-level people: Associates tend to hold MBAs and have spent time working for investment firms as well as with entrepreneurial ventures prior to joining the firm.

KLEINER PERKINS CAUFIELD & BYERS

Assets under management: The firm does not disclose total assets under management, but it is currently focused on investing a $700 million fund (KPCB XIII Fund) focused on greentech, IT, and life sciences, as well as a $500 million Green Growth Fund.

Establishment: Founded in 1972

Investment focus: Early-stage investments in life sciences, information technology, especially e-commerce, pandemic preparedness, and clean energy.

Notable investments: Google, Palm, Travelocity, Amazon, AOL, Electronic Arts, Netscape, Sun Microsystems

Leadership: The firm has thirty-one partners. Of the four namesake partners only Brook Byers is still active. He is a graduate of Georgia Tech and received an MBA from Stanford. Perhaps the firm's most famous partner, however, is John Doerr. Since joining KPCB in 1980, he has led investments in Amazon, Google, and Sun Microsystems, among others. Prior to joining KPCB, he worked in sales and marketing at Intel and founded a software company as well as a broadband cable firm.

MATRIX PARTNERS

Assets under management: $3 billion

Establishment: Paul Ferri founded Matrix Partners in 1982 after establishing the precursor firm Hellman Ferri Investment Associates in 1977.

Investment focus: Software, communications equipment, semiconductors, storage, internet and wireless.

Notable investments: Apple, SanDisk, Tivoli, Sycamore Networks

Leadership: Founding partner Paul Ferri still works at the firm. Matrix's India office is run by its two cofounders, one of whom ran India's largest online marketplace. The other has worked at Sequoia Capital India, J.P. Morgan, and McKinsey. In the United States, Partner Timothy Barrows worked in mergers and acquisitions at Merrill Lynch before joining Matrix. He graduated from Williams College and holds an MBA from Stanford.

Profile of junior-level people: The firm hires associates who do not have MBAs. They typically have banking or consulting backgrounds, as well as startup experience.

SEQUOIA CAPITAL

Assets under management: The firm does not disclose AUM.

Establishment: Donald Valentine started Sequoia Capital in 1972 after working for almost fifteen years in the semiconductor business at Fairchild Semiconductor and National Semiconductor. Sequoia Capital was incubated out of the Capital Group.

Investment Focus: Provides seed ($100,000–$1 million), early ($1 million–$10 million) and growth ($10 million–$100 million) stage investments in the consumer, financial services, healthcare services, infrastructure services, internet, mobile, outsourcing, and technology sectors through offices in China, India, Israel, and the United States.

Notable Investments: Apple, Cisco, Electronic Arts, YouTube, PayPal, eHarmony, Oracle, Atari, Yahoo, Google

Leadership: Founder Donald Valentine still works at the firm and is in the office every day. The firm's most well-known partner is Michael Moritz. He joined the firm in 1986 after working at *Time* magazine and starting Technologic Partners, a technology conference company. He has been involved in many of the biggest technology–venture capital successes including Google, Cisco, PayPal, and YouTube. He is a graduate of Oxford University and the Wharton School of Business.

Profile of junior-level people: Most of the associates held jobs at other growth investment firms, such as Summit Partners.

SUMMIT PARTNERS

Assets under management: $6 billion

Establishment: Founded in 1984 as a venture firm, but now commits the majority of its capital to later-stage growth equity investments.

Investment focus: Summit Partners invests in growing, profitable companies through its venture-capital, private-equity, and subordinated-debt funds. It invests in companies in a wide array of industries.

Notable investments: McAfee, Unica, CMGI

Leadership: Bruce Evans is a managing director of the firm. (See interview)

Profile of junior-level people: Associates are hired directly out of college or with one or two years of finance experience. Many have some technical or business background, but a significant number majored in fields outside of engineering or business.

TA ASSOCIATES

Assets under management: $6 billion

Establishment: Founded by Peter Brooke as an early-stage venture firm, though like Summit, the firm now focuses most of its capital on later-stage growth equity investments and buyouts.

Investment focus: Invests across a number of sectors, including technology, finance, and healthcare. Investments range from $50 million to $600 million.

Notable investments: Asurion, Apex, ImmunoGen

Leadership: Chairman Kevin Landry joined the firm in 1967 while he was still at Wharton Business School. Nearly all of the firm's U.S. managing directors had experience at another finance firm prior to joining TA. Some also had industry experience in the sector in which they focus their investments.

Profile of junior-level people: Associates are hired after completing an investment banking analyst program.

ENTREPRENEURS

The professional and educational backgrounds of America's most successful entrepreneurs are incredibly varied. Below are profiles of three recent megasuccessful entrepreneurs.

Steve Jobs: Attended Reed College in Oregon, but dropped out after one semester.[5] He worked at Atari with Steve Wozniak with whom he founded Apple Computer. After being ousted by Apple's board in 1985 he started NeXT Software and Pixar Animation Studios. In 1996 when Apple bought NeXT, Jobs returned to the company he founded to run the business.

Larry Page: Graduated from the University of Michigan and went to Stanford to study computer engineering, where he met Sergey Brin. As a research project, the two created a search engine that would generate results based on the most frequently visited sites. The IPO of their company, Google, made them both billionaires.[6]

Pierre Omidyar: Graduated from Tufts University with a degree in computer science in 1988. Upon graduating he developed software for a division of

Apple Computer. In 1991 he started Ink Development Corp. with three friends, which he worked at through 1994. He then became a developer services engineer for the mobile communication company General Magic. In 1995 he started a website, which he called Auction Web, to allow direct person-to person auctions over the Internet. The company was renamed eBay in 1997 and went public in 1998.[7]

PRIVATE EQUITY

There are over one hundred U.S. private equity firms with more than $1 billion to invest. Some specialize in certain industry areas (e.g., media and telecom, manufacturing), many focus on companies of a certain size, and others look for businesses in specific situations (for example, those in bankruptcy or in need of financial restructuring). Listed below are twelve of the largest U.S.-based firms. One or more of these firms has been involved in nearly every major U.S. leveraged buyout of the past few years.

APOLLO MANAGEMENT

Assets under management: $38 billion

Establishment: Founded in 1991 by Leon Black in order to make investments based on the expertise he developed working on private equity deals at Drexel Burnham Lambert.

Firm structure: The firm utilizes its financial restructuring expertise to invest in distressed businesses as well as to complete leveraged buyouts of profitable companies and take minority positions in growth-oriented companies.

Major deals: Harrah's Entertainment, Claire's Stores, Realogy (Coldwell Banker and Century 21)

Leadership: Founder and chairman Leon Black ran the Mergers and Acquisitions Department at Drexel Burnham Lambert from 1977 to 1990. He majored in philosophy and history at Dartmouth and received an MBA from Harvard.

BAIN CAPITAL

Assets under management: $60 Billion

Establishment: Founded in 1984 by Bain & Co. partners with the intent to utilize the expertise they had built advising companies on strategy in order to identify, invest in, and improve companies.

Firm structure: Bain Capital now consists of five investment groups: private equity, public equity, fixed income and credit instruments, venture capital, and global macro asset investments.

Major deals: Hospital Corporation of America, Dunkin' (Donuts) Brands, Domino's, Toys "R" Us, Burger King

Leadership: Managing director Josh Bekenstein attended Yale and Harvard Business School before joining Bain & Co. He has worked at Bain Capital since its inception. Managing director John Connaughton joined the firm in 1989 after working at Bain & Co. He received a BS from the University of Virginia and an MBA from Harvard Business School. Managing director Paul Edgerley graduated from Kansas State and Harvard Business School. He was an accountant before doing consulting work at Bain & Co. Managing director Mark Nunnelly attended Centre College and Harvard Business School. He worked at Proctor & Gamble and several startups and was a partner at Bain & Co. before joining Bain Capital. Managing director Steve Pagliuca worked at an accounting firm before attending Harvard Business School. He consulted at Bain & Co. before joining Bain Capital in 1989 (see interview). He took a leave of absence from the firm in September 2009 to run for the U.S. Senate.

THE BLACKSTONE GROUP

Assets under management: $94 billion

Establishment: Founded in 1985 by Steve Schwarzman and Pete Peterson with $400,000 to invest.

Firm structure: Private equity, real estate, alternative asset management (hedge funds, corporate debt), and financial advisory services (advising clients on mergers and acquisitions, restructuring and raising capital).

Major deals: Equity Office Properties, Hilton Hotels, Michaels

Leadership: CEO Steve Schwarzman started his career at Lehman Brothers after attending Yale and Harvard Business School. At Lehman he rose to head of the mergers and acquisitions department before leaving to start Blackstone. President Tony Hamilton joined DLJ as an investment banking associate after graduating from Harvard Business School. Seven years later he became head of the firm's global mergers and acquisitions group. After Credit Suisse bought DLJ in 2000 he became chairman of global investment banking and private equity at Credit Suisse. He joined Blackstone as vice chairman in 2002.

THE CARLYLE GROUP

Total assets under management: $85 billion

Establishment: Founded in 1987 by David Rubenstein, William Conway, Daniel D'Aniello, and a fourth partner who has since left the firm.

Firm structure: Has sixty-four funds, the most of any large private equity
firm, and offices around the world. Investment funds include buyout,
growth capital, real estate, and leveraged finance.

Major deals: Kinder Morgan (energy infrastructure), Nielsen Media, Hertz
Rent-A-Car[8]

Leadership: Cofounder David Rubenstein practiced law and served in the
Carter administration before starting Carlyle (see interview). Cofounder
William Conway worked at First National Bank of Chicago in corporate
finance for ten years and then served in a variety of other executive roles,
including CFO at MCI Communications. Cofounder Daniel D'Aniello
worked in the finance departments of PepsiCo and TWA before becoming vice president of finance and development at Marriott.

Cerberus Capital

Total assets under management: $22 billion[9]

Establishment: Founded in 1992 by Stephen Feinberg and William Richter
with $10 million.

Firm structure: Highly secretive hedge-fund/buyout firm. The organization
manages roughly a dozen funds, most of which include an array of investments, such as debt, LBOs, real estate, and public equities.

Major Deals: Chrysler, ANC Rental Corporation (National and Alamo Car[10]
Rental), GMAC, Albertson's (grocery chain)[11]

Leadership: Cofounder Stephen Feinberg served in the Reserve Officers' Training Corps (ROTC) before taking a job as a trader at Drexel Burnham. He
later worked at the investment firm Gruntal & Co. before starting
Cerberus at the age of thirty-two. Senior managing director William
Richter ran his own brokerage firm before cofounding Cerberus. Chair-
man John W. Snow assumed his position at the firm after serving as U.S.
Treasury secretary. Previously, he was CEO of CSX, a transportation
company, where he worked for twenty years. He graduated from the
University of Toledo, has a JD from George Washington University and a
PhD in economics from the University of Virginia.[12]

CCMP Capital

Assets under management: $10 billion

Establishment: CCMP Capital was formed in March 2005 by the senior buyout and growth equity professionals of J.P. Morgan Partners (the private
equity division of JP Morgan Chase). CCMP Capital now manages the
investments made by J.P. Morgan Partners, which was formed in 1984.
After the merger of J.P. Morgan and Bank One, the newly formed bank

decided to retain One Equity as the firm's internal private equity investment unit and to spin off J.P. Morgan Partners. One Equity was much
smaller, but the types of deals it completed posed less of a potential conflict of interest with the investment banking division than J.P. Morgan
Partners' transactions.

Firm structure: The firm invests in buyout and growth equity opportunities
in consumer retail and services, energy, healthcare infrastructure, industrials, media, and telecom.

Major deals: Aramark, JetBlue, Quizno's Subs

Leadership: Chairman Greg Brenneman joined the firm after serving as CEO
of Quizno's and Burger King. Earlier in his career he was a partner at
Bain & Co. and served as president of PwC Consulting. He holds degrees
from Washburn University and Harvard Business School. President and
CEO Stephen Murray worked in the Lending Division of Manufacturers
Hanover before joining J.P. Morgan Partners in 1989. He attended
Boston College and has an MBA from Columbia.

GOLDMAN SACHS CAPITAL PARTNERS

Assets under management: $37 billion[13]

Establishment: Goldman Sachs was the first major investment bank to establish its own private-equity group. The fund is one of the largest in the
world, but generally takes minority positions alongside other private-
equity firms.

Major Deals: Burger King, Alltel Wireless, TXU

Leadership: Managing director Joseph Gleberman began his career at Goldman Sachs in the investment banking division. He graduated from Yale
and has an MBA from Stanford.

KOHLBERG KRAVIS ROBERTS & CO.

Assets under management: $51 billion, $38 billion dedicated to private equity

Establishment: The firm was established in 1976 by cousins Henry Kravis and
George Roberts and their mentor Jerome Kohlberg, all of whom worked
together at Bear Stearns.

Major deals: RJR Nabisco, Texas Genco, Toys "R" Us, Dollar General, Hospital
Corporation of America

Leadership: Cofounders Henry Kravis and George Roberts, who still run the
firm, both worked at Bear Stearns before starting the organization.
Kravis attended Claremont McKenna College and received his MBA
from Columbia. Cofounder Jerome Kohlberg left the firm in 1987 to
found Kohlberg & Co. a separate private equity firm.

PROVIDENCE EQUITY PARTNERS

Assets under management: $22 billion

Establishment: Founded in 1989 by Jonathan Nelson.

Firm structure: Makes investments in media, entertainment, communications and information companies.

Major deals: Voice Stream Wireless (which became T-Mobile), MGM, Warner Music Group

Leadership: Prior to founding Providence Equity, CEO Jonathan Nelson was a managing director at Narraganset Capital, a private equity firm, which made investments in cable television, broadcasting, and publishing. He graduated from Brown University and Harvard Business School.

THL PARTNERS (THOMAS H. LEE PARTNERS)

Assets under management: $15 billion

Firm structure: Engages in leveraged buyouts of large, growth-oriented companies with enterprise values of $1 billion to $15 billion.

Major deals: Warner Music Group, Clear Channel, Dunkin' (Donuts) Brands, Houghton Mifflin

Leadership: Co-president Scott Schoen started at the firm after working in the private finance department of Goldman Sachs. He was a history major at Yale and has an MBA and a JD from Harvard. Co-president Scott Sperling worked at the Boston Consulting Group before spending ten years helping to invest Harvard's endowment. He holds a BS from Purdue University and an MBA from Harvard. Co-president Anthony DiNovi worked in corporate finance at Goldman Sachs and Wertheim Schroeder & Co. He graduated from Harvard and Harvard Business School. Managing director and head of the Strategic Resources Group Richard Bressler began his career as an accountant before joining Time Inc. He was a senior officer of AOL Time Warner and later the CFO of Viacom. He holds a degree in accounting from Adelphi University. Founder Thomas H. Lee no longer works at the firm. He has started a new fund, Lee Equity Partners.

TPG (TEXAS PACIFIC GROUP)

Assets under management: $45 billion

Establishment: Founded in 1992 by David Bonderman and Jim Coulter under the name Texas Pacific Group. The firm recently changed its name to TPG, which makes sense given that the firm's headquarters are in San Francisco.

Firm structure: Private equity, venture capital, public equity, and debt investing

Major deals: Continental Airlines, Burger King, J. Crew

Leadership: Founding Partner David Bonderman received a law degree
   from Harvard and worked in the U.S. Attorney General's office and
   later for a Washington, D.C., law firm, where he specialized in corporate and securities litigation. He joined the Robert M. Bass Group, a
   private equity firm in 1983 and was Chief Operating Officer when he
   left in 1992 to start his own firm.[14] Founding Partner Jim Coulter
   managed money for the Bass family with David Bonderman before
   cofounding TPG. He is a graduate of Dartmouth and Stanford's Graduate School of Business.

WARBURG PINCUS

Assets under management: $30 billion

Establishment: The 1966 merger of the investment bank E. M. Warburg with
   Lionel I. Pincus & Co., a venture capital and financial consulting firm,
   created Warburg Pincus.

Firm structure: Firm invests in all stages of a company's development from
   venture capital to leveraged buyouts. The firm was an investor in the
   Aramark LBO, but generally invests in deals under $1 billion.[15]

Major deals: Aramark, Avaya

Leadership: Co-president Charles Kaye has worked at Warburg Pincus since
   1986 and played a significant role in the development of the firm's Asian
   operations. He graduated from the University of Texas. Co-president
   Joseph Landy has worked at Warburg Pincus since 1985. He graduated
   from Wharton and received an MBA from the Stern School at New York
   University.

HEDGE FUNDS

Many large-asset managers, including the investment banks, operate some
type of hedge fund. J.P. Morgan, Goldman Sachs, and UBS operate particularly large funds. Similarly, some private-equity firms operate funds focused
on public markets employing the strategies described in the chapter on hedge
funds. The firms profiled here are all organizations that focus primarily on
operating one or more hedge funds. Their investment strategies vary, as do
the size of the funds, but they all have distinguished themselves as influential
players in the public markets.

THE BAUPOST GROUP

Assets under management: $14 billion[16]

Establishment: Baupost was formed in 1982 as an investment manager for four families. The firm was originally set up to invest the families' money with outside fund managers, but soon decided to become its own fund and execute all investment decisions. Though the firm has expanded its investor base beyond the original families, it is closed to new investors.

Investment focus: The firm invests across a wide array of asset classes (international and domestic equities, bonds, and real estate) and seeks to deploy its value-based approach wherever there are profitable opportunities.

Leadership: President Seth Klarman joined the firm at its founding after graduating from Harvard Business School. Despite the fact that his previous professional experience was limited to summer analyst roles at investment firms, he is largely responsible for the exponential growth of Baupost (see interview).

BRIDGEWATER ASSOCIATES

Assets under management: $72 billion, $39 billion in hedge fund assets

Establishment: Ray Dalio started Bridgewater out of his New York City apartment in 1975. However, he did not launch his hedge fund portfolio until 1990 when he received capital from Loews Corporation and Kodak. Unlike most funds that accept individual investors, Bridgewater exclusively serves institutional clients.

Investment focus: Bridgewater offers five investment strategies to its clients: Pure Alpha, All Weather, currency overlay, global fixed income, and inflation indexed bonds. The Pure Alpha fund is focused on creating maximum return for shareholders by making investments across asset classes. All Weather seeks high risk-adjusted returns and is designed to perform well in any market condition. Currency overlay is a vehicle through which fund managers can limit their exposure to currency fluctuations from international equities. The firm deploys a heavily quantitative strategy in identifying investment opportunities.

Leadership: Founder and president Ray Dalio graduated from Long Island University and received an MBA at Harvard. He worked in commodities, currencies, and futures for a few different firms before starting his own consultancy to help companies hedge currency and interest-rate risk.[17]

CITADEL INVESTMENT CORPORATION

Assets under management: $11 billion[18]

Establishment: CEO and founder Ken Griffin developed bond arbitrage models and began trading in the late 1980s when he was still a student at Harvard College. He launched Citadel in 1990, one year after graduating.

Investment focus: In addition to its primary role as an alternative asset manager, Citadel also provides investment bank–type services: hedge fund administration, market making, and order execution.

Leadership: The firm is managed by founder Ken Griffin. The organization is known for having nearly twice as many investment professionals as firms of comparable size in order to execute Citadel's complex trading strategies.

D. E. SHAW

Assets under management: $29 billion

Establishment: The firm was founded in 1988 by David E. Shaw, who applied his computer science background to the fields of computational finance. Through lengthy research projects and complex mathematical models, the firm has consistently produced large financial returns.

Investment focus: The firm's original investment approach focused exclusively on quantitative strategies, utilizing research and models to capture profitable arbitrage opportunities. The firm has expanded its approach to include qualitative strategies that involve valuations of securities and market conditions.

Leadership: Founder David Shaw received his PhD from Stanford and was a professor of computer science at Columbia University. He left teaching in 1986 to focus on computational finance research and started his firm two years later. Though he remains involved with the firm, he devotes a significant portion of his time to scientific research pursuits.

FORTRESS INVESTMENT GROUP

Assets under management: $31 billion

Establishment: Founded in 1998, the firm went public in 2007.

Investment focus: The firm has multiple hedge funds and a private-equity investing division. The internal hedge funds invest primarily in the derivatives, fixed income, currency, equity, and commodity markets. Their hybrid funds function somewhat like fund-of-funds and can invest with managers outside of the firm.

Leadership: CEO Daniel Mudd joined Fortress in 2009. Previously he was CEO of Fannie Mae and before that the head of GE Capital, Japan. He holds an MPA degree from the Kennedy School of Government and a BA from the University of Virginia. Cochairman Wesley Edens was a cofounder of the firm and runs its private equity arm. Prior to Fortress, he worked at UBS, BlackRock, and Lehman Brothers. He holds a BS from Oregon State University. Cochairman Peter Briger is responsible for the hybrid hedge fund business. Prior to Fortress he worked at Goldman Sachs in a variety of senior trading positions. He holds a BA from Princeton and an MBA from Wharton.

PAULSON & CO.

Assets under management: $29 billion

Establishment: John Paulson founded the firm in 1994.

Investment focus: Paulson & Co. utilizes primarily event-driven investment strategies. The firm's most well-known investment success was foreseeing the collapse in the subprime mortgage market and using credit default swaps to make billions as the value of debt securities plummeted. The value of these instruments rose as the underlying security values declined. The fund uses limited leverage in its investments.

Leadership: Founder John Paulson was a managing director in Mergers & Acquisitions at Bear Stearns before starting his firm. He is a graduate of New York University and Harvard Business School.[19]

RENAISSANCE TECHNOLOGIES

Assets under management: $17 billion[20]

Establishment: James Simons founded the firm in 1982, applying his mathematical acumen to financial markets.

Investment focus: The firm hires a large number of PhDs to develop computer-driven models that identify profitable trading opportunities. Renaissance is best known for its Medallion Fund, which charges some of the highest fees in the industry (justified by the fund's exceptional long-term performance). Renaissance has a number of other funds focused on specific markets and asset classes.

Leadership: Founder and chairman James Simons taught mathematics at Harvard and MIT and conducted research in math prior to entering the financial world. He holds a BA from MIT and a PhD from the University of California at Berkeley. Co-presidents Peter Brown and Robert Mercer are speech-recognition experts who worked at IBM. They both joined the firm in 1993 and identified patterns in public markets similar to speech-recognition technologies, which provided the basis for profitable trades.

SAC CAPITAL

Assets under management: $12 billion

Establishment: Steven A. Cohen started the firm in 1992 with $25 million.

Investment focus: SAC traditionally employed a long-short equity strategy, but has broadened its approach. The firm has a number of different funds; strategies range from convertible and statistical arbitrage to quantitative trading approaches.

Leadership: Founder Steven Cohen still runs operations at the firm and stays heavily involved in daily trading activities. Cohen graduated from the Wharton School at the University of Pennsylvania where he actively traded stocks. After college he went to work at the investment brokerage firm Gruntal & Co. Within six years he was running his own trading group and after fourteen years at the firm, he left to start SAC Capital.[21]

TUDOR INVESTMENTS

Assets under management: $11 billion

Establishment: The firm was founded in 1980 by Paul Tudor Jones.

Investment focus: The firm utilizes event-driven strategies to invest in domestic and international public equity, fixed income, currency, and commodities markets.

Leadership: Chairman and founder Paul Tudor Jones worked at the investment brokerage firm E. F. Hutton after graduating from the University of Virginia. He later worked for the famed commodity trader Eli Tullis. President and vice chairman Mark Dalton worked at the investment firm Kidder Peabody before joining Tudor Investments in 1988. He received a BA from Denison University and a JD from Vanderbilt University Law School.

MANAGEMENT CONSULTING

The consulting industry is comprised of a plethora of firms. Their specialties are as diverse as the industries, practices, and problems of the businesses and investment firms they serve. The firms below are large, generalist management-consulting practices that serve clients across a wide array of industries. Since most consulting firms are private companies, it can be difficult to ascertain their true size. For the profiles below we have listed revenue, where possible, and/or the number of consultants the firm employs.

ACCENTURE

Establishment: Accenture had its origins in the Arthur Anderson accounting firm. Arthur Anderson had an internal consulting division for decades, but in 1989 Anderson Consulting became a separate entity and grew to exceed its former parent company. In 2000, Anderson Consulting sued Arthur

Anderson over its obligation to continue paying royalties despite the fact that Arthur Anderson's new consulting practice now competed with Anderson Consulting. In 2000, the companies severed ties completely and Anderson Consulting became Accenture. Arthur Anderson was dissolved shortly afterward as a result of its involvement in illicit accounting practices at Enron. Accenture became a publicly traded company in 2001.

Leadership: CEO William D. Green has worked at Accenture for over thirty years in a broad array of the company's business areas. He is a graduate of Dean College and has a BS and an MBA from Babson College.

Reputation: Accenture is known for its technology services and outsourcing expertise; however it also has a large management consulting practice.

Size: Accenture has 47,000 consultants[22] and annual revenue of $23 billion.[23]

BAIN & COMPANY

Establishment: Founded in 1973 by Bill Bain and six other former consultants from the Boston Consulting Group.

Leadership: Chairman Orit Gadiesh has worked at Bain & Company since she graduated from Harvard Business School. Worldwide managing director Steve Ellis founded a Silicon Valley–based consulting firm before joining Bain. He graduated from the University of California at Berkeley and has an MBA from Stanford.

Notable alumni: Kevin Rollins (former CEO of Dell Computer), Meg Whitman (former CEO of eBay), Mitt Romney (cofounder of Bain Capital, former governor of Massachusetts), Ken Chenault (CEO of American Express)

Reputation: The most collegial of the top consulting firms; leader in serving private equity clients

Size: 3,500 consultants[24]

BOOZ & COMPANY

Establishment: Founded in 1914 by Edwin Booz, with the name The Business Research Service. The company conducted research and advised businesses in Chicago. Allen brought on partners George Fry, Jim Allen, and Carl Hamilton to help build the business into a large sustainable entity. The company created its government practice during World War II and experienced rapid growth. In 2008 The Carlyle Group purchased a majority stake in the government practice of the firm for $2.5 billion.[25] The government consultancy maintained the name Booz Allen Hamilton and the commercial consulting practice took the name Booz & Company.

Leadership: Chairman Joe Saddi attended ESSEC in Paris and Cornell Business School. He worked at Bain & Co. prior to joining Booz Allen. CEO Shumeet Banerji holds a PhD from the Kellogg Graduate School of Management at Northwestern University and was a professor at the University of Chicago Business School before joining Booz Allen.

Size: 3,300 consultants

Boston Consulting Group

Establishment: Founded by Bruce Henderson in 1963 as a division of the Boston Safe Deposit and Trust Company.

Leadership: CEO Hans-Paul Bürkner has worked at BCG since 1981. He holds degrees from the University of Bochum and Yale as well as a DPhil from Oxford University.

Notable alumni: Indra Nooyi (CEO of PepsiCo.), Benjamin Netanyahu (prime minister of Israel), John Legend (musician)

Reputation: The firm is known for its innovative strategy work and a somewhat more academic culture than its major competitors.

Size: 4,500 consultants[26]

Deloitte

Establishment: Deloitte Consulting is a division of Deloitte, a global accounting firm. It is the largest consulting practice that still operates as a division of an accounting firm. In 1995 Deloitte acquired ICS to increase its SAP technology integration service offerings.

Leadership: Deloitte CEO Barry Salzberg is a CPA with deep experience in the firm's tax practice. He has degrees in accounting and law from Brooklyn College and holds an LLM in taxation from New York University Law School. Doug Lattner is the CEO of Deloitte Consulting. He joined the firm in 1975. He graduated from the University of Oklahoma and has an MBA from the University of Dallas.

Reputation: Similar to Accenture, Deloitte Consulting has expertise in technology integration and outsourcing, as well as in strategy and operations.

Size: 25,000 consultants. The consulting division generates annual revenues of $3.5 billion.[27]

IBM Global Business Services

Establishment: IBM Global Business Services is the professional service arm of the IBM Corporation. It started as a service for clients of its computer

products and services and expanded dramatically in 2002 when IBM
purchased the consulting practice of Price Waterhouse Cooper.

Leadership: Ginni Rometty is the senior vice president of IBM Global Business Services. Prior to starting at IBM, she worked in a technology systems function at General Motors. At IBM she has held leadership roles
within the company's insurance and business services divisions. She has
a BS in computer science and electrical engineering from Northwestern
University.

Reputation: IBM Global Business Services began as a way for the company to
sell more computer products, but it has grown into a large multiservice
business. It frequently competes with Accenture and Deloitte Consulting,
particularly for technology business cases.

Size: $20 billion in annual revenue[28]

McKINSEY & COMPANY

Establishment: Founded in 1926 by Professor James McKinsey.

Leadership: Worldwide managing director Dominic Barton has worked at the
firm for over two decades. Prior to becoming head of the organization he
ran the company's Asian operations. He holds an MPhil from Oxford
University.

Notable alumni: Lou Gerstner (former CEO of IBM and American Express),
Jim McNerney (CEO of Boeing), Harvey Golub (chairman of AIG),
Jonathan Schwartz (CEO of Sun Microsystems).

Reputation: The largest and most global management-consulting firm in the
world, slightly more formal and travel intensive than its peers.

Size: 8,400 consultants

MONITOR GROUP

Establishment: Founded in 1983 by Mark and Joe Fuller as well as Harvard
Business School professor and strategist Michael Porter. The firm sought
to create a consulting practice out of the innovative new business ideas
that Porter and the Fullers helped create.

Leadership: Chairman Mark Fuller taught at Harvard Business School prior
to cofounding the firm. CEO Joe Fuller worked briefly at Bain & Company after graduating from Harvard Business School (see interview).

Notable alumni: Michael Porter (HBS professor, business strategy author),
Richard Dearlove (former Head of British Intelligence Service), Ian
Smith (CEO of Reed Elsevier)

Reputation: The name Monitor Group refers to the collection of areas within
the firm, including Monitor Action Group, Monitor University, and

Monitor Clipper Partners (the private-equity arm of the firm). The firm is known for its innovative global structure and focus on developing consulting success through applications of new business theory.

Size: 1,500 consultants

OLIVER WYMAN

Establishment: Oliver Wyman is a division of Marsh & McLennan Companies, a publicly traded organization that owns five businesses providing insurance and consulting services. Oliver Wyman is itself the product of the integration of three consulting practices controlled by Marsh & McLennan. The original company, Oliver, Wyman & Company, was formed by former Booz Allen consultants.

Leadership: CEO John Drzik has worked at Oliver Wyman since 1984, the year the firm was founded. He is a graduate of Princeton University.

Notable alumni: David Morrison (partner at Lee Equity Partners), Premal Shah (president of Kiva.org)

Reputation: Oliver Wyman offers consulting services across industries, but it is known as a leader in serving the financial services industry.

Size: Annual revenues of $1.6 billion[29]

APPENDIX B

FEATURED INTERVIEWEES' BACKGROUNDS

Jamie Dimon
CEO of JPMorgan Chase & Co.
   Education:
        Tufts University, 1978
        Harvard Business School, 1982
   Professional Experience:
        American Express, 1982–1985
        Citigroup (and predecessor companies), 1985–1998
        Bank One, 2000–2004
        JPMorgan Chase & Co. 2004–Present

Suzanne Nora Johnson
Former vice chairman of Goldman Sachs
   Education:
        University of Southern California, 1979
        Harvard Law School, 1982
   Professional Experience:

U.S. Fourth Circuit Court of Appeals, law clerk, 1982–1983
Simpson, Thacher & Bartlett (law firm), 1983–1985
Goldman Sachs, 1985–2007
    Positions included: head of Global Healthcare Investment
        Banking, founder of Latin American Business, head of
        Global Investment Research, chairman of Global Markets
        Institute, vice chairman of the firm

VENTURE CAPITAL AND ENTREPRENEURSHIP

Bruce Evans
Manager director of Summit Partners
    Education:
        Vanderbilt University, B.E., 1981
        Harvard Business School, 1986
    Professional Experience:
        IBM salesman, 1981–1983
        Salomon Brothers, 1985
        Summit Partners, 1986–Present

Noah Glass
Founder and CEO of GoMobo
    Education:
        Yale University, 2003
    Professional Experience:
        Shutterfly.com, 2000
        Braun Consulting, 2003–2004
        Endeavor Global (development nonprofit), 2004–2005
        GoMobo (mobile service startup), 2005–Present

Sam Clemens
CEO of Models from Mars, formerly of Greylock Partners
    Education:
        Yale University, 1997
        Harvard Business School, 2004
    Professional Experience:
        Booz Allen & Hamilton (management consulting), 1997–1999
        Elance Inc (software startup), 1999–2002
        Amazon.com, 2003
        Greylock Partners, 2004–2006
        BzzAgent Inc (software startup), 2006–2008
        Models for Mars (technology startup), 2008–Present

PRIVATE EQUITY

David Rubenstein
Cofounder of The Carlyle Group
    Education:
        Duke University, 1970
        University of Chicago Law School, 1973
    Professional Experience:
        Paul, Weiss, Rifkind, Wharton & Garrison (law firm), 1973–1975
        U.S. Senate Judiciary Committee's Subcommittee on Constitutional Amendments, 1975–1976
        Deputy assistant to the president for domestic policy, 1977–1981
        Shaw, Pittman, Potts & Trowbridge (law firm), 1982–1986
        The Carlyle Group, 1987–Present

Steve Pagliuca
Managing director of Bain Capital
    Education:
        Duke University, 1977
        Harvard Business School, 1982
    Professional Experience:
        Peat Marwick Mitchell & Co. (accounting firm), 1977–1980
        Bain & Company, 1982–1989
        Bain Capital, 1989–Present

HEDGE FUNDS

Julian Robertson
Founder of Tiger Management
    Education:
        University of North Carolina at Chapel Hill, 1955
    Professional Experience:
        Kidder, Peabody & Co., 1957–1980
        Tiger Management, 1980–Present

Seth Klarman
President of The Baupost Group
    Education:
        Cornell University, 1980
        Harvard Business School, 1982
    Professional Experience:
        The Baupost Group, 1982–Present

Tim Jenkins
Cofounder of Marble Arch Investments
    Education:
        Washington and Lee University, 1997
        Harvard Business School, 2003
    Professional Experience:
        Morgan Stanley Capital Partners, 1997–1999
        Madison Dearborn Partners, 1999–2001
        Tiger Management, 2003–2007
        Marble Arch Investments, 2007–Present

MANAGEMENT CONSULTING

Chuck Farkas
Senior director of Bain & Company
    Education:
        Princeton University, 1976
        Brandeis University, graduate program in history
        Harvard Business School, 1980
    Professional Experience:
        Bain & Company, 1982–Present

Joe Fuller
CEO and cofounder of the Monitor Group
    Education:
        Harvard College, 1979
        Harvard Business School, 1981
    Professional Experience:
        Bain & Company, 1981–1983
        Monitor Group, 1983–Present

Ron Daniel
Former worldwide managing director of McKinsey & Company
    Education:
        Wesleyan University, 1952
        Harvard Business School, 1954
    Professional Experience:
        McKinsey & Company, 1957–Present

MANAGEMENT OF FORTUNE 500 COMPANIES

Chris Galvin

Former CEO of Motorola, chairman of Harrison Street Capital

    Education:

        Northwestern University, 1971

        Kellogg School of Management, 1973

    Professional Experience:

        Motorola, 1973–2003

        Harrison Street Capital, 2005–Present

Peter Nicholas

Cofounder and chairman of Boston Scientific Corporation

    Education:

        Duke University, 1964

        Wharton School of Business, 1968

    Professional Experience:

        U.S. Navy, 1964–1966

        Eli Lilly, 1968–1978

        Millipore Corporation, 1978–1979

        Boston Scientific, 1979–Present

Shona Brown

Senior vice president of business operations at Google

    Education:

        Carleton University, 1987

        Oxford University, 1989

        Stanford University, 1995

    Professional Experience:

        Stanford University, Department of Industrial Engineering and En-
            gineering Management, 1989–1995

        McKinsey & Company, 1995–2003

        Google, 2003–Present

ACKNOWLEDGMENTS

We are grateful to a large number of people who contributed their wisdom, experiences and insights for this project. Conversations in 2003 with Jeff Bloomberg, Jim Sloman, and Jon Lee, about the evolution of their careers in business and the intricacies of the industries in which they work, sparked the initial idea for this book. Joel Fleishman's early enthusiasm and magnanimous introductions to many wise business veterans were hugely helpful in giving us the confidence to pursue the book. Frank Binswanger, Mary V. Bell, Mike Galvin, Suzy Welch, and Joe Tessitore all provided entrée to the publishing community, and Suzy and Joe helped us hone the focus of our endeavor. Through a serendipitous series of introductions (thank you, Auren Hoffman and Ben Casnocha) we had the great privilege of working with our agent, Lisa DiMona of Lark Productions. We could not have asked for a better advisor and representative.

The dozens of interviewees were exceptionally generous with their time and the thoughtfulness of their comments. This book would not have been possible without them. Lastly, we would like to thank all of the people who put pen to paper and commented on early chapter drafts to ensure their accuracy, thoroughness, and readability. Jessica Wheeler, Jonathan Snider, Andy and Jody Snider, Jeff Bloomberg, Chuck McMullan, Ben Steiner, Tim Jenkins, Chuck Farkas, Joe Fuller, Nick Beim, Tom Seeman—we are grateful for your assistance in revising and refining the text.

NOTES

INTRODUCTION

1. "Remarks by the President on 21st Century Financial Regulatory Reform," June 17, 2009.

CHAPTER ONE

1. Jamie Dimon, "Letter to Shareholders," 2008. J.P. Morgan Annual Report.
2. Bryan Burrough, "Bringing Down Bear Stearns," *Vanity Fair,* August 2008.
3. Ibid.
4. "Investment Banking," Microsoft® Encarta® Online Encyclopedia, 2008, http://encarta.msn.com © 1997–2008 Microsoft Corporation.
5. Floyd Norris, "Ex-Salomon Chiefs' Costly Battle," *New York Times,* August 19, 1994.
6. Peter Truell, "Jett, Ex-Kidder Trader, Must Repay Millions," *New York Times,* July 22, 1998.
7. PBS, "Inside the Meltdown," *Frontline,* February 17, 2009.
8. Interview with Jeff Bloomberg, June 28, 2009.
9. Amar Bhidé, "Why Bankers Got So Reckless . . ." *Business Week,* February 9, 2009.
10. Daisy Maxey, Jaime Levy, & Ian Salisbury, "Wall Street Employee owners shudder as Bear Stearns implodes," Dow Jones Newswire, March 17, 2008.
11. Jamie Dimon, "Letter to Shareholders," 2008. J.P. Morgan Annual Report.
12. Goldman Sachs 2008 10-K financial statement.
13. The Goldman Sachs fiscal year ran through November until 2008 when the firm switched to the calendar year.

CHAPTER TWO

1. Susan is a composite based on interviews with associates at top venture firms.
2. Scott Shane, *The Illusions of Entrepreneurship* (New Haven: Yale University Press, 2008).
3. Howard Means, *Money and Power* (New York: John Wiley, 2002), p. 8.
4. David Hsu and Martin Keeney, "Organizing Venture Capital: The Rise and Demise of American Research & Development," December 1, 2004.
5. Ibid.

6. William Hambrecht, "Venture Capital and the Growth of Silicon Valley." *California Management Review*, Winter 1984.
7. Andreas Boquist and J. Dawson. " U.S. Venture Capital in Europe in the 1980s and the 1990s." *Journal of Private Equity* 39, no. 1 (Winter 2004).
8. Hambrecht, "Venture Capital."
9. Ibid.
10. Boquist and Dawson, "U.S. Venture Capital."
11. Ibid.
12. The data for the graphs in this chapter are from Thomson, the Venture Capital Association, Yearbook 2008.
13. Richard Waters, "Technology Boom Venture Capital Leaders Named," *Financial Times*, February 18, 2003; NVCA/ Thomson Reuters, Venture Capital Performance Statistics Decline across All Time Horizons in the Fourth Quarter," April 27, 2009
14. Pui-Wing Tam, "Venture Capitalists Head for the Door," *Wall Street Journal*, June 5, 2009.
15. Michael Mandel, "Lessons from Credit Disasters Past," *Business Week*, August 13, 2007, and a lecture delivered by Mitch Mumma.
16. Spencer Ante, "These Angels Go Where Others Fear to Tread," *Business Week*, June 1, 2009.
17. Connie Loizos, "Tim Draper Aims to Take Startups 'Public' Beginning in September," Reuters, May 22, 2009.
18. Spencer Ante, "These Angels Go Where Others Fear to Tread."
19. Interview with Jeff Hurst.
20. Paul A. Gompers, Anna Kovner, Josh Lerner, and David S. Scharfstein, "Performance Persistence in Entrepreneurship." Harvard Business School, July, 2008.
21. Interview with Sam Clemens.
22. "The Midas List." *Forbes*, January 24, 2008 and January 25, 2007.

CHAPTER THREE

1. John is a composite based on interviews with associates at a number of top private equity firms.
2. Keynote speech delivered by Henry R. Kravis at the Private Equity Analyst Conference, New York City, September 22, 2004.
3. "The 400 Richest Americans," *Forbes*, September 30, 2009.
4. "Top Ten Deals: The Biggest Private Equity Deals of All-time," *Fortune*, February 23, 2007.
5. Keynote speech delivered by Henry R. Kravis at the Private Equity Analyst Conference.
6. "Private Equity Fund Raising up in 2007: Report," Reuters, January 8, 2008.
7. "Judge Says Linens 'n Things Can Close More Stores," Reuters, August 15, 2008.
8. Andrew Ross Sorkin and Michael J. de la Merced, "Debt Linked to Buyouts Tightens the Economic Vise," *New York Times*, November 3, 2008.
9. The Carlyle Group, 2008 Annual Report.
10. Andrew Martin, "Private Equity Firm Buys 17% of Whole Foods," *New York Times*, November 5, 2008.
11. Scott Lanman and Sarah Mulholland, "Fed Says TALF Loan Requests Increase to $10.6 Billion," Bloomberg, May 5, 2009.
12. Warren Buffett, "Chairman's Letter," Berkshire Hathaway 2008 Annual Report.

13. World Economic Forum, "The Global Economic Impact of Private Equity Investment Investigated in Most Comprehensive Report," January 25, 2008.

14. The Boston Consulting Group and IESE, "Get Ready for the Private-Equity Shakeout," December 2008.

15. Peter Carbonara and Jessica Silver-Greenberg, "How Private Equity Could Rev Up the U.S. Economy," *Business Week,* May 7, 2009 (citing the research firm Preqin).

16. Most private equity funds have return thresholds below which they do not earn performance fees. For example, if a fund's threshold is 7 percent, and the fund earns only 5 percent, the fund would not charge a performance fee.

17. In the interview about the roofing company (discussed in the text), the interviewer would expect the interviewees to be able to break down the market between residential and commercial roofing as well as new and replacement roofing material demand. Other considerations might be the locations in which the company sells its products, its market share and how it distributes. Key concerns would likely be the effect of fluctuations in material prices and a decline in new housing.

CHAPTER FOUR

1. Jack is a composite based on interviews with associates at a number of hedge funds.

2. Roger Lowenstein, *When Genius Failed: The Rise and Fall of Long-Term Capital Management.* (New York: Random House, 2000), p. 25.

3. Tyler Cowen, "Bailout of Long-Term Capital: A Bad Precedent?" *New York Times,* December 26, 2008.

4. Louise Story, "Hedge Funds, Unhinged," *New York Times,* January 18, 2009.

5. Hedge Fund Research data, cited by MSNBC, "Once-invincible Hedge Funds Brace for Bad 2009," January 13, 2009.

6. "Alternative Social Investments," *Economist,* June 26, 2009.

7. Jessica Silver-Greenberg, "An X-Rated Hedge Fund," *Business Week,* May 22, 2008.

8. Interview with Lee Ainslie from Beverly Chandler, *Investing with Hedge Fund Giants: Profit Whether Markets Rise or Fall* (Harlow, U.K.: Pearson Education Limited, 2002).

9. Interview with Seth Klarman, November 30 2007.

10. "What's Bigger than Cisco, Coke or McDonald's?" *Business Week,* October 3, 2005.

11. Jack Schwager, *Stock Market Wizards.* (New York: Harper Business, 2001).

12. Marcia Vickers, "The Most Powerful Trader on Wall Street You've Never Heard Of," *Business Week,* July 21, 2003.

13. Interview with David Shaw from Jack Schwager, *Stock Market Wizards* (New York: Harper Business, 2001).

14. "Top Hedge Fund Manager Had Take-Home Pay of $1.5 Billion in 2005 on 5% Fee and 44% of Gains," FinFacts Ireland, May 26, 2006, citing data from *Alpha* Magazine.

15. "Top Earning U.S. Hedge Fund Manager Made $3.7bn in 2007 from Subprime Crisis," FinFacts Ireland, April 16, 2008, citing data from *Alpha* Magazine.

16. Andrew Ross Sorkin, "Running a Hedge Fund is Harder than It Looks," *New York Times,* August 19, 2008.

17. "Madoff's Victims," *Wall Street Journal,* March 6, 2009.

18. Lowenstein, *When Genius Failed,* p. 24.

19. Harvard Business School Alumni Bulletin, December 2008.

CHAPTER FIVE

1. Laura is a composite based on interviews with associates at a number of top consulting firms.
2. Nancy J. Perry, "A Consulting Firm too Hot to Handle?" *Fortune*, 4/27/1987.
3. "Management Consulting: Giving Advice in Adversity," *The Economist*, October 15, 2008.
4. Ibid.
5. Accenture's 2008 revenues were approximately $25.3 billion.
6. Consulting firms try to log all their insights from cases and research in an internal database in order to help future case teams.

CHAPTER SIX

1. The name of the person in this story has been changed.
2. "Largest U.S. Corporations," *Fortune*, May 4, 2009. The 2009 list uses 2008 revenue figures. The unprofitable businesses failed to make money because their overhead expenses, costs of goods sold, interest expenses, depreciation, and taxes exceeded their revenues.
3. Charles Morris, *The Two Trillion Dollar Meltdown* (New York: Public Affairs, 2008), p. 3.
4. Karen Brettell, "U.S. Companies Buy Back Loans as Prices Plunge," *Business Week*, March 27, 2009.
5. Robert Guest, "Surviving the Slump," *The Economist*, May 30, 2009.
6. Robert Kaplan and David Kiron. "Accounting Fraud at WorldCom." Harvard Business School Case 104–071, September 14, 2007.
7. Larry Bossidy and Ram Charan, "Execution: the Discipline of Getting Things Done." (New York: Crown Business, 2002).
8. Spencer Stuart, "Route to the Top," *Chief Executive* magazine, November 5, 2008.
9. Based on the top 100 S&P 500 companies.
10. Stuart, "Route to the Top."
11. Daniel Dornbusch and Christopher B. Howard, "Blueprint for a Great Leader." *Pharmaceutical Executive*, 4/1/2004.
12. Clifford, Donald K. Jr., "Managing the Threshold Company: A report to Management"(New York: McKinsey & Company, 1973).
13. Kenji Hall, "CEO Pay: Don't Look to Japan for Answers," *Business Week*, February 23, 2009. [Data for 2004–2006, collected by Towers Perrin.]
14. Shareholder anger caused the benefit to be reduced to $100 million; Mark Maremont & Cari Tuna, "Nabors Cuts CEO's Death Benefit," *Wall Street Journal*, May 1, 2009.

APPENDIX A: FIRM PROFILES

1. All data in this appendix is from firm documents, unless otherwise cited. Assets are as of the end of the second quarter of 2009, data from Thomson Reuters. Asset totals for banks which report their financials in currencies others than USD have been converted into dollars.
2. Worldwide Announced M&A H1 2009.
3. Udayan Gupta. *Done Deals* (Harvard Business School Press: Cambridge, Mass., 2000), p.18.
4. Interview with Sam Clemens, April 6, 2009.

5. Darren Vader, "Biography: Steve Jobs," The Apple Museum, www.theapple museum.com/index.php?id=49.
6. "Larry Page," www.Biography.com
7. Academy of Achievement, "Pierre Omidyar," http://www.achievement.org/auto doc/page/omi0bio–1.
8. Emily Thornton, "Carlyle Changes its Stripes," *Business Week,* February 12, 2007.
9. "Who's Who in Private Equity," *The Wall Street Journal Online,* http://online.wsj .com/public/resources/documents/info-pequity0607–12.html.
10. "What's Bigger Than Cisco, Coke or McDonald's?" *Business Week,* October 2, 2005.
11. "Private Equity Power List," *Fortune,* 2007.
12. "John W. Snow, Secretary of the Treasury," www.whitehouse.gov/government/ snow-bio.html.
13. This is the aggregate value of the four Goldman Sachs Capital Partners Funds that have not yet been liquidated.
14. World Air Transport Summit, "David Bonderman," 2006, www.iata.org.
15. "Private Equity Power List," *Fortune,* 2007.
16. *Alpha* magazine 2009 hedge fund rankings
17. Brian O'Keefe, "The World's Biggest Hedge Fund," *Fortune,* March 19, 2009.
18. *Institutional Investor,* 2009.
19. Statement of John Paulson to the U.S. House of Representatives Committee on Oversight and Government Reform, November 13, 2008.
20. Jenny Strasburg and Scott Patterson, "Renaissance's Simons Delays Retirement Plans," *Wall Street Journal,* June 12, 2009.
21. Marcia Vickers, "The Most Powerful Trader on Wall Street You've Never Heard Of," *Business Week,* July 21, 2003.
22. Data on total billable consultants by firm is from *Consulting Magazine,* September/October 2009.
23. Fiscal year 2008.
24. *Consulting Magazine,* September/October 2008.
25. Zachary Goldfarb, "Booz Allen Details Plan to Split Firm," *Washington Post,* May 22, 2008.
26. *Consulting Magazine,* September/October 2008.
27. Annual revenues for 2008.
28. IBM company financials.
29. Marsh & McLennan company financials.

INDEX

MONEY MAKERS

244

Cerberus Capital Management, 93, 100, 108, 128, 220
Cherry, JB, 8, 97, 105
Chrysler, 93, 182, 220
Circuit City, 182
Cisco, 182, 216
Citigroup, 21, 31, 36, 39, 46, 158, 209, 211
Clark, Megan, 8, 59, 64, 196
Clemens, Sam, 8, 68, 71, 74–75, 82–83, 233
Clifford, Donald, 197
commercial banks, 2, 21, 48
Commonwealth Capital Ventures, 8, 49, 56, 71, 214
Cooke, Jay, 11
Corzine, Jon, 41
Cramer, Jim, 33
Crédit Agricole, 137
credit default swaps, 2, 30–31, 226

Daniel, Ron, 8, 158, 161, 170, 172–174, 177, 235
D'Aniello, Daniel, 109, 219, 220
D.E. Shaw, 130–131, 225
derivatives, 28–30
Dimon, Jamie, 10–11, 17, 20–21, 39, 44–47, 211, 233
Drexel Burnham, 12–13, 218, 220

economic downturn
big business and, 182–184
compensation and, 41
hedge funds and, 124
impact of, 157–158
loss of confidence and, 120–121
managment consulting and, 154–158
private equity investment and, 90, 94
trends spurring, 18–19
venture capital and, 59
Eli Lilly, 196, 236
Enron, 71, 109, 228
entrepreneurship. see also venture capital
explanation, 51–53
history, 50–51
equities, 29, 33, 121, 125–127, 133
European Exchange Rate, 117–118
Evans, Bruce, 7, 55, 72, 74, 76, 78, 79–80, 216, 233
event-driven strategies, 131
Evercore Partners, 7, 34, 39
Exxon Mobil, 182, 207

Fairfield Greenwich Advisors, 137
Fannie Mae, 17, 147, 225
Farkas, Charles, 7, 159, 161, 166, 170, 172, 175, 184, 235, 237
FDIC, 45
Foley, Craig, 7, 57, 61, 64, 72
Freddie Mac, 17, 147
Frey, Kip, 8, 67, 70, 72, 73, 77–79
Fuller, Joe, 8, 154, 156–159, 161, 164, 170, 173, 176–177, 184, 230, 235

Galvin, Chris, 7, 187–191, 198–199, 237
Geithner, Tim, 11, 46
General Motors, 182, 189, 230
Glass, Noah, 8, 52, 69, 80–82, 233
Glass-Steagall Act, 19
global macro funds, 131–132
globalization, 18, 158, 195
Goldman Sachs, 8, 17, 20, 26, 35, 37–39, 41–42, 47–48, 90, 98, 156, 208, 210–211, 213, 221, 222, 223, 226, 232–233
Google, 51, 102, 164, 191, 194–195, 201–202, 215, 216, 217, 236
Graham, Benjamin, 116, 143
Greenhill, Robert, 34

headhunters, 105
hedge funds
activist shareholders, 133
analysis, 134–135
arbitrage and, 118–119, 130–131
characteristics for success, 140
compensation, 141
creation of, 116–117
current state of, 121–122
description, 114–115
economic downturn and, 120–121
event-driven strategies, 131
expansion of industry, 119–120
fees, 135–137
global macro funds, 131–132
hiring practices, 141–142
history, 114–116
industry leaders on, 142–147
investment strategies, 126–133
long-short funds, 128–130
managed futures, 132
organizational culture and lifestyle, 138–140
positive externalities, 122–124
promotion and mobility, 140–141
regulation, 137
Soros and Bank of England, 117–118
starting and running, 124–126
value investing vs. speculation, 127–128
Howard, Chris, 194, 196
HSBC, 137
Hurst, Jeff, 8, 49, 56, 58, 60, 71, 72–74, 77–78

Icahn, Carl, 89
Insana, Ron, 136–137
investment banks
arbitrage and, 119
big business and, 181
boutique banks, 33–34
characteristics for success, 37–38
compensation, 41–42
consulting firms and, 154, 156–157, 171
current state of, 19–20
definition, 21
description, 10–11